Communicating in Small Groups

Principles and Practices

Third Edition

Steven A. Beebe
Southwest Texas State University

John T. Masterson
University of Miami

 HarperCollins*Publishers*

An Instructor's Manual for this text is available. It may be obtained through a local Scott, Foresman representative or by writing to: Speech Editor, Scott, Foresman/Little Brown Higher Education Division, Scott, Foresman and Company, 1900 E. Lake Avenue, Glenview, IL 60025.

Library of Congress Cataloging-in-Publication Data

Beebe, Steven A.
   Communicating in small groups: principles and practices / Steven A. Beebe, John T. Masterson—3rd ed.
      p.   cm.
   Includes bibliographical references.
   ISBN 0-673-38874-3
   1. Small groups.   2. Communicating in small groups.   3. Group relations training.
   I. Masterson, John T.   II. Title
HM133.B43   1989
302.3′4—dc20   89-39558

Credit lines for the photos, illustrations, and other copyrighted materials
appearing in this work are placed in the acknowledgments section on page 299–300
of this book. The acknowledgments section is to be considered an extension
of the copyright page.

Preface

The first two editions of *Communicating in Small Groups: Principles and Practices* have enjoyed widespread success with both teachers and students. Our challenge in writing the third edition has been to retain the goals of the first two editions—to be relevant, practical, and useful—and to incorporate cutting-edge research.

Some group texts emphasize the theory of group interaction. Theory without application, however, can result in knowledgeable group participants who lack the skills to tap their new-found knowledge. Other books emphasize skills; group members who are armed with techniques and informed only about the mechanics of group interaction may not understand when and how to apply their skills. The underlying premise of this book is that effective group communication requires knowledge of both the principles and dynamics that characterize group interaction, and practice in applying those principles. We review small group communication theory and research in a variety of group contexts, and accompany this information with exercises that allow students to translate information into action. In each chapter we suggest ways of converting principles into practice.

Instructors using the third edition will recognize features from the previous two editions: chapter objectives, a glossary, discussion questions, and chapter-end activities and exercises, as well as the same lively writing style and use of relevant examples. This edition also includes expanded coverage of several small group concepts, plus new features to make the book even more useful. Additions include:

- Liberal use of review boxes that summarize key terms, skills, and concepts
- Research-based distinctions between problem solving and decision making
- New material on team building
- New research applications of group problem solving
- A new description of the use of focus groups
- The latest research applications of situational leadership models
- A new appendix on improving research skills
- A new appendix on meeting management, including parliamentary procedure
- A new approach to developing active listening skills
- A greatly expanded Instructor's Manual that includes additional activities, exercises, overhead transparency masters, chapter outlines, and a new test bank

- An accompanying videotape that provides examples of the problem-solving process

We appreciate the useful suggestions made by users of the second edition which have helped to make the third edition a better book. Specifically, we wish to thank: Gail A. Hankins, North Carolina State University; Ted Zorn, University of North Carolina; Kathie Leeper, Northwest Missouri State University; Rodney Cole, University of Maine–Augusta; Theresa McGinnis, College of DuPage; William Yaremchuk, Monmouth College; Donna Graham, De Anza College; Jerry Salley, Merced College; Jill O'Brien, DePaul University; Dan DeStephen, Wright State University; Dean Tomlinson, University of Evansville; Cynthia Stohl, Purdue University; Thomas Harris, University of Evansville; Jane Elvins, University of California–Santa Barbara; and Samuel Dudley, Mississippi State University.

We wish to acknowledge those who provided suggestions for the second edition of the book: Isa N. Engleberg, Prince George's Community College; Don Friar, American River College; Theodore Hopf, Washington State University; Richard Kaough, Southern Oregon State College; Elaine Lashley, University of Cincinnati; Patrick A. Sciarra, College of DuPage; and Victor D. Wall, Jr., The Ohio State University. We also would like to thank our colleagues who reviewed the first edition: Randall Alderson, Wagner College; Kimberly Buckingham, San Jose State University; April Christian-Schmidlapp, Edison State Community College; Ray Collins, San Jose City College; Gay Lumsden, Kean College of New Jersey; and John L. Vohs, University of California–Davis.

Our editors at Scott, Foresman have continued to provide excellent assistance to us. We are especially appreciative of the guidance and leadership of Vikki Barrett, the acquisitions editor, and Louise Howe, the developmental editor who worked on this project. We appreciate the feedback and helpful suggestions we received from Russ Wittrup, producer of the videotape which accompanies this text, and Cathy Fleuriet, author of the Instructor's Manual for the third edition. Both Russ and Cathy are faculty members at Southwest Texas State University. We also want to acknowledge the expertise of our friends and colleagues, Dennis and Laurie Romig of Performance Resources, Inc., of Austin, Texas. Their insight and advice about the group communication process have helped to shape the direction of many of our revisions.

Finally, we offer our thanks and gratitude to our families for their support. Our sons, Mark and Matthew Beebe and John and Noah Masterson, sacrificed time with their dads so this book could be written. Nancy Masterson contributed countless hours as proofreader and encourager. Susan Beebe was invaluable as typist, editor, proofreader, co-author of the first edition of the Instructor's Manual, and author of Appendix A.

Steven A. Beebe
John T. Masterson

Contents

——— Chapter One ———

An Introduction to Small Group Communication   1

WHAT IS SMALL GROUP COMMUNICATION?   3
Meeting with a Common Purpose ▪ Feeling a Sense of
Belonging to the Group ▪ Exerting Influence Upon One
Another ▪ Communicating Face-to-Face

WHY LEARN ABOUT SMALL GROUPS?   5

ADVANTAGES AND DISADVANTAGES OF WORKING
IN SMALL GROUPS   7
Advantages ▪ Disadvantages

TYPES OF SMALL GROUPS   12
Primary Groups ▪ Study Groups ▪ Therapy Groups ▪
Problem-Solving Groups ▪ Decision-Making Groups

PUBLIC COMMUNICATION FORMATS   16
Panel Discussions ▪ Symposium Presentations ▪
Forum Presentations

AN INTRODUCTION TO SMALL GROUP
COMMUNICATION: PUTTING PRINCIPLE
INTO PRACTICE   19

PRACTICE   20

NOTES   22

——— Chapter Two ———

Small Group Communication Theory   24

THE NATURE OF THEORY AND THE
THEORY-BUILDING PROCESS   25

THEORY: A PRACTICAL APPROACH TO GROUP COMMUNICATION 27

Explanatory Function ▪ Predictive Function

THE POWER OF THE SPOKEN WORD 29

Uncertainty ▪ Complexity ▪ Small Groups: More Complexity and More Uncertainty

THEORETICAL PERSPECTIVES FOR THE STUDY OF SMALL GROUP COMMUNICATION 31

Social Exchange Theory and Small Group Communication ▪ Rules Theory and Small Group Communication ▪ Systems Theory and Small Group Communication ▪ A Task-Contingency Theory of Small Group Communication

A THEORETICAL MODEL OF SMALL GROUP COMMUNICATION 36

SMALL GROUP COMMUNICATION THEORY: PUTTING PRINCIPLE INTO PRACTICE 39

PRACTICE 39

NOTES 40

───────── **Chapter Three** ──────────────────

Group Formation 42

WHY DO PEOPLE JOIN GROUPS? 44

INTERPERSONAL NEEDS 44

Maslow's Hierarchy ▪ Schutz's Theory

INDIVIDUAL GOALS 49

GROUP GOALS 49

Establishing Mutuality of Concern

INTERPERSONAL ATTRACTION 53

Similarity ▪ Complementarity ▪ Proximity/Contact/ Interaction ▪ Physical Attractiveness

GROUP ATTRACTION 55

Group Activities ▪ Group Goals ▪ Group Membership

GROUP FORMATION: PUTTING PRINCIPLE INTO PRACTICE 56

PRACTICE 58

NOTES 59

──────── Chapter Four ────────────────────────

Relating to Others in Small Groups   60

ROLES   62
Self-Concept Development: Role Formation ▪ Diversity
of Roles in Small Groups ▪ Group Task Roles ▪ Group
Building and Maintenance Roles ▪ Individual Roles

NORMS   67
Identifying Group Norms ▪ How Do Norms Develop? ▪
Conforming to Group Norms

STATUS   70
Privileges Accorded to High-Status Group Members ▪
Effects of Status Differences ▪ Observing Status
Differences to Predict Group Dynamics

POWER   73
Power Bases ▪ Effects of Power on Group Process

TRUST   76
Developing Trusting Relationships ▪ Self-Disclosure ▪
The Johari Window

THE DEVELOPMENT OF GROUP RELATIONSHIPS
OVER TIME   82

RELATING TO OTHERS IN SMALL GROUPS:
PUTTING PRINCIPLE INTO PRACTICE   83
Roles ▪ Power ▪ Trust ▪ Norms ▪ Status ▪
Self-Disclosure

PRACTICE   85

NOTES   88

──────── Chapter Five ────────────────────────

Improving Group Climate   90

A CASE STUDY   91

DEFENSIVE COMMUNICATION   93

DEFENSIVE AND SUPPORTIVE CLIMATES   93
Evaluation *Versus* Description ▪ Control *Versus* Problem
Orientation ▪ Strategy *Versus* Spontaneity ▪ Neutrality
Versus Empathy ▪ Superiority *Versus* Equality ▪ Certainty
Versus Provisionalism

DISCONFIRMING AND CONFIRMING RESPONSES   97
Disconfirming Responses ▪ Confirming Responses

DEFENSIVENESS AND UNCERTAINTY   99

LISTENING   100
Types of Listening   ▪   Barriers to Effective Listening   ▪
A Guide to Active Listening

VERBAL DYNAMICS IN THE SMALL GROUP   105
Words as Barriers to Communication

GROUP COHESIVENESS   107
Composition and Cohesiveness   ▪   Individual Benefits
and Cohesiveness   ▪   Task Effectiveness and
Cohesiveness   ▪   Communication and Cohesiveness   ▪
Suggestions for Building a Cohesive Team

COMMUNICATION NETWORKS   111

ANOTHER FACTOR: GROUP SIZE   112

GROUP CLIMATE AND PRODUCTIVITY   113

**IMPROVING GROUP CLIMATE: PUTTING PRINCIPLE
INTO PRACTICE   114**

PRACTICE   115

NOTES   119

Chapter Six

Nonverbal Group Dynamics   120

**THE IMPORTANCE OF NONVERBAL COMMUNICATION
TO GROUP COMMUNICATION   122**

**FRAMEWORKS FOR DESCRIBING AND ANALYZING
NONVERBAL CUES   124**
Categories of Nonverbal Communication   ▪   Dimensions of
Nonverbal Meaning

**APPLICATIONS OF NONVERBAL COMMUNICATION
RESEARCH   127**
Body Posture and Movement   ▪   Eye Contact   ▪   Facial
Expression   ▪   Vocal Cues   ▪   Territoriality and Personal
Space   ▪   Personal Appearance   ▪   Communication
Environment

**NONVERBAL GROUP DYNAMICS: PUTTING PRINCIPLE
INTO PRACTICE   139**
Interpreting Nonverbal Behavior   ▪   Body Posture and
Movement   ▪   Eye Contact   ▪   Facial Expression   ▪   Vocal
Cues   ▪   Territoriality and Personal Space   ▪   Personal
Appearance   ▪   Communication Environment

PRACTICE   142

NOTES   144

——— Chapter Seven ———

Understanding Decision Making and Problem Solving in Small Groups   147

DECISION MAKING *VERSUS* PROBLEM SOLVING   148
Group Decision Making ▪ Characteristics of Good
Decisions ▪ Methods of Group Decision Making ▪
Group Problem Solving ▪ Characteristics of Effective
Group Problem Solvers

FORMULATING DISCUSSION QUESTIONS   156
Questions of Facts ▪ Questions of Value ▪ Questions
of Policy

TYPES AND TESTS OF EVIDENCE   161
Facts ▪ Examples ▪ Opinions ▪ Statistics ▪ Using
Evidence Effectively

TWO APPROACHES TO GROUP PROBLEM
SOLVING   163

THE DESCRIPTIVE APPROACH   164
Phase One: Orientation ▪ Phase Two: Conflict ▪ Phase
Three: Emergence ▪ Phase Four: Reinforcement ▪ The
Process Nature of Group Phases

UNDERSTANDING PROBLEM SOLVING IN SMALL
GROUPS: PUTTING PRINCIPLE INTO PRACTICE   169
Group Decision Making ▪ Group Problem Solving ▪
Formulating Discussion Questions ▪ Two Approaches to
Group Problem Solving

PRACTICE   171

NOTES   175

——— Chapter Eight ———

Small Group Problem-Solving Techniques   177

A TRADITIONAL APPROACH TO PROBLEM SOLVING:
REFLECTIVE THINKING   179
Step One: Identify and Define the Problem ▪ Step Two:
Analyze the Problem ▪ Step Three: Suggest Possible
Solutions ▪ Step Four: Suggest the Best Solution(s) ▪
Step Five: Test and Implement the Solution ▪ Applying
Reflective Thinking

A CREATIVE APPROACH TO PROBLEM SOLVING: BRAINSTORMING   184

Applying Brainstorming

QUESTION-ORIENTED APPROACHES TO PROBLEM SOLVING   187

Ideal-Solution Format ▪ Single-Question Format ▪ Applying Question-Oriented Approaches

AGENDAS FOR PARTICIPATIVE GROUP PROBLEM SOLVING   191

Buzz Sessions ▪ RISK Technique ▪ Nominal Group Technique ▪ Quality Circles: A Participative Decision-Making Agenda ▪ Focus Groups

SMALL GROUP PROBLEM-SOLVING TECHNIQUES: PUTTING PRINCIPLE INTO PRACTICE   195

Reflective Thinking ▪ Brainstorming ▪ Ideal Solution and Single Question ▪ Participative Decision Making

PRACTICE   198

NOTES   205

─────── Chapter Nine ──────────────────────────

Conflict Management in Small Groups   207

WHAT IS CONFLICT?   208

Myths About Conflict

MANAGING DIFFERENT TYPES OF CONFLICT   211

Managing Pseudo-Conflict: When Misunderstandings Occur ▪ Managing Simple Conflict: Disagreeing on Issues ▪ Managing Ego-Conflict: Unraveling Personality Clashes

GROUPTHINK: WHEN CONFLICT DOES NOT OCCUR   215

Symptoms of Groupthink ▪ Suggestions to Reduce Groupthink

CONSENSUS: A GOAL OF TASK-ORIENTED SMALL GROUPS   222

Nature of Consensus ▪ Suggestions for Reaching Consensus

CONFLICT MANAGEMENT IN SMALL GROUPS: PUTTING PRINCIPLE INTO PRACTICE   226

Groupthink ▪ Consensus

PRACTICE   227

NOTES   234

Chapter Ten

Leadership 236

WHAT IS LEADERSHIP? 237

TRAIT PERSPECTIVE 238

FUNCTIONAL PERSPECTIVE 238
Task Leadership ▪ Process Leadership

SITUATIONAL PERSPECTIVE 244
Leadership Style ▪ Situational Factors in Leadership
Behavior: A Case Study ▪ A Contingency Model of
Leadership Effectiveness ▪ Hersey and Blanchard's
Situational Model ▪ Some Observations on the Situational
Approach to Leadership

EMERGENT LEADERSHIP IN SMALL GROUPS 252

LEADERSHIP TRAINING 254

LEADERSHIP: PUTTING PRINCIPLE
INTO PRACTICE 254

PRACTICE 257

NOTES 258

Chapter Eleven

Observing and Evaluating Group Communication 260

THEORY AND OBSERVATION: A NATURAL
RELATIONSHIP 261

OBSERVING COMMUNICATION NETWORKS:
INTERACTION DIAGRAMS 262

OBSERVING GROUP CLIMATE 263
Confirming and Disconfirming Responses

OBSERVING ROLES AND ROLE PERCEPTIONS 266
Group Role Inventory ▪ Functional Roles

OBSERVING GROUP COHESIVENESS 268
Self-Report Measure: A Cohesiveness Index

OBSERVING GROUP INTERACTION 268
Interaction Process Analysis

OBSERVING GROUP LEADERSHIP   270
Leadership Rating Scale ▪ Feedback Rating Instrument

EVALUATING GROUP MEETINGS   274
Post-Meeting Reaction Sheet

OBSERVATING AND EVALUATING GROUP
COMMUNICATION: PUTTING PRINCIPLE
INTO PRACTICE   276

PRACTICE   278

NOTES   278

─────── Appendix A ───────────────────────────────────────

Conducting Research: Preparing for Group Discussion   279

LIBRARY RESEARCH   279
The Card Catalog ▪ Computer Access System ▪ The
Stacks ▪ Periodical and Newspaper Indexes and
Holdings ▪ The Reference Section ▪ Government
Documents

SURVEY RESEARCH   282
Sample Questions

NOTE   284

─────── Appendix B ───────────────────────────────────────

Meeting Management   285

MANAGING MEETINGS EFFECTIVELY   285
Planning the Meeting ▪ Leading the Meeting

CONDUCTING FORMAL MEETINGS: PARLIAMENTARY
PROCEDURE   288
Types of Motions ▪ Chairing a Formal Meeting

NOTES   291

Glossary   292

Acknowledgments   299

Index   301

Chapter One

An Introduction to Small Group Communication

After studying this chapter, you should be able to:

☐ Define small group communication.

☐ Explain the importance of studying small group communication.

☐ List and describe the advantages of working with others in small groups.

☐ List and describe the disadvantages of working with others in small groups.

☐ Identify different types of small groups.

☐ Organize and implement the following public small group communication formats: (1) panel discussion, (2) symposium presentation, and (3) forum presentation.

Using a variety of research methods, communication scholars, sociologists, psychologists, and anthropologists have reached a similar conclusion about humankind. Their universal, but perhaps not so startling, conclusion is that humans are social creatures. We need to establish meaningful relationships with others. We need to associate with others in groups. We are reared in family groups. We are educated in groups. We worship in groups. We are entertained in groups. We work in groups. When an important problem arises, we seek others' advice and meet with problem-solving and decision-making groups in order to help find answers to important issues.

This book is about groups. More specifically, it is about communication in small groups.

"Why study small group communication?" You have probably already asked yourself that question. Or maybe you have asked, "What can a systematic study of small group communication do for me? How will it help me with my career? Will it really help me be a better committee member? Will studying small group communication improve my interpersonal relationships with my family and my friends?"

Studying small group communication may help you in many ways, but the main purpose of this book is to help you become a better communicator in the context of a small group. The book will strive to give you both a broad understanding of group communication processes and practical advice to help you be a better small group participant. Note that the book will primarily deal with **task-oriented small groups**—groups with a specific objective to achieve, a problem to solve, or a decision to make.

The communication that occurs in a group will be this book's focus. In discussing its importance in an organization, Goldhaber describes communication as:

> the lifeblood of the organization
> the glue that binds the organization
> the oil that smooths the organization's functions
> the thread that ties the system together
> the force that pervades the organization
> the binding agent that cements all relationships.[1]

These metaphors apply to small groups as well as to large corporations. Regardless of a group's size, its members must be able to talk, listen, and respond to one another. They must be sensitive to the needs and feelings of other group members. Ideally, group members should have some training in the way groups function most efficiently. Without an understanding of the group communication process, members may become frustrated, and meetings may degenerate into unpleasant, unproductive experiences.

WHAT IS SMALL GROUP COMMUNICATION?

As the nation becomes more concerned about the growing nuclear arms race, the President of the United States meets with his chief arms negotiators to discuss arms control.

The city commission has finally decided to begin formulating plans for a new cultural arts center. The commissioners appoint a subcommittee to help develop the project.

The Board of Directors of General Motors believes that in order to compete with the foreign automobile industry, American automakers must produce a new low-cost, high-quality automobile. The board decides to appoint a group of the company's top-level executives and engineers to develop plans for a new car.

Each of these three situations involves a group of people meeting for a specific purpose. Although the purposes are quite different, these groups share something in common—something that distinguishes them from, for example, a cluster of people waiting for a bus or riding in an elevator. Just what is that "something"? What are the characteristics that make a group a group?

Several scholars have developed definitions of **small group communication** and group discussion. Here are a few of their definitions:

. . . a group of few enough members for each to perceive all others as individuals, who meet face-to-face, share some identity or common purpose, and share standards for governing their activities as members.[2]

. . . a number of persons who perceive each other as participants in a common activity, who interact dynamically with one another, and who communicate their responses chiefly through words.[3]

. . . the process whereby two or more people exchange information or ideas in a face-to-face situation to achieve a goal.[4]

. . . three or more people working together to do a clearly specified job or to reach a common goal.[5]

. . . two or more persons who are interacting with one another in such a manner that each person influences and is influenced by each other person.[6]

. . . the purposeful, systematic, primarily oral exchange of ideas, facts, and opinions by a group of persons who share in the group's leadership.[7]

Despite the differences among these definitions, they have several characteristics in common that may help sharpen your perception of small group communication.

Meeting with a Common Purpose

The President's disarmament advisers, the city commission, and the Board of Directors of General Motors have one thing in common—their members have a specific purpose for meeting. They share a concern for the objectives of the group. While a group of people waiting for a bus or riding in an elevator may share the goal of transportation, they do not have the same *collective* goal. Their individual destinations are different. Their primary concerns are for themselves, not for others. As soon as their individual goals are realized, they leave the bus or elevator. On the other hand, a goal keeps a committee or discussion group together until that goal is realized. Many groups fail to remain together because they never identify their common purpose. While participants in small groups may have somewhat different motives for their membership, a common purpose cements the group together.

Feeling a Sense of Belonging to the Group

Not only do group members need a mutual concern to unite them, but they also need to feel that they belong to the group. Commuters waiting for a bus probably do not feel part of a collective effort. Members of a small group, however, need to have a sense of *identity* with the group; they should be able to feel that it is *their* group.

Exerting Influence Upon One Another

Although some groups have an elected or appointed leader, members of most groups share leadership responsibilities. To assist in leading the group toward its goal, members may keep the group on schedule, provide information, ask questions to keep the group moving forward, or take notes of the group's meetings. Even in a small group with an appointed leader, all members should share leadership responsibilities. Regardless of its size, a group achieves optimal success when each person accepts some leadership responsibilities.

Communicating Face-to-Face

Group members must be able to respond immediately, both verbally and nonverbally, to the discussion at hand. To have a sense of belonging to the group, they need to interact with one another on a personal, face-to-face basis. In this age of telephone conference calls, FAX machines, and overnight mail, communicating over a great distance has become increasingly easy. Such communication may, nonetheless, be hindered by sluggish feedback or delayed replies that are not a problem when meeting face-to-face.

In summary, **small group communication** is defined as face-to-face communication among a small group of people who share a common purpose or goal, who feel a sense of belonging to the group, and who exert influence upon one another.

WHY LEARN ABOUT SMALL GROUPS?

Besides defining small group communication, one of this book's first objectives is to help you understand the value of studying the principles of effective communication in a small group. Consider these reasons for learning about small groups.

1.   *You will spend a significant portion of time working in small groups.* Stop reading for just a moment, and count how many different groups you are involved with this week. What is your total? Perhaps you thought of only one or two groups you're currently associated with, such as a committee or a work group. But did you consider your friends? How about fraternities, sororities, or religious groups? Your family? If you're employed, did you consider the groups you participate in while on the job? Mosvick and Nelson report:

- Most business in the United States is accomplished in group meetings.
- The average manager or professional spends almost one-fourth of every workweek in meetings.
- Evidence suggests that the number of meetings being held is increasing. Over the next five years, business organizations may expect a 5 to 9 percent increase in the number of meetings they hold.[8]

Human beings need to socialize. We have a need to congregate, to associate with others. Unless you're a hermit living in an isolated cave, you communicate with others in groups. Chances are, you will continue to do so. Work groups, social groups, educational groups, family groups, and therapy groups occupy a significant portion of our communication time. While this book will emphasize small groups that exist for the purpose of making decisions and solving problems, it will also discuss many principles that are applicable to most of the groups with which you associate.

2.   *You will need to understand how groups make decisions and solve problems.* You may not consider many of the groups you belong to as decision-making or problem-solving groups. You join some groups just for the fun of socializing and being with others. You may think that problem solving or decision making occurs only in groups that have a very specific task. Even in your social groups, however, problems arise and decisions need to be made. This book will discuss various

approaches to group problem solving and decision making. An increased understanding of what happens when people make decisions in groups should improve your ability to arrive at better decisions and, consequently, should enhance your enjoyment of working in a group.

3.   *You can reduce the uncertainty and anxiety you may have about working with others in small groups.* You often fear what you do not understand. Your first day on a new job provokes fear and anxiety. You're not sure what to expect. You probably experience some uncertainty on your first day in a new class or new school. Often, anxiety and uncertainty can inhibit you so that you do not make the most of your situation, whether it is a new job, a new class, or a new group. Most colleges and universities have orientation programs to help reduce your uncertainty about your new environment. On a new job, you are usually given time to get broken in or to learn the ropes, and you may go through extensive training programs to help you do a better job. Learning the principles of small group communication and applying specific suggestions for improving its quality can reduce (though not necessarily eliminate) some of the uncertainty and discomfort you may feel working with others in small groups. It helps to know what to expect. Armed with communication theory, you should be in a better position to explain and predict what happens when people communicate in small groups.

4.   *You will better understand your own communication behavior.* After participating in a small group discussion, have you ever said to yourself, "Now why did I say that?" or "I don't know why I feel so tense and uncomfortable in this group"? Have you ever wondered why you always seem to disagree with someone or why you are not an effective committee leader? Studying small group communication should help you answer these questions. This book will discuss relationships and leadership, as well as nonverbal communication, conflict management, and reasons for joining groups. As you work with others, a knowledge of small group communication principles and theory will expand your understanding of yourself.

5.   *You can help groups in which you participate function more effectively.* Mounting evidence indicates that many group meetings are poorly run. It has been estimated that over 50 percent of the productivity of the billions of hours Americans spend in meetings is wasted. One company estimated that it lost 71 million dollars a year because of inept management of meetings. Another study reported that one-third of the chief executive officers of some companies studied thought meetings were of "marginal value or not worth the time."[9] While one course in small group communication cannot cure all of the problems that plague group meetings, learning about effective group principles and practices can make a difference.

Individuals trained in small group communication have the opportunity to improve many of the group situations in which they may find themselves. Because most groups are not run effectively, skillfully, and diplomatically, you will stand out as a valuable member of any group. While you do not need to announce your superior expertise to the group or use other heavy-handed approaches, you can use your skills subtly and helpfully to nudge the group into functioning effectively.

ADVANTAGES AND DISADVANTAGES OF WORKING IN SMALL GROUPS

"What's so great about working in groups?" mutters an exasperated member of the student entertainment committee, after spending two hours in a meeting with the other committee members. "I could have solved the problem in fifteen minutes. Why do we have to spend two hours rehashing old information?"

"I'm really looking forward to our committee meeting this evening," says an enthusiastic member of an ecology group. "There is always such a great spirit of unity and cohesiveness during each meeting. Even though we sometimes disagree, each group member really seems to respect the ideas and opinions of the others. I think it's because we really enjoy working together as a group."

What are your feelings about working in groups? Maybe you dread attending group meetings. Perhaps you agree with the observation that a committee is a group that keeps minutes but wastes hours. You may believe that groups bumble and stumble along until some sort of compromise is reached—a compromise with which no one is pleased. "To be effective," said one committee member, "a committee should be made up of three people. But to get anything done, one member should be sick, and another absent."

Conversely, you could be one of those people who enjoy group work. You may relish the challenge of trying to solve problems, make decisions, and accomplish tasks while working with others. If you're lucky, you've had more pleasant than unpleasant encounters with group work, but most likely you've had both.

People can easily become disgruntled with a group if it does not meet their expectations of how a good group should function. An important purpose of this book is to help you appreciate the advantages of working with other people; as many advantages as there are, you will also encounter problems that may lead to frustration and anxiety. By understanding both the advantages and the potential pitfalls of working in groups, you will form more realistic expectations about small group work.[11]

Some people view groups as a cure-all for complex problems. If they need a solution to a problem, they form a group or committee. The work of small groups can result in good solutions, sound decisions, and well-executed projects. Some situations and problems, however, are best not handled by a group at all.

Advantages

1. *Groups have greater information resources than individuals do.* Because of the variety of backgrounds and experiences that individuals bring to a group, the group as a whole has more information and ideas from which to seek solutions to

REVIEW BOX

What's Wrong with Group Meetings

Two recent studies suggest there is a need for greater skill in participating in group delibera-tions.[10] The most frequently reported problems in group meetings are:

Rank	Problem
1	Getting off the subject
2	No goals or agenda
3	Too lengthy
4	Poor or inadequate preparation
5	Inconclusive
6	Disorganized
7	Ineffective leadership/lack of control
8	Irrelevance of information discussed
9	Time wasted during meetings
10	Starting late
11	Not effective for making decisions
12	Interruptions from within and without
13	Individuals dominate
14	Rambling, redundant, or digressive discussion
15	No published results or follow-up actions
16	No premeeting orientation/canceled or postponed meetings

a problem than one person would have alone. With more information available, the group is more likely to discuss all sides of an issue and is also more likely to arrive at a better solution. Groups foster all sides of an issue to be discussed. For example, when a manufacturer ponders whether to develop and market a new product, it seeks input from individuals with expertise in finance, marketing, advertising, personnel, engineering, and management. Only after considering vari-ous viewpoints will the manufacturer reach a well-informed decision.

2.   *Groups can employ a greater number of creative problem-solving methods.* Research on groups generally supports the maxim that "two heads are better than one" when it comes to solving problems. Groups usually make better decisions than individuals working alone do because groups have more approaches to or methods of solving a specific problem. A group of people with various back-grounds, experiences, and resources can more creatively consider ways to solve a problem than one person can. Whether the problem is an issue that concerns the local ecology group or a major decision that confronts the Board of Directors of General Motors, people who work on problems with other people can capitalize on one another's experiences.

3. *Working in groups fosters improved learning and comprehension of ideas discussed.* Imagine that your history professor announces that the final exam next week is going to be comprehensive. History is not your best subject. You realize you need help. What do you do? You may form a study group with other class-mates. Your decision to study with a group of people is a wise move; education theorists claim that when you can take an active role in the learning process your comprehension of information will be improved. If you studied for the exam by yourself, you would not have the benefit of asking and answering questions posed by other study group members. By discussing a subject with a group, you learn more and improve your comprehension of the subject.

4. *Members' satisfaction with the group decision increases because they partic-ipate in the problem-solving process.* Group problem solving provides an opportu-nity for group members to participate in the decision-making process. Several research studies suggest that individuals who help solve problems in a group will be more committed to the solution and more satisfied with their participation in the group.

Imagine that while working with a group of other construction workers building a new apartment complex you've been asked to increase your productivity. You will probably be much more responsive to the suggestion if it has evolved from group discussions than if your supervisor simply tells you that you need to increase your rate of productivity. If you are consulted, you will be more committed to implementing the recommendation. That way, you have some responsibility in governing your own behavior. Thus, when individuals work together in small groups, they are more satisfied with the group decision that they helped to shape.

5. *Group members gain a better understanding of themselves as they interact with others.* Working in groups helps you gain a more accurate picture of how others see you. Because of the feedback you receive, you become aware of personal characteristics that are not known to you but that are known to others. Whether the interaction is advantageous or disadvantageous depends largely on how you respond to the feedback others provide. If someone tells you that you are obnoxious and difficult to work with, you may respond by ignoring the comment, disagreeing with the observation, or examining your behavior to see if the criticism is justified. By becoming sensitive to feedback, you can better understand yourself (or at least better understand how others perceive you) than you would if you worked alone. Group interaction and feedback can be useful in helping you examine your inter-personal behavior when interacting with others and in helping you determine whether you want to change your communication style.

Disadvantages

The discussion thus far suggests that working in small groups can be beneficial for several reasons. Groups make well-informed and better decisions more often than do individuals because of the varied experiences individual members bring to a group. With these extra resources, groups can consider more creative methods of solving problems. Group interaction can enhance members' comprehension of a project and improve their satisfaction in working on it. Members also learn about themselves when they work with others because they receive feedback. For these reasons, groups and committees are formed to help solve problems. As noted earlier, however, problems occur when people congregate. Consider some of the disadvantages of working in groups. Identifying these potential problems can help you avoid them.

1.   *Group members may pressure others to conform to the majority opinion.* Most people don't like conflict; they generally try to avoid it. This tendency to avoid controversy in relationships can affect the quality of a group decision. What's wrong with group members reaching agreement? Nothing, unless group members are agreeing to conform to the majority opinion or even to the leader's opinion. Group members may agree on a bad solution just to avoid conflict. Social psychologist Irving Janis calls this phenomenon *groupthink*—when groups agree primarily to avoid conflict.[12] Chapter Nine discusses conflict in small groups, talks about groupthink in more detail, and suggests how to avoid it.

Have you ever had a professor ask your class a question, only to have no one respond? Perhaps you thought you knew the answer, yet you did not raise your hand, either because you could have been wrong or because no one else was raising a hand and you didn't want to be a know-it-all. You didn't contribute because of what others may have thought about you. Thus, you conformed to the standards set by the rest of the group. This happens not only in classrooms but also in other group settings, such as board meetings and committee discussions. One disadvantage of working with others in a group is that some members tend to conform to group pressure or to what other group members are doing (or not doing).

2.   *An individual group member may dominate the discussion.* In some groups it seems as if one person must run the show. That member wants to make the decisions and, when all is said and done, insists that his or her position on the issue is the best one. "Well," you might say, "if this person wants to do all the work, that's fine with me. I won't complain. It will sure be a lot easier for me." Yes, if you permit a member or two to dominate the group, you may do less work yourself, but you then forfeit greater availability of knowledge and of more creative approaches to the group's task. You also lose the advantage of other members' satisfaction because they may feel alienated from the decision making. They may not enjoy working on the project, and the group then suffers from their lessened input.

Try to use the domineering member's enthusiasm to the group's advantage. If an individual tries to monopolize the discussion, other group members should channel that interest more constructively. The talkative member, for example, could be given a special research assignment. Of course, if the domineering member continues to monopolize the discussion, other group members may have to confront that person and suggest that others be given an opportunity to present their views.

3. *Some group members may rely too much on others to get the job done.*

"Charlie is a hard worker. He'll see that the job is done right."
"Lilian seems to really like taking charge. She is doing such a good job. The group really doesn't need me."
"No one will miss me if I don't show up for the meeting this afternoon. There will be enough people to do the work."

These kinds of statements occur when group members are not aware of the importance of each individual in the group. A danger of working in groups is that you may be tempted to rely on others rather than to pitch in and help. Working together distributes the responsibility of accomplishing a task. But if the responsibility is spread among all group members, shouldn't this shared responsibility be an advantage of group work? It should be. When some group members develop an attitude that others can carry the work load, however, problems can develop. Just because you are part of a group, don't think you can get lost in the crowd. Your input is needed. Don't abdicate your responsibility to another group member. To avoid this problem, try to encourage less talkative group members to contribute to the discussion. Also, make sure each person knows the goals and objectives of the group. Encouraging each member to attend every meeting helps, too. Poor attendance at group meetings is a sure sign that members are falling into the "Let Charlie do it" syndrome. Finally, see that each person knows and fulfills his or her specific responsibilities to the group.

4. *Solving a problem takes longer as a group than as an individual.* For many people, one of the major frustrations about group work is the time it takes to accomplish tasks. Not only does a group have to find a time and place where everyone can meet (sometimes a serious problem in itself), but a group simply requires more time to define, analyze, research, and solve problems than do individuals working by themselves. It takes time for people to talk and listen to others. Still, such input usually results in a better solution. You have to remind yourself and the group, "If we want a better solution, it is going to take time, patience, and understanding."

If you determine that solving problems in groups takes too much time, you may decide that problems requiring an immediate decision may be better handled by individuals. In the heat of battle, commanders usually do not call for a committee meeting of all their troops. True, the troops may be more satisfied with the decision if they participate in making it, but the obvious need for a quick decision overrides any advantages that may occur from meeting as a group. Thus, though small group communication can be extremely effective, you should also know when it may be more efficient to solve problems individually. Remember that solving problems in groups requires more time.

TYPES OF SMALL GROUPS

So far you have read about the key characteristics of a small group, the importance of studying small group communication, and several advantages and disadvantages of working in groups. Besides understanding what a small group is and why you should study it, you need to keep in mind that small group communication can range from a relatively unstructured, spontaneous discussion of an issue to a more formal, planned presentation.

Groups are formed for several reasons. As you will find in Chapter Three, some groups originate to fulfill our basic needs for association and fellowship. Others are formed to solve a specific problem, to make a decision, or to gather information. To give you an idea of the variety of purposes and formats for group meetings, the following sections will identify several types of groups and three types of public group communication formats.

Primary Groups

In "The Death of the Hired Man," poet Robert Frost mused, "Home is the place where, when you have to go there / They have to take you in." Your family provides one of the best illustrations of a **primary group**, a group whose main purpose is to fulfill the basic need to associate with others. Family communication does not usually follow a prescribed agenda; family conversation is informal. Conversation is also informal within other primary groups, such as informal cliques of friends or workers who interact over an extended period of time. Primary group members associate with one another for the joy of fellowship—to fulfill the basic need to associate with others.

The main task of the primary group is to perpetuate the group so that members can continue to enjoy one another's companionship. Because people want to maintain these ties, they may be eager to conform to the behavior of the group. Teenagers who embrace the latest clothing style or current music group often do so not only because they genuinely enjoy what's currently in vogue but also because they need to fit in with their peers. Primary groups do not meet regularly to make decisions unless a meeting is needed to perpetuate the social patterns of the group. As with any group, some members may assert more influence than others. The key reward of belonging to a primary group, however, is simply the satisfaction of being a member.

Study Groups

As a student, you are no doubt familiar with **study groups**. The primary purpose of these groups is to gather information and learn new ideas. One advantage of participating in a group is that you learn by being involved in a discussion. With several individuals, a study group also has the advantage of sharing a greater amount of information and ideas.

Study groups are not formed just for learning the facts taught in a classroom.

In small groups individuals have access to more information and resources to help them in solving a problem than they would have working alone.

Often members of a study group may try to gather information about particular issues or problems. Their prime purpose is not to solve problems but to research ideas so that others may make informed choices. Staff meetings and briefing sessions are examples of nonclassroom groups in which the primary purpose is to learn and study.

While, strictly speaking, a study group is formed only to learn about a topic, often such groups are formed to promote a particular belief or point of view. Churches, political parties, and organizations that focus on drug or alcohol abuse are examples of organizations that may sponsor study groups to promote changes in attitudes or behavior.

Therapy Groups

A **therapy group,** also called an encounter group or T-group, strives to provide treatment for the personal problems of those who belong to the group. Such groups are led by professionals who are trained to help members overcome, or at least

Problem-solving groups are formed to overcome an obstacle or to resolve an issue, such as the question of how to create a winning play for the sports team shown here.

manage, individual problems in a group setting. Group therapy takes advantage of the self-understanding that members gain as they communicate with others in the group. This is an important reason why group therapy exists. Members learn how they are perceived by others. By participating in a therapy group, people with similar problems can benefit from how others learned to cope. Groups such as Weight Watchers and Alcoholics Anonymous also provide positive reinforcement when members have achieved their goals. By experiencing therapy with others, members of a T-group take advantage of the greater knowledge and information available to the group.

Problem-Solving Groups

A **problem-solving group** exists to resolve an issue or overcome some unsatisfactory situation or obstacle. While the goal of therapy groups and many learning groups is to help the individual, the goal of a problem-solving group is to solve a problem with which the entire group identifies.

Many, if not most, groups in business and industry are problem-solving groups. The typical problem for-profit organizations face is finding a way to make more money. Chapters Seven and Eight will review principles and suggestions for improving your group problem-solving ability.

A **committee** is often formed to solve a problem. A committee is a small group that can be formal or informal. Brilhart and Galanes define a committee as a "small

Types of Small Groups

Group Type	Group Purpose
Primary Group	A group, such as a family, whose main purpose is to fulfill the basic need to associate with others.
Study Group	A group organized to gather information and learn new ideas.
Therapy Group	A group designed to provide treatment to help solve the personal problems of group members; also called encounter group or T-group.
Problem-Solving Group	A group that meets to resolve an issue or overcome an obstacle.
Decision-Making Group	A group whose purpose is to make a choice among several alternatives.

group of people given an assigned task or responsibility by a larger group (parent organization) or person with authority."[13] Most of you have probably sat through meetings of such groups. You may react to serving on a committee negatively; many people do. They regard committee work as time-consuming, tedious, and ineffective—except in increasing the sale of aspirin! Organizations such as schools, churches, businesses, and hospitals often set up committees when they have problems to solve. While they can have several different objectives (to gather information, make decisions, implement policies), committees often attempt to identify or solve a problem. Some committee members are appointed to a **standing committee** (one that remains active for several years); others serve on an **ad hoc committee** (one that disbands when its special task has been completed).

Decision-Making Groups

The task of a **decision-making group** is to make a choice among several alternatives. The group must identify what the possible choices are, discuss the consequences of the choices, and then select the alternative that meets a need or achieves the goal of the group or parent organization. A search committee that screens applicants for a job has the task of making a decision. The group must select one person from among the many alternatives available. A city council that must decide where to build a new airport looks at the alternatives recommended by a consulting firm. The council's job is to choose one site from the several that are recommended.

Decision making is usually a part of the problem-solving process. Groups that have a problem to solve must usually identify several possible solutions and decide on the one that best solves the problem. While all group problem solving involves making decisions, not all group decision making solves a problem.

The most frequently used public group discussion format, a panel discussion is held before an audience in order to help audience members understand an issue or solve a problem.

PUBLIC COMMUNICATION FORMATS

The types of groups discussed thus far may not have audiences listening to their deliberations. Some groups, however, are designed so that others can listen to the discussion. **Public communication formats** help an audience understand all sides of an issue, particularly if individuals with diverse viewpoints are involved in the discussion. The three public communication formats considered in the following sections are **panel discussions, symposium presentations**, and **forum presentations**.

Panel Discussions

A panel discussion is the most frequently used group discussion format. It is usually selected to inform an audience about an issue or a specific problem. A panel discussion is defined as a group discussion that takes place before an audience with the purpose of (1) informing the audience about issues of interest, (2) solving a problem, or (3) encouraging the audience to evaluate the pros and cons of a controversial issue.

An appointed chairperson or moderator usually organizes a panel discussion. The moderator's job is to keep the discussion on track. The moderator usually opens by announcing the discussion question. Most panel discussions include at least three panelists; if they include more than eight or nine panelists, the panelists have difficulty participating equally. Since the panel is presented for the benefit of an audience, organizers should take care that the audience can see and hear the discussion clearly. Panelists usually sit in a semicircle or behind a table. While they should be informed about the subject they will discuss, they should not rehearse their discussion; the conversation should be extemporaneous. Panelists may use notes to help them remember facts and statistics, but they should not use a prepared text.

After announcing the discussion topic, the moderator briefly introduces the panel members, perhaps noting each one's qualifications for being on the panel. To begin the discussion, the moderator may then direct a specific question to one or more panelists. An effective moderator encourages all panelists to participate. If one panelist seems reluctant, the moderator may direct a specific question to that person. If a panelist tends to dominate the discussion, the moderator may politely suggest that other panel members be given an opportunity to participate. Rather than let the discussion continue until the group has nothing more to say on the issue, a specific time limit should be set on the discussion. Most panel discussions last about an hour, but the time limit can be tailored to the needs of the audience and the topic. At the conclusion of the discussion, the moderator may either summarize comments made by the group members or ask another group member to do so. Often, the summary is followed by an invitation to the audience to ask the panel questions.

Symposium Presentations

A symposium is another public discussion format in which a series of short speeches is presented. Usually a central theme or issue pervades all of the speeches. Unlike participants in a panel discussion, participants in a symposium either come with prepared speeches or speak extemporaneously from an outline. The speakers are usually experts who represent contrasting points of view. For example, imagine that your physics instructor has invited four experts in the field of nuclear energy to speak to your class. Each expert has selected a specific aspect of nuclear energy to present. Your instructor will probably give a brief introduction of the speakers and announce the central topic of discussion. The speakers may be asked to address themselves to a discussion question. Then each will speak from eight to ten minutes. The speakers will probably not talk informally between speeches; they will most likely know in advance what general areas the other speakers will discuss. After the speeches, your instructor may summarize the major ideas presented and allow the audience to participate in an open forum.

Public Communication Group Formats

Format	Description
Panel	An unrehearsed discussion that takes place before an audience to inform, solve a problem, or make a decision.
Symposium	A series of short speeches unified by a central theme or issue.
Forum	Audience members are invited to question or respond to a group. Forum presentations frequently follow panel or symposium presentations.

Technically, a symposium is not really a form of group discussion because there is little or no interaction among the participants. But a symposium often concludes with a more informal panel discussion or forum. A major advantage of the symposium lies in the ease of organizing it: Just line up three or four speakers to discuss a designated topic. In addition, when speakers with contrasting viewpoints present their ideas, a lively discussion often follows. Make sure that the speakers know their time limits and address their assigned topics. An able moderator can prevent a symposium from digressing into irrelevant issues. Also announce a time limit for the audience forum following a symposium.

Forum Presentations

Group discussion encourages more interaction and participation than other forms of communication (such as public speaking). A forum presentation takes maximum advantage of the principle that when many people participate improved decisions can result. The word *forum* originated with the Romans. The forum was the public marketplace where Roman citizens could assemble and voice their opinions about the issues of the day. A forum discussion generally follows a panel discussion or symposium. It can also come after a single speaker's presentation. A forum permits an audience to get involved in the discussion. Rather than play a passive role, as they would in a panel discussion, the audience directs questions and responses to a chairperson or to a group of individuals. When holding a news conference, the president of the United States presents a prepared statement, followed by questions and responses from reporters—a forum. Some talk radio stations have forum discussions on issues of the day. Many communities still conduct town meetings in which citizens can voice their opinions about issues affecting the community. The audience in a forum has an opportunity to provide feedback. Comments from audience members can sometimes be used to determine how successfully a speaker or panel enlightened the audience. The questions and responses also give the featured speakers an opportunity to clarify and elaborate their viewpoints.

AN INTRODUCTION TO SMALL GROUP COMMUNICATION: PUTTING PRINCIPLE INTO PRACTICE

Groups are an integral part of society. This chapter has noted why studying small group communication is important. To help summarize how you can apply some of the principles of groups, consider these suggestions:

- Work in small groups to benefit from the knowledge and information that others have but that you lack.
- Work in small groups to take advantage of other members' creative approaches to problem solving and decision making.
- When you want to improve your understanding and comprehension of a subject or issue, form a discussion group and talk about the topic with others.

- If it is important that people are satisfied with decisions that affect them, work in small groups so that they can participate in making decisions. They will be more likely to support the decision if they have an opportunity to contribute to the discussion.
- You can usually learn something about yourself when you work with others in small groups.
- Try not to let others pressure you to conform to the group's majority opinion just for the sake of agreement.
- When working in a small group, don't let one or two members dominate the discussion. If you do, you lose many of the advantages of working in groups.
- Don't fall into the trap of relying too much on other group members. Assume your fair share of the responsibility for getting things done.
- You will probably be less frustrated if you realize that groups take more time to work together to accomplish a task than you do when you work alone.
- There are five types of small groups: (1) primary groups, (2) study groups, (3) therapy groups, (4) problem-solving groups, and (5) decision-making groups.
- If you are given the task of organizing a public group discussion, consider one of the following formats: (1) panel discussion, (2) symposium presentation, or (3) forum presentation.

PRACTICE

Get-Acquainted Activities

The following activities are designed to help you get to know your classmates better. These discussion starters can be used in most small group situations.

Activity 1: If you were in a gift shop, what kind of gift would you buy for the various members of your group to make them feel good about themselves as well as about you? Share with the group. React to the gifts others give you. Try to be honest. Would the gifts really make you feel good about yourself? About them?

Activity 2: Describe the kind of house you think each member now lives in or may live in later. If group members are not married, what kinds of husbands or wives would the members choose? How would they rear their children? What kind of work would they do? What hobbies would they have? How would they entertain themselves? Share with the group. React to others' perceptions of you.

Activity 3: Each member can give a five-minute soliloquy about himself or herself.

Activity 4: Describe to the group what your name means to you.

Activity 5: If members of the group could change their names and be someone else, whom do you think they would choose to be? The figure can be from the past or the present or can be a character from a play or novel. Share with the group. React to others' insights of you. Would you really like to be such a person?

Activity 6: Describe what you do least well. Members take turns. Then describe what you do best.

Activity 7: Try to picture each member of the group at age eight or nine. What kind of person was he or she? Aggressive? Shy? A leader? A follower? It may help to close your eyes and develop a mental image of the person. Share with the group.

Activity 8: Each member of the group should draw or symbolize his or her family tree. Explain how you see yourself in comparison to your mother, father, brother, sister, son, daughter, etc.

Activity 9: Each member of the group should draw or symbolize his or her lifeline. Use symbols and pictures to illustrate your life; symbolize where you have been and where you think you are going.

Agree-Disagree Statements

Read each statement once. Mark whether you agree (A) or disagree (D) with each statement. Take five or six minutes to do this.[14]

_____ 1. A primary concern of all group members should be to establish an atmosphere in which all feel free to express their opinions.

_____ 2. In a group with a strong leader, an individual is able to achieve greater personal security than in a leaderless group.

_____ 3. Often individuals who are part of working groups should do what they think is right regardless of what the groups decide to do.

_____ 4. It is sometimes necessary to use autocratic methods to obtain democratic objectives.

_____ 5. Sometimes it is necessary to change people in the direction you think is right, even if they object.

_____ 6. It is sometimes necessary to ignore the feelings of others in order to reach a group decision.

_____ 7. When leaders are doing their best, one should not openly criticize or find fault with their conduct.

_____ 8. Democracy has no place in a military organization, an air task force, or an infantry squad when actually in battle.

_____ 9. Much time is wasted talking when everybody in the group has to be considered before making a decision.

_____ 10. Almost any job that can be done by a committee can be done better by having one individual responsible for the job.

_____ 11. By the time most people reach maturity, it is almost impossible for them to increase their skills in group participation.

After you have marked the above statements, break up into small groups and try to agree or disagree unanimously with each statement. Try especially to find reasons for differences of opinion. If your group cannot reach agreement or disagreement, you may change the wording in any statement to promote unanimity.

"Group Communication Is . . ."

Scholars have developed various definitions of group communication in order to explain the group communication process. The purpose of this exercise is to allow you to analyze critically different definitions of group communication so that you may more clearly understand the most important components of the group process. The class will divide into groups of five to seven members and do the following:[15]

1. Each group member will choose one of the definitions on pages 3 and 4. Without interacting with other group members, study the definition so that you can explain it clearly to the other members.

2. Name three examples that meet the criterion contained in the definition.

3. Name three examples of two or more people in close proximity who do not meet the criterion contained in the definition. Allow about ten minutes for this part of the exercise.

4. Discuss any changes that you think would improve the definitions you have discussed, and derive your own definition of group communication. Be ready to share it with the rest of the class.

5. Look at the types of groups discussed on pages 12-18 (study groups, therapy groups, problem-solving groups, decision-making groups, panel discussions, symposium presentations, and forum presentations). As a group, decide whether or not each type of group can adequately carry out your group's definition of group communication. Be ready to give reasons for your answer.

6. Now look at the definition on page 5. Does this definition cover the components of group communication that your group believes are important? Discuss any changes you would make, and share them with the rest of the class.

7. After each group has completed its discussion, it should choose a member(s) to read the group's definition in front of the class and state the group's conclusions about the most important components of the group.

Notes

1. Gerald M. Goldhaber, *Organizational Communication,* 5th ed. (Dubuque, Iowa: Wm. C. Brown, 1986), p. 5.

2. John K. Brilhart and Gloria J. Galanes, *Effective Group Discussion,* 6th ed. (Dubuque, Iowa: Wm. C. Brown, 1978), p. 5.

3. Dean C. Barnlund and Franklyn S. Haiman, *The Dynamics of Discussion* (Boston: Riverside Press, 1960), p. 20.

4. R. Victor Hamack, Thorrel B. Fest, and Barbara Schindler Jones, *Group Discussion: Theory and Technique,* 2nd ed. (Englewood Cliffs, New Jersey: Prentice-Hall, 1977), p. 12.

5. Ernest G. Bormann and Nancy Bormann, *Effective Small Group Communication,* 3rd ed. (Minneapolis: Burgess Publishing Company, 1980), p. 15.

6. Marvin E. Shaw, *Group Dynamics: The Psychology of Small Group Behavior,* 3rd ed. (New York: McGraw-Hill, 1981), p. 8.

7. David Potter and Martin P. Anderson, *Discussion in Small Groups: A Guide to Effective Practice,* 3rd ed. (Belmont, California: Wadsworth Publishing Company, 1976), p. 1.

8. Roger K. Mosvick and Robert B. Nelson, *We've Got to Start Meeting Like This! A Guide to Successful Business Meeting Management* (Glenview, Illinois: Scott, Foresman and Company, 1987).

9. *Ibid.*

10. *Ibid.*

11. The discussion of the advantages and disadvantages of working in small groups is based, in part, on Norman R. F. Maier, "Assets and Liabilities in Group Problem Solving: The Need for an Integrative Function," *Psychological Review* 74 (1967): 239–249.

12. Irving L. Janis, "Groupthink," *Psychology Today* 5 (November 1971): 43–46, 74–76.

13. John K. Brilhart and Gloria J. Galanes, *Effective Group Discussion,* p. 4.

14. Developed by Alvin Goldberg, University of Denver.

15. Developed by Cathy Fleuriet, Southwest Texas State University.

——— Chapter Two ———

Small Group Communication Theory

After studying this chapter, you should be able to:

☐ Discuss the nature and functions of both theory and theory construction.

☐ Explain the relevance of theory to the study of small group communication.

☐ Explain the model of small group communication presented in this chapter.

☐ Identify some of the components of small group communication.

☐ Discuss four general theories that apply to small group communication.

"Well it sounds good in theory, but in reality . . ."
"Theoretically speaking . . ."
"Yes, but that's only a theory."

Theory. It is a word people encounter almost daily in their casual conversations, in classrooms, and on news broadcasts. They discuss and evaluate theories of evolution, the theory of relativity, quantum theory, social exchange theory, the continental drift theory. Fictitious criminal investigators on television develop theories about what took place at a crime scene. Psychologists and parents create theories of personality development and theories of child-rearing (in fact, there are practically as many theories of child-rearing as there are parents). In short, theories abound—some are simple, some complex; some are formal, some informal; some are scientific, some unscientific. Yet few people take the time to think about what theory is. What are theories? What good are they? Where do they come from? How are they built? What do people do with them after they've got them?

Many people are intimidated by the word **theory**. To them, studying theory is an esoteric activity that has no real relevance except for the scientist or the academician. Today's students are interested in relevant, practical kinds of knowledge, and seem to assume that theory is neither relevant nor practical. Dance and Larson disagree, claiming that "theorizing is a very basic form of human activity."[1] Theory is *very* practical. Theorizing helps to explain or predict the events in people's lives. On a rudimentary level people theorize when they reflect on their past experiences and make decisions based on these experiences. Theory, then, has two basic functions: to explain and to predict. These functions are discussed more fully later in the chapter.

This chapter examines some of the central issues of group communication theory. First, the discussion of the nature of theory and the theory-building process will be continued. Second, attention will turn to the relevance and practicality of theory in the study of small group communication. Third, four theoretical perspectives for the study of small groups will be discussed. Finally, a theoretical model of small group communication will be presented.

THE NATURE OF THEORY AND THE THEORY-BUILDING PROCESS

Theories are very practical. Suppose, for example, that you do your weekly grocery shopping every Thursday after your late afternoon class. On each visit to the store you are pleased to see that several checkout lanes are open with no lines of people behind any of them. "Ah," you say, "I'll be out of here in short order." With your cart before you, you proceed up one aisle and down the next. To your dismay you notice that each time you pass the checkout lanes, the lines have grown. By the time you have filled your cart, at least six people are waiting in each lane. You now have a twenty-minute wait at the checkout.

If the situation described above were to occur once, you would probably curse your luck and chalk it up to fate. If you find, however, that the same events occur each time you visit the market, you begin to see a consistency in your observations that goes beyond luck or fate. In noticing this consistency, you take the first step in building a theory. You have observed a *phenomenon.* You have witnessed a *repeated pattern* of events for which you feel there must be some *explanation.* So you ponder the situation. In your mind you organize all of the facts available to you: the time of your arrival, the condition of the checkout lanes when you enter the store each time, and the length of the lines when you complete your shopping. Lo and behold, you discover that you have been arriving at the store at approximately 4:45 each afternoon and reaching the checkout lanes about twenty-five minutes later. Between the time you arrive and the time you depart, thousands of workers have headed for home, some of them stopping off at the store on the way. *Voilà*—you have a theory. You have organized your information to explain the phenomenon.

Assuming that your theory is accurate, it is now very useful for you. Having *explained* the phenomenon, you may now reasonably *predict* that under the same set of circumstances events within the phenomenon will recur. In other words, if you continue to do your weekly shopping after your late class on Thursday, you will repeatedly be faced with long checkout lines. Given this knowledge, you can adapt your behavior accordingly, perhaps by doing your shopping earlier or later in the day.

Life is very theory-directed. When you call the weather service to get the latest forecast before an outing, the information you receive is a prediction based on a theoretical explanation of the relationships among various geographic, atmospheric, and astronomic conditions. On a more immediate level your theory about yourself—your **self-concept**—influences the choices you make throughout the day. You tend to do things that you see as being consistent *(predictable)* with your self-concept. In essence, this self-concept or "self-theory" serves to explain yourself to yourself, thereby allowing you to predict your behavior and to successfully select realistic goals. This is theory at its most personal and pervasive.

Theory building is a common, natural process of human communication. You notice consistencies in your experience and examine relationships among the consistencies. You then build an explanation of the phenomenon that allows you to predict future events and, in some cases, to exercise some control over situations. Some theories, of course, are very elaborate and formal, but even in these the fundamental features of explanation and prediction can be seen. In George Kelly's definition of theory we find reference to these features:

A theory may be considered as a way of binding together a multitude of facts so that one may comprehend them all at once. When the theory enables us to make reasonably precise predictions, one may call it scientific.[2]

Theory is crucial to the study of small group communication. The explanatory power of good theory helps make sense of the processes involved when people interact with others in a group. The predictive precision of theory allows people to anticipate probable outcomes of various types of communicative behavior in the group. Armed with this type of knowledge, people can adjust their own communicative behavior to help make group work more effective and rewarding.

THEORY: A PRACTICAL APPROACH TO GROUP COMMUNICATION

As pointed out earlier, the development of theory is a very practical pursuit. Theory, both formal and informal, helps people make intelligent decisions about how to conduct themselves. Working in small groups is no exception. Each person brings a set of theories to small group meetings—theories about herself or himself, about other group members, and about groups in general. Once in the group, people regulate their behavior according to these theories. They behave in ways consistent with their self-concepts. They deal with others in the group according to their previous impressions (theories) of them. If they believe (theorize) that groups are essentially ineffectual, that "a camel is a horse designed by a committee" or that "if you really want something done, do it yourself," then they will probably act accordingly and their prophecy will be fulfilled. If, on the other hand, they come to the group convinced that groups are capable of working effectively, and if they know how to make the group work, they will behave very differently and contribute much more to the group's effectiveness.

Explanatory Function

To be practical, theories of small group communication must suggest ways in which participants can make group discussion more efficient and rewarding. The **explanatory function** of theory is important in this regard. If people understand why some groups are effective while others are not, or why certain styles of **leadership** are appropriate in some situations but not in others, then they are better prepared to diagnose the needs of their own groups. Studying theories of group interaction can help people understand that process and the ways in which different facets of it are related.

Predictive Function

While people derive satisfaction from understanding a process, the **predictive function** of theory is even more useful for them. Consider the hypothetical situation that follows:

The dean of student affairs at your college has become sensitive about reports from students that the activities scheduled for orientation week each year are silly. Specifically, students have been reacting to two of the dean's favorite activities at the first orientation mixer—a pass-the-orange-under-your-chin race and a find-your-own-shoes-in-the-middle-of-the-room relay race. Students claim to feel undignified during these activities, as if they are being treated more as children than as adults. Bewildered, the dean remembers how much the Class of '53 enjoyed these activities and is at a loss about what to do. Therefore, the dean has appointed a group of students to investigate the matter. You are one of those students.

The committee is composed mostly of juniors and seniors. The dean thinks they have been around long enough to know the ropes. As president-elect of next year's sophomore class, you are the youngest of the six committee members. The chairperson is a graduating senior.

At the first meeting you arrive ready to work. The committee is to plan activities that are "more closely aligned with the needs of today's college men and women." You are excited about being a part of a decision-making process that will have a real effect. To your dismay, the other members of the group seem to disregard their task and spend the meeting discussing the prospects for the basketball team, hardly mentioning orientation week activities for next fall. You leave the meeting confused, but hope that the next meeting will be more fruitful. You resolve to take a more active role and to try to steer the meeting more toward the committee's task.

At the second meeting you suggest that the committee really should discuss orientation week. Members concur, then make jokes about past orientation week activities. When the chairperson makes no effort to keep the group on the track, you feel overwhelmed and bewildered.

Many theories, if you were familiar with them, might help you understand what is going on in this group—leadership theories, theories of group growth and development, problem-solving theories, various theories of interpersonal interaction, and so on. Basing your observations on theory, you might say, for example, that your inferior status as the youngest committee member reduces your ability to influence the group process. You might also say that the chairperson's leadership style is inappropriate to the task and situation. You might say that every group goes through an orientation period and that the time spent on trivia is a necessary part of the group process.

All of these theories might be correct to a degree. At least you have a way of describing your group experience systematically. However, you have not met the test of practicality. While understanding a process is satisfying, the more important question is what do you do with your understanding? Once you know something about group communication, how do you use what you know to help the group function more effectively?

In medicine a diagnosis is useless unless it suggests some course of treatment. Nevertheless, diagnosis—*explanation*—is a necessary first step. *Understanding* the process leads toward ways to *improve* the process, and herein lies the usefulness of the predictive quality of theory. By understanding a specific group and group communication in general, and by being aware of the alternative behaviors that are possible, you can use theory to select behaviors that will help you achieve the goal of your group. In other words, if you can reasonably predict that certain outcomes will follow certain types of communication, you can regulate your behavior to achieve the most desirable results. If, in the example of the dean's advisory committee, participants know that a necessary orientation period is coming to a close and that some task-oriented statements will help the group achieve its goal, they can choose to make such statements. In this way, theory *informs* communicative behavior in small groups. Group members no longer behave randomly; they behave with understanding and purpose.

Some theories presented in this book explain small group phenomena. These descriptive theories are referred to as *process theories.* Other theories, called *method theories,* take a prescriptive approach to small group communication. These how-to-do-it theories are particularly useful in establishing formats for solving problems and resolving conflicts in a group. Both types of theories add to the knowledge and skills that can make you a more effective communicator. The ability to use spoken words, which is the subject of the next section, is central to your effectiveness as a communicator.

THE POWER OF THE SPOKEN WORD

A group cannot function without spoken words; **speech communication** is the vehicle that allows a group to move toward its goals. Spoken words call into being the realities, or potential realities, that they represent. Thus, a verbal description of an idea for a new product at a manufacturing company's board meeting creates a vision of that product for board members. Presented effectively, the description may result in new or changed attitudes and behaviors; the idea may be adopted. Words, then, have the power to create new realities and change attitudes; they are immensely powerful tools. While this may seem obvious, it is a truth that often goes unnoticed. People spend so much of each day speaking, listening, reading, and writing that language seems commonplace to them. It is not. Through language people reduce uncertainty and unravel the immense complexity that is their world.

Uncertainty

Dean Barnlund and others have proposed that the aim of speech communication is to reduce uncertainty.[3] According to this principle, speech communication organizes and makes sense out of all the sights, sounds, odors, tastes, and sensations in the environment. As Barnlund states, "Communication occurs any time meaning is assigned to an internal or external stimulus."[4] Thus, when people arrive at a meeting room and begin to shiver, the sensation brings to their minds the word *cold.* Within themselves, or on an *intrapersonal level,* they have reduced uncertainty about the nature of an experience. The room is too cold. Giving verbal expression to an experience organizes and clarifies that experience.

At the *interpersonal level* of speech communication the reduction of uncertainty principle is even more clearly evident. As you get to know someone, you

To reduce your uncertainty in interacting with people in a new environment, you must get to know others by studying their beliefs, attitudes, and behavior.

progressively discover what it is that makes that person unique. You reduce uncertainty about him or her. By developing an explanation of that person's behavior, you can predict how he or she is likely to respond to future communication and events. You base your predictions on what you know about the person's beliefs, attitudes, values, and personality. In essence, you build a theory that allows you to explain another person's behavior, to predict that person's future responses, and to control your own communicative behavior accordingly. In other words, theories help reduce people's uncertainty about others.

Complexity

Getting to know someone is a process of progressively reducing uncertainty—and a lot of uncertainty exists, especially at the outset of a relationship. Think back to your first day at college or to your first day in group communication class. You were probably surrounded by many unfamiliar faces. At times such as these, you feel tentative and think "What am I doing here?" and "Who are all of these other people?" Your feelings of uncertainty soar. You encounter a person you find attractive in the cafeteria line. You say, "Hi! Are you a freshman? What do you think of school so far?" This takes a bit of courage because you don't know what kind of response you will get. So you are tentative. You make small talk and look for signs in the other person's behavior that might indicate whether that person desires further communication. You communicate, observe the response, and base further communication on your interpretation of that response. This is a complex process, particularly because both individuals communicate, observe, respond, and interpret simultaneously!

The process's complexity creates uncertainty. Many communication theorists have noted that whenever an individual communicates with another person at least six people are involved: (1) who you think you are, (2) who you think the other person is, (3) who you think the other person thinks you are, (4) who the other person thinks he or she is, (5) who the other person thinks you are, and (6) who the other person thinks you think he or she is. All six of these people influence and are influenced by the communication—a very complex matter indeed, and one that contributes to people's uncertainty about interpersonal relationships. Nevertheless, people persist in communicating and find that, on the interpersonal level, communication reduces their uncertainty about others.

Small Groups: More Complexity and More Uncertainty

If six people are involved when two people interact, how many are involved when eight people interact? Mathematically inclined readers probably already know that the numbers grow exponentially rather than arithmetically with the addition of each new member to a group. When eight people interact, literally thousands of factors influence communication and are influenced by it—factors such as "who I think Ted thinks Sally thinks George is" or "who I think Bonnie thinks Tom thinks I am."

Fortunately, people don't consciously think about all of these factors all of the time. They would be horribly debilitated if they did so. Nevertheless, these dynamics subtly influence people whenever they interact. The number of factors influencing people interacting in groups is staggering.

THEORETICAL PERSPECTIVES FOR THE STUDY OF SMALL GROUP COMMUNICATION

Thus far this chapter has discussed the nature of theory and its relationship to effective small group communication. It has pointed out that certainty and complexity are pervasive characteristics of small groups, while speech communication is the driving force that moves groups toward their goals.

Small group communication theory attempts to explain and predict small group phenomena. Given the complexity of the process and the number of variables that affect small group communication, no single theory can account for all of the variables involved, nor can one theory systematically relate the variables to one another. Therefore, a number of approaches to group communication theory have emerged in recent years. Each seeks to explain and predict group behavior while focusing on different facets of the group process. Individually and in concert,

Table 2-1   Increase in Potential Relationships with an Increase in Group Size

Size of Group	Number of Relationships
2	1
3	6
4	25
5	90
6	301
7	966

Reprinted from "A Quantitative Analysis of Intragroup Relationships" by William M. Kephart, *American Journal of Sociology* 60 (1950), by permission of The University of Chicago Press.

these theories provide insight into the subject. Four of these theoretical perspectives are described briefly here: social exchange theory, rules theory, systems theory, and task-contingency theory.

Social Exchange Theory and Small Group Communication

Exchange theory is a simple but powerful attempt to explain human behavior in terms that sound like a blend of behavioral psychology and economic theory. According to this theory, relationships can be described in terms of their rewards and costs, profits and losses. Rewards are pleasurable outcomes associated with particular behaviors; costs include such things as mental effort, anxiety, or even embarrassment.[5] Profit equals rewards minus costs; as long as rewards exceed costs, a relationship remains attractive.

Rewards and costs can take many forms in a group. Fellowship, job satisfaction, achievement, status, and meeting personal needs are all rewards that a group can provide. On the other hand, group work takes time and effort and may be frustrating—all forms of cost. Exchange theory predicts that as long as rewards exceed costs—that is, as long as group membership is profitable—group membership will continue to be attractive.

Small group variables such as cohesiveness and productivity are directly related to how rewarding the group experience is to its members. The basics of exchange theory are useful in their descriptiveness. Keep them in mind as you read the remaining chapters and as you observe working groups.

Rules Theory and Small Group Communication

Rules theory assumes that for successful communication to take place, interactants must share rules that structure communicative behavior. The rules of grammar that order words in a logical sequence are one example. However, people also share rules about how to greet others, how to take turns speaking, and how to be insulting or sarcastic.

Understanding the attitudes of others in a small group helps members work together for a common purpose.

Susan Shimanoff defines a rule as "a followable prescription that indicates what behavior is obligated, preferred, or prohibited in certain contexts."[6] A rule, to be a rule, must be *followable.* This implies that people have a choice about whether or not to follow a rule. If they had no choice, they would be conforming to a law of nature, not a rule. A rule is also *prescriptive;* that is, failure to conform may result in some form of penalty, such as criticism or social ridicule. Furthermore, a rule dictates behavior. It tells people what to do or what not to do, but it does not dictate how people should think, feel, or interpret.[7] Finally, a rule is *contextual.* While some rules are relatively stable (such as the rule that says one should apologize for stepping on someone's toe), others vary from one situation to another.

In groups, rules indicate what behaviors are appropriate or inappropriate. They apply to behaviors that the group wishes to encourage or discourage. Shimanoff suggests that most "rules can be classified in one of seven categories: (1) who says, (2) what, (3) to whom, (4) when, (5) with what duration and frequency, (6) through what medium, and (7) by what decision-procedure."[8] In the literature of group theory and research, rules are usually referred to as *norms,* behaviors that will be considered further later in this chapter.

Systems Theory and Small Group Communication

Perhaps the most prevalent approach to small group communication is that of systems theory. In many respects, systems theory represents the most promising perspective on small group communication because it is flexible enough to encompass the vast array of variables that influence small group interaction.

One way to approach the concept of **system** is to think of your own body. The various organs of your body make up systems (digestive, nervous, circulatory) that, in turn, make up the larger system which is you. Each organ depends on the proper functioning of other organs; a change in one part of the system causes changes in the rest of the system. Furthermore, the physiological system cannot be isolated from the environment that surrounds it; to maintain the proper functioning of your physiological systems, you must adjust to changes outside of the body. A decrease in oxygen at a higher elevation will cause you to breathe more rapidly; a rise in temperature will make you perspire, and so forth. In other words, your body is an *open* system composed of interdependent elements. It receives *input* from the environment (food, air, water), *processes* that input (digestion and oxygenation), and yields an *output* (elimination of waste materials, such as carbon dioxide). Like the human body, a small group is an open system, composed of interdependent variables, that receives input, processes the input, and yields an output.

An Open System. A group does not operate in isolation; it is continually affected by interactions with its environment. New members may join, and former members may leave; demands from other organizations may alter the group's goals. Even the climate may affect the group's ability to work.

Interdependence. The various components of the group process are interrelated in such a way that a change in one component may alter the relationships among all other components. A shift in **cohesiveness** can change the group's productivity level. The loss of a group member or the addition of a new member effects a change felt throughout the system. **Interdependence** in the small group makes the study of small group communication so fascinating and so difficult: None of the variables involved may be understood properly in isolation.

Input Variables. By viewing them as parts of subsystems, the variables of small group communication can be categorized according to the systems theory concept of input, process, and output. Input variables in the small group system include such things as group members and group resources (funds, tools, knowledge, purposes, relationships to other groups or organizations, and the physical environment).[9]

Process Variables. These variables relate to the procedures the group follows to reach its goals. Many of these variables are represented in the model in the next section.

Output Variables. Output variables, the outcomes of the group process, range from problem solutions and decisions to personal growth and satisfaction.

Although systems theory does not explain small group phenomena, it serves as a useful organizational strategy. Indeed, all of the theories identified in this section are incomplete pictures of human behavior. Each does, however, provide insight into the maze of forces that affect small group communication.

The next theory focuses on the relationship between communication and the type of task before a group.

A Task-Contingency Theory of Small Group Communication

Communication scholar Randy Y. Hirokawa is developing a new and promising perspective on small group communication based on a three-factor description of a group's task.[10] His theory grew out of a need to explain inconsistent findings in the research relating communication to group performance. Some studies show that open discussion prior to decision making significantly improves the quality of decisions.[11] However, other studies indicate that groups in which members do not interact or interact only slightly produce decisions that are of equal or even better quality than those of freely interacting groups.[12] Hirokawa found that these inconsistencies may be explained by differences in tasks:

> In general, studies finding communication to be unrelated to group performance have typically utilized *simple, means-independent tasks*—that is, tasks which possess a single correct answer and can be easily and successfully accomplished by competent, informed individuals independent of interaction with other group members. However, studies employing more *complex, means-interdependent, open tasks* (i.e., tasks which do not possess a single, correct answer, and require collaboration and social interaction in order to be successfully completed) have tended to discover that the opportunity for communication is positively related to decision performance.[13]

From this discovery, Hirokawa concluded that the relationship between communication and group performance is a function of the task situation. He identified three facets of that situation: task difficulty, cooperation requirement, and solution multiplicity.

Task difficulty refers to the mental effort required to solve the problem or complete the task. Research suggests that communication in a group is relatively unimportant for success when the task is an easy one but becomes increasingly important for success when the task gets more difficult.

Cooperation requirement is the degree to which success depends on utilizing the resources members bring to a group. For example, effective decision making at the highest level of many corporations is based on interdependence and cooperation among executives from sales, marketing, research and development, manufacturing, and public relations. Each member of the management team has information and expertise that the whole group depends on. As this kind of interdependence increases, the need for communication increases.

Solution multiplicity is the number of available choices that will successfully solve a problem. When a group has only one acceptable solution available to it, communication tends to be less important in arriving at that solution. When a group has many acceptable solutions available to it, however, communication is essential to ensure the group's satisfaction with and support for the final choice.

Using these three facets of a task situation, Hirokawa described eight possible group decision-making scenarios. These are summarized in Table 2-2, along with Hirokawa's summary of the role of communication in each.

This theory is introduced here for several reasons. First, it exemplifies some of the most recent thinking of group communication scholars. Second, it demonstrates how a new theory develops to explain phenomena—in this case, to explain inconsistencies in research findings. Most important, the predictive function of this theory yields not only hypotheses that can be tested in further research but also knowledge that can help you judge how much and what kind of communication is important in different tasks you encounter. In short, it's useful.

A THEORETICAL MODEL OF SMALL GROUP COMMUNICATION

A theoretical model that takes into account sender, receiver, and message variables in a small group would be hopelessly complicated even before it could be designed to include other variables central to the study of small group communication. Students must, then, settle for a less comprehensive model but one that

Table 2-2 Summary of Task Situations

Situation	T.D.	C.R.	S.M.	Role of Communication
1	Low	Low	Low	Announce correct choice; confirm correct choice
2	Low	Low	High	Obtain insights regarding alternative choices and consequences
3	Low	High	Low	Centralize important information; announce correct choice; confirm correct choice
4	Low	High	High	Centralize important information; obtain insights regarding alternative choices and consequences
5	High	Low	Low	Integrate individual competences; develop decision-making strategy; announce and confirm correct choice
6	High	Low	High	Understand problem; obtain insights regarding choices and consequences
7	High	High	Low	Centralize important information; integrate individual competences; develop decision-making strategy; announce and confirm correct choice
8	High	High	High	Centralize important information; understand problem; obtain insights regarding choices and consequences

From R. Y. Hirokawa, "The Role of Communication in Group Decision-Making Efficacy: A Task-Contingency Perspective." Paper presented at the annual meeting of the Central States Speech Association, Schaumberg, IL, April 14–16, 1988.

How well members communicate and assume various required roles in small groups will determine how well the group works toward achieving its goal.

suggests the features and relationships critical to an understanding of small group communication.

Figure 2-1 represents such a descriptive model. This framework depicts small group communication as a constellation of variables, each related to every other. Speech communication—what you say and how you say it—establishes and maintains the relationships among these variables. The model includes only essential variables. This book will present an in-depth discussion of these variables in a later chapter; for now, note the brief discussion that follows.

- *Speech Communication.* Speech communication comprises what people say, how they say it, and to whom they say it. This is the primary object of study in small group communication research.
- *Leadership.* In Chapter One, part of the definition of small group communication concerned mutual influence. Leadership refers to behavior that exerts influence upon the group.
- *Goals.* All groups have goals. A goal may be to provide therapy for members, to complete some designated task, or simply to have a good time. Individual group members also have goals. Often individual goals complement the group goal; sometimes, though, they do not.
- *Norms.* Norms are rules that establish which behaviors are permitted or encouraged within the group and which are forbidden or discouraged. Every

Figure 2-1   Constellation of Variables in Small Group Communication

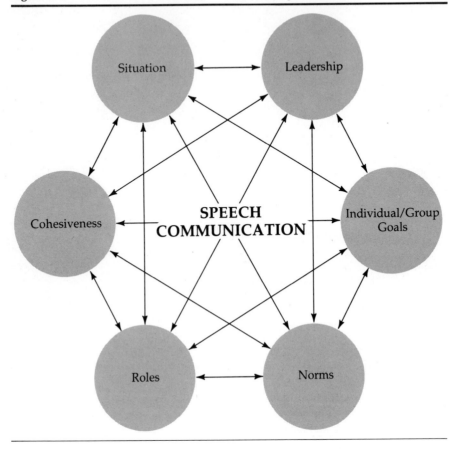

group, from your family to the president's cabinet, develops and maintains norms or rules. Some norms are formal, such as when a group uses parliamentary procedure. Others are informal, such as when a group always begins meetings fifteen minutes late.

- *Roles.* Roles are sets of expectations people hold for themselves and for others in a given context. Different people play different roles in different groups. Researchers have identified several roles that need to be filled in order for a small group to reach maximum satisfaction and productivity.

- *Cohesiveness.* Cohesiveness is the degree of attraction group members feel toward one another and toward the group. Feelings of loyalty help unite the group.

- *Situation.* The context in which group communication occurs is of paramount importance. The task situation is significant, but many other important situational variables exist, such as group size, the physical arrangement of group members, the location or setting, the group's purpose, even the amount of stress placed on the group by time constraints or other internal or external pressures. Each of these situational variables will be examined later in the book.

Small group communication theory seeks to explain the relationships among these and other variables and to make predictions based on such explanations. Thus, the theories presented in this book help eliminate most of the complexity and uncertainty that surface at every level of group interaction.

SMALL GROUP COMMUNICATION THEORY: PUTTING PRINCIPLE INTO PRACTICE

Theorizing is a basic form of human activity, not an esoteric endeavor reserved for scientists and academicians. The theories discussed throughout this book explain consistencies in communicative behavior that researchers have observed within small groups. If people can attain a theoretical grasp of small group communication, they can more successfully predict and control their behavior.

At the present, no single theory of small group communication systematically relates all of the major variables involved. However, each theory presented in this book adds insight and power to influence the process. In this chapter, for example, the discussion of exchange theory explains that members are more likely to be satisfied if the rewards the group provides exceed the costs of membership in the group. This knowledge can help people to seek ways of identifying and maximizing the rewards and minimizing the costs of membership in a group. Likewise, Hirokawa's explanation of the relationship between communication and group performance can help members adopt the type of communication most effective in each task situation.

As you read through the book continue to look for ways to apply what you're learning. The power of good theory is in the way it guides effective behavior.

PRACTICE

1. Make a list of informal theories you have about an ordinary day (e.g., Professor X is boring, I'm afraid of speaking in class, etc.). On what basis did you formulate these theories? How do they affect your behavior? What might cause you to alter these theories?
2. Make a list of your beliefs about working in small groups. How do these beliefs affect your behavior in small groups?
3. Based on your experience in groups and the model presented in Chapter Two, make predictions about how changes in one facet of small group communication affect the other facets.

4. What areas of uncertainty can you identify within the small group context? How does communication function to reduce uncertainty in these areas?

5. The purpose of small group communication theory is to explain and predict small group phenomena. This exercise attempts to relate each of the theories discussed in this chapter (i.e., social exchange theory, rules theory, systems theory, task-contingency theory) to a specific group communication situation so that you may more clearly understand how theory can explain everyday communication.

The following procedure will be used:[14]

a. The class will divide into groups of five to seven members.

b. Each group will choose one of the theories outlined in this chapter and discuss it until each member is comfortable with the theory's meaning.

c. As a group, think of an example of a specific group communication situation where the theory could appropriately explain the group interaction. For example, rules theory may appropriately explain a newly formed group where members have never met. The group situation may be a meeting to plan a school social event.

d. After the group communication situation has been chosen, members may share ideas as to how the communication theory explains the group communication situation your group has outlined.

e. After the group has accomplished this task, members should discuss the following questions: Do you think the theory could explain all group communication situations? Why or why not? What are the strengths of the theory? The weaknesses?

f. Relate your findings to the group communication model shown on page 38. What aspects of the model relate directly to the theory your group has discussed? Choose members of your group to be ready to explain your findings to the class.

g. After all groups have concluded their discussion on theory, each group may explain the theory to class members and answer any questions that the class may have.

Notes

1. Frank E. X. Dance and Carl E. Larson, *The Functions of Human Communication: A Theoretical Approach* (New York: Holt, Rinehart & Winston, 1976), p. 4.

2. George A. Kelly, *A Theory of Personality: The Psychology of Personal Constructs* (New York: W. W. Norton & Company, 1963), p. 18.

3. Dean Barnlund, *Interpersonal Communication: Survey and Studies* (Boston: Houghton Mifflin Company, 1968).

4. Dean Barnlund, "Toward a Meaning Centered Philosophy of Communication," in Johnson et al., (eds.), *Nothing Never Happens* (Beverly Hills: Glencoe Press, 1974), p. 213.

5. Stephen W. Littlejohn, *Theories of Human Communication* (Belmont, California: Wadsworth Publishing Company, 1989), p. 185.

6. Susan B. Shimanoff, *Communication Rules: Theory and Research* (Beverly Hills: Sage Publications, 1980), p. 57.

7. Littlejohn, *Theories of Human Communication,* p. 63.

8. Susan B. Shimanoff, "Group Interaction via Communication Rules," in R. S. Cathcart and L. A. Samovar (eds.), *Small Group Communication,* 5th edition (Dubuque, Iowa: Wm. C. Brown, 1988), p. 50–62.

9. John K. Brilhart, *Effective Group Discussion,* 5th edition, (Dubuque, Iowa: Wm. C. Brown, 1986), p. 26.

10. Randy Y. Hirokawa, "The Role of Communication in Group Decision-Making Efficacy: A Task-Contingency Perspective." Paper presented at the annual meeting of the Central States Speech Association, Schaumberg, Illinois, April 14–16, 1988.

11. Brant Burleson, B. J. Levine, and Wendy Samter, "Decision-Making Procedure and Decision Quality," *Human Communication Research* 10 (1984): 557–574.

12. J. E. McGrath, *Groups: Interaction and Performance* (Englewood Cliffs, New Jersey: Prentice-Hall, 1984).

13. Randy Y. Hirokawa, p. 7.

14. Developed by Cathy Fleuriet, Southwest Texas State University.

—— Chapter Three ——

Group Formation

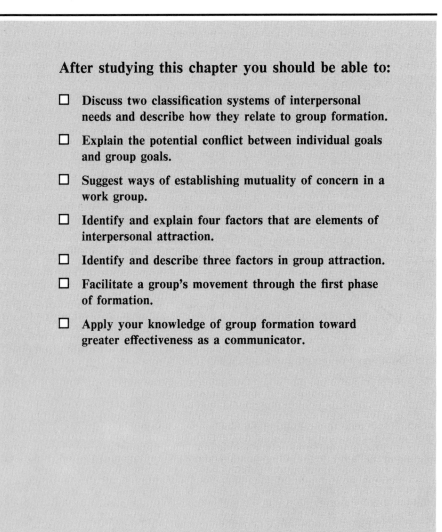

After studying this chapter you should be able to:

☐ Discuss two classification systems of interpersonal needs and describe how they relate to group formation.

☐ Explain the potential conflict between individual goals and group goals.

☐ Suggest ways of establishing mutuality of concern in a work group.

☐ Identify and explain four factors that are elements of interpersonal attraction.

☐ Identify and describe three factors in group attraction.

☐ Facilitate a group's movement through the first phase of formation.

☐ Apply your knowledge of group formation toward greater effectiveness as a communicator.

Are you considering or being considered for membership in any particular group right now? A fraternal organization? A sports club? A political action group? Are you thinking about getting married? Granted, a marriage starts with only two people, but it has a way of becoming a group of three or more.

To which groups do you already belong? Can you identify a circle of friends you might refer to as "your group"? Do you belong to clubs? Teams? You can probably generate a rather long list of groups, from the past and in the present, to which you belong. From the moment you are born into your first group, your family, you belong to a succession of groups. Some are formally organized, some are loosely structured; some you choose; others you are assigned to. But *membership in groups does not happen randomly.* Groups meet specific needs and perform special functions. To understand group formation, then, requires that you examine the needs and functions around which groups form.

Upon learning of the plans for this book, a friend remarked, "I don't know how you can even stand to think about it. I hate committee work. I'll do anything I can to avoid working in groups. I'd rather do things my own way." This fairly prevalent attitude toward groups ignores the pervasive influence that groups have on people's lives (discussed in Chapter One). When asked if there wasn't at least one group in his life that provided him with some pleasure, the friend faltered, "There is my bowling team . . . and, come to think of it, I enjoyed working with a group of political strategists in the last election. My religion and human rights discussion group at the church is pretty interesting, . . . and of course there is my family." He added, "But there's a difference between *those* groups and the committees I have to serve on as part of my job." Although this person might be in the wrong job, groups people choose to belong differ from those they are assigned to. Even the groups and committees people are assigned to at work or in school are the result of choices they have made. Professors do not enjoy every university committee they are required to serve on, but these committees are a part of the larger group that they *did* choose—the academic community. You may not have selected the group you work with in class, but you *did* select that class. Therefore, it is safe to say that all of the groups people belong to reflect *personal decisions.* Some groups they chose directly; others resulted from prior choices they made.

WHY DO PEOPLE JOIN GROUPS?

Understanding the many reasons that draw people to groups can help explain the complexity of small group interaction. Groups are many things to many people. To one member of a committee the group's problem is an exciting vehicle toward greater self-understanding. To another member it is merely an uninteresting but necessary obstacle on the way to reaching a personal goal. These individuals differ dramatically in their motivation for joining the group and in their commitment and contribution to it. This chapter will first examine the needs and goals that lead individuals to join small groups; then it will explore the impact of these needs and goals on small group communication.

The answer to the question "Why do people join groups?" has many dimensions. These dimensions can be placed into several broad categories: (1) **interpersonal needs**, (2) individual goals, (3) group goals, (4) interpersonal attraction, and (5) group attraction.

INTERPERSONAL NEEDS

Maslow's Hierarchy

Abraham Maslow asserts that all humans have basic needs and that these needs can be arranged in a hierarchy; that is, people do not concern themselves with higher-level needs until lower-level needs are satisfied.[1] Maslow termed the two levels of needs at the bottom of the hierarchy *physiological needs* and *safety needs.* People's physiological needs are for air, water, and food. Their safety needs are for security and protection. Maslow called these two levels *survival needs;* satisfaction of these needs is necessary to basic human existence. During childhood years the family satisfies these needs.

Once survival needs are fulfilled, the higher-level needs that Maslow called *psychological needs*—the need to belong, the need for esteem, and the need for self-actualization—become more important. These needs may affect people's group memberships throughout their lives. See Figure 3-1 to understand how interpersonal needs form a hierarchy.

Belongingness Need. Maslow posits that once people have satisfied their basic survival, physiological, and safety needs, they turn their attention to a social or belongingness need. People need to feel that they are a part of some group. Here again, the family provides a sense of belonging for children, but as they get older they begin to look outside the family to satisfy this need. Peer groups gain importance during adolescence. Think about the "in" group and the "out" group in high school. At that time, people's need for affiliation was at its strongest. To be a social pariah seemed a fate worse than death. Consequently, teams, clubs, and cliques take care of this need for teenagers.

Figure 3-1   Maslow's Need Hierarchy

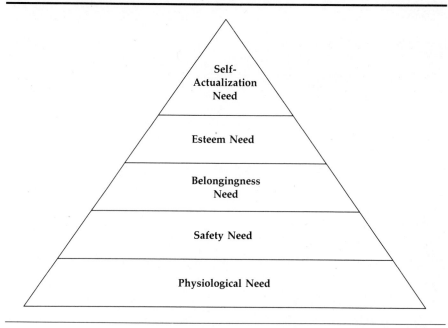

Self-
Actualization
Need

Esteem Need

Belongingness
Need

Safety Need

Physiological Need

Esteem Need. Once people have developed a sense of belonging, Maslow says that they have a need for respect or esteem. They need to feel not only that they are accepted, but also that they are worthwhile and valued by others. People cannot, of course, receive this positive feedback from others if they are isolated. They need a group of people whose opinions they value to tell them they're OK.

Self-Actualization Need. Finally, Maslow says that people have a need for self-actualization. This need differs from the first four needs. The former needs Maslow calls "deficiency needs" because individuals perceive them as a void to fill by drawing on the resources of other people. Maslow calls self-actualization a "being" need. Basically, it involves people trying to be all that they can be and living life to its fullest potential. Having taken care of deficiencies by drawing on others, people are ready to give of themselves. They are ready to function as autonomous beings, operating independently in quest of their own full potential. They no longer need groups to take care of their deficiencies; instead, they need groups in which to find and express their wholeness. While this need level is, perhaps, the most difficult to grasp conceptually, Maslow's hierarchy is consistent: People need groups to satisfy interpersonal needs. People also clearly differ from one another in their motivations for joining groups. Their differing motivations may be reflected in their communicative behavior in the group. Those who simply want to belong may interact differently from those who need the group's esteem and respect.

Groups usually form because the individuals comprising them share similar goals; in groups they find a way to meet their interpersonal needs.

Schutz's Theory

In an elaborate theory of interpersonal behavior, William Schutz suggests that three basic human needs influence individuals as they form and interact in groups. These needs are **inclusion, control**, and **affection**.[2]

Inclusion Need. Just as Maslow postulates in his belongingness need, Schutz says people join groups to fulfill their need for inclusion. They need to be recognized as unique individuals and need to feel understood. When people try to understand someone it implies that the individual is worthy of their time and effort. In this respect, Schutz's inclusion need is also related to Maslow's esteem need.

Control Need. The need for control is a need for status and power. People need to have some control over themselves and over others and, sometimes, to give others some control over them, such as when they seek guidance and direction.

REVIEW BOX:

Maslow's Hierarchy of Interpersonal Needs

Survival Needs

physiological needs: the fundamental needs for air, water, and food

safety needs: the need for security and protection

Psychological Needs

belongingness need: the need to feel part of some group

esteem need: the need to feel worthwhile and valued by others

self-actualization need: the need to realize one's full potential; groups are seen as arenas for expressing personal wholeness rather than means for making up deficiencies

---

Affection Need. The need for affection drives people to give and receive emotional warmth and closeness. Individuals' needs for inclusion, control, and affection vary, but groups provide them settings in which such needs can be satisfied.

In a broad sense, groups are more than collections of people with common goals; they are arenas in which individual needs are satisfied or frustrated. Schutz asserts that people join groups to satisfy needs for inclusion, control, and affection and that these needs influence group process throughout the life of the group. He has observed that in the initial stages of group formation, communication aims primarily toward inclusion needs. Group members are friendly but cautious as they try to evaluate one another and try to be accepted by other members. As the group develops, control needs become more evident: members contest issues and vie for leadership. Schutz observes that as conflicts are resolved people turn toward affection needs. Members characteristically express positive feelings in this phase. The progression, Schutz says, is cyclical.

Continuing Cycle of Group Process. From Schutz's perspective group formation is a process not limited to the initial coming together of the group. Rather, formation patterns repeat themselves as the group develops over time. Group decision making involves a series of smaller decisions on the way toward achieving the group's primary goal. For example, a group of engineers planning a bridge must make decisions about the location and frequency of their meetings as well as the design and materials for the bridge. A group progresses through developmental phases throughout its life (as will be discussed in Chapter Seven), and this cyclical pattern of formation and reformation occurs whenever the group approaches each new meeting and each new decision. If this process could be visualized it might look something akin to a large jellyfish moving through the water. The jellyfish floats in the water in a relatively disorganized state until it needs to move forward; then it organizes itself, contracts, and propels itself through the water until it

People often form groups simply because they enjoy the same activities, as do the crew members of the racing yacht shown here.

returns to a restful, less organized state. Group process moves through a similar series of contractions until it reaches its ultimate goal.

A group is defined, in part, by a common purpose. Within that purpose are several smaller goals. As a group reaches each of these goals, it momentarily loses a bit of its definition until a new goal replaces the old. As people accomplish each new goal, they begin a new cycle of inclusion, control, and affection behaviors. Following is an example:

Harv:	Well. It's been hard, but we've finally found a date for the banquet that we can all agree on.
Juanita:	For sure. For a while I thought we'd never agree but I think we've made the best decision now.
Betsy:	Yeah. We're over the major hurdle. Feels good, doesn't it?
Phil:	Amen. We're organized now and ready to go for it! This is getting to be fun.
	(Laughter, followed by a pause)
Juanita:	Well, here we are. What do we do next?
Phil:	I guess we ought to talk about the theme and the speakers.

Harv: Hold on there! The speakers are irrelevant if no one is there to hear them. We've got to talk first about how we're going to publicize.

Phil: C'mon, Harv. How can we publicize if we don't even have a theme?

Betsy: Here we go again.

In this example you can see the end of one cycle and the beginning of the next. Members expressed positive feelings about the group and its accomplishments and halted a little in their conversation before regrouping for another attack on a new facet of their problem. The sense of cohesiveness peaks during the affection phase and then falls off, only to rebuild around the next task. Like the jellyfish, which coordinates its processes around its task of propulsion, the small group does not end up back where it started. The whole process moves forward. To say that the phases are cyclical, then, is somewhat misleading. Certain types of communicative behaviors recur, but the whole process moves forward. Frank E. X. Dance captured the essence of this process when he described human communication as being like a helix.[3] Like a bedspring, the helix is both linear and circular. It turns in on itself and yet always moves forward. Seen in this light, group formation does not cease but pulses throughout the life of the group.

INDIVIDUAL GOALS

Theories of interpersonal needs provide some of the psychological bases for group formation. So, too, do individual goals. Goals have a more tangible and obvious effect on people's selection of group memberships. What is it that you want out of life? Prestige? Status? Power? Anonymity? Recreation? Education? Personal growth? In other words, what goals do you have that exist apart from any particular group membership?

Individual goals are instrumental in determining which groups people join. Obviously, if people enjoy arranging flowers and wish to improve their skills, they may join garden clubs. If personal growth is an aim, people will join a T-group or encounter group. If they desire status and power they will seek a group that they think will bring such status and power. Sometimes the prestige associated with a particular group is enough to make membership attractive to some people. This is often a motivation for joining a particular sorority or fraternity. Whatever their individual goals may be, people bring those goals with them when they join groups.

GROUP GOALS

Group goals are identifiable goals that transcend the group members' individual goals. Certain professional and fraternal organizations serve community needs. For example, the Lions Club is well-known for its contributions toward finding cures for eye diseases and preventing blindness. Individual members have many different goals for joining the club: the chance to rub elbows with other professionals from the community, camaraderie and fellowship, the prestige of membership, the sense of belonging, or the genuine interest in serving the community. While individual goals may vary, the group goal takes precedence over them.

Of course, somewhere along the way an individual or small group of individuals proposed the group goals, which suggests some initial commonality of purpose among individual goals. Once individuals adopt group goals, however, their individual goals are superceded. The many needs and goals that individuals bring to small groups may be incompatible with the group's goal. This is a potential source of problems in small group communication. Consider the following situation:

The First Church in the town of Roseville has a Building and Grounds Committee. This committee, charged with overseeing the regular maintenance and upkeep of the church building and surrounding property, makes sure that the lawns are mowed, the hedges trimmed, the furnace maintained, the roof patched, and so forth. The committee consists of the following members:

Robert Bomblast. Robert has been an accountant for a local firm for twenty-three years. He has always felt that his firm has never given him a chance to show his true leadership ability. He sees this committee, of which he is chairperson, as his big chance to prove himself and show the world what a truly fine administrator he is. He has another ulterior motive: He wants very much to be the new part-time business manager for the church when "Old George," the present manager, dies or becomes too senile to do the job. This committee, then, is Robert's stepping-stone to greatness.

"Marmalade." No one is sure of "Marmalade's" real name. Found ten years ago wandering around the sanctuary saying, "Wow . . . wow . . . wowwwww . . . wowwwwwwwww," he is your basic burnout. The church members took him under their wing. He has been sweeping floors and doing other odd jobs around the church since that time. The pastor thought it would "do Marmalade some good" to get involved with a responsible committee, so he assigned him to this one.

Polly Prim. Polly is the president of Roseville's Garden Club. She has been complaining that the landscaping around the church "lacks imagination." She has struggled for the last three years trying to get on the committee. Finally, she is on it.

Merry Midwest. In all of her forty-seven years, Merry has not been outside of her home state. She loves her country, her state, her community, her home, and her family. She especially loves her church because of the sense of warmth and community she feels there. She has served on every committee in the Church and when she is not serving on a committee she misses a sense of fellowship. Merry has high needs for inclusion. She is pleased to be on this committee.

Thurman Jester. Ever since his vacation trip to Dallas, Thurman wears a white belt and off-white shoes to work every day (and strongly urges his employees at the insurance office to do the same). He is committed to keeping up with the trend setters, and Dallas, he feels, is where trends are set. Thurman was also impressed by a forty-foot neon cross he spotted outside a church in Dallas. Thurman is highly motivated by control needs.

Imagine that this group has come together for its first monthly meeting, that the church custodian has just resigned, and that the roof of the church leaks. The group's goal is to maintain the building and grounds. All of the members are, to some degree, committed to the goal. However, this commitment means different things to different members. An individual need or goal shapes each person's perception of what the group should be doing. Group members are aware of their personal goals, but most members are not aware that their behavior is motivated by desires to satisfy interpersonal needs. Merry Midwest may interpret her own behavior as a desire to serve, while her underlying, unconscious motive may be her need for inclusion. Thurman Jester wants to put a neon cross outside the church, but he may not be aware of his need to control others.

Needs and goals influence individuals' perceptions of group members and the group's task. Some individual goals are likely to overlap with group goals, while other individual goals will emerge from the group's focus. If a group goal is the desired end result of a group, and an individual goal is the desired end result of an individual, then individual and group goals will likely overlap in any given group. Differences between these goals may help or hinder the group. The conflict between individual and group goals is often the reason why some groups can't get off the ground.

Returning to the example of the church committee, try to imagine what the first meeting or two might be like. Even better, ask some friends or classmates to play the roles of the various characters: Each has a personal agenda—an individual goal—that will have a profound effect on his or her behavior in the group. Robert seeks personal gain; "Marmalade" is unpredictable; Polly will attempt to get the committee busy on landscaping projects; Merry just wants to feel a part of something; and Thurman wants to make his mark on the world with a forty-foot neon cross. Each of these characters will direct his or her communication in the group toward a particular goal; but none of their five goals is compatible with the more immediate need for fixing the leaky roof and hiring a new custodian. While all the characters have come together ostensibly for the same purpose, each has a different idea of what the group should be doing. If each member pulls in a different direction, the results could be disastrous. The group may go nowhere, and, to compound matters, each member will probably perceive the others as being un-cooperative. For this reason, groups must question their members' **mutuality of concern**—the degree to which members share a concern for a group's task needs—during the initial stages of group formation.

Establishing Mutuality of Concern

When people join groups they often assume that other group members share their commitment to their group's task. If a problem is to be solved they take for granted that others view the problem in much the same way they do. However, as in the earlier example of the building and grounds committee, each person may view the problem differently. Many small groups function poorly because they begin to propose solutions before they have defined the problem to everyone's mutual satisfaction. Chapter Eight will explore this further.

Groups can also be frustrated because people bring different levels of commitment or concern to them. Suppose that you have been appointed to a student government group whose task is to recommend whether your college should institute a plus/minus grading system or continue with a straight A,B,C, and D grading policy. If you are a freshman or sophomore, this policy change could have a direct effect on your grade point average over your four years in college. If you are a graduating senior, a policy change would have little or no effect on you. Hence the level of concern over the problem can vary from member to member. Once again, individual goals interact with a group goal. Those affected directly by the problem will probably become more active in the group than those who are not as concerned with the problem. This can lead to needless conflict, as when some members resent having to carry the bulk of the work load.

The degree to which members are concerned with the group's task needs to be clarified at the outset. Each group member should state clearly her or his personal needs and goals regarding the topic area. Patton and Giffin make some suggestions about how to begin this process in your group:

> To clarify a mutual concern with others you start with tentative, trusting behavior, clearly stating your personal view of the situation and how you feel about it. Your comment may be something like this: "I see a need to reconsider course requirements for the English major, and I feel this need is very important." The keynote elements are "I see . . ." and "I feel. . . ." These elements indicate a personal viewpoint (not the only possible viewpoint) and signify that another group member may see or feel differently.
>
> At this stage your interpersonal manner, way of stating your viewpoint and attitude toward other members can indicate a good, or poor, understanding of this phase of the decision-making process. You must state clearly and honestly your viewpoint and your feelings; by all means be genuine and sincere. But show your expectation that others in the group will do the same, comfortably disagreeing as necessary. Your manner of stating your viewpoint and feelings should be genuine and honest, but it should deliberately and overtly tell other members you can tolerate expressed differences of viewpoints or feelings when they state their position.
>
> As each group member in effect says "This is the way I see it . . ." and "This is how I feel about it . . . ," the nature and degree of common concern can be diagnosed. If honesty prevails, it will become apparent whether a group can work well together on the problem previously thought to be of mutual concern. All members must be prepared to discover that others do not share their view and concern. In fact, it may be discovered that there is no common concern at all. In such case it is better to discover this early than late; it can save time, energy and, possibly, interpersonal emotional wear and tear.[4]

While individual needs and goals may bring a group together in the first place, they can also break a group apart. The success or failure of a group depends, in part, on the degree to which its goal is assumed by individuals as their own. Unsatisfied or unclarified individual needs and goals can become hidden agendas—goals individuals work toward while seeming to work toward the group goal. Such hidden agendas can be extremely disruptive to the group. Establishing mutuality of concern can help reduce this disruptive influence.

In any given situation the interaction of individual and group needs will cause one of four possible outcomes:

> (1) Individual and group needs may be so diverse that they interfere with each other with no positive effects accruing either to individuals within the group or to the group as a whole. (2) Group interaction may result in the realization of goals desired by the group as a whole, while individuals needs are not met. (3) Individual needs may be realized by one or more group members to the detriment or destruction of the group. (4) Individual and group needs may blend so completely that the needs realized by the group as a whole are the same needs individuals wish to realize.[5]

In the ideal, fully integrated group this fourth alternative is realized. Mutuality of concern can merge individual and group needs and goals.

Aside from the relationships among interpersonal needs, personal goals, and group goals, two other factors have an influence on people's selection of groups: interpersonal attraction and group attraction.

INTERPERSONAL ATTRACTION

Often people are attracted to groups because they are attracted to the people who compose them. While many factors influence interpersonal attraction, four of these are especially significant: similarity, complementarity, proximity/contact/interaction, and physical attractiveness.

Similarity

One of the strongest influences in interpersonal attraction is **similarity**. Remember your first day on campus? That feeling of newness, strangeness, and aloneness? You needed a friend, and you probably found one. Who did you look for to be your friend? Did you seek out someone you perceived to be very different from you? Probably not. If the principle of similarity in interpersonal attraction applies here, you probably looked for someone to talk to who appeared to be in the same situation—another lonely newcomer, or perhaps someone dressed in a style similar to yours.

Who are your closest friends? Do you share many of the same attitudes, beliefs, and values? Do you enjoy the same activities? More than likely you do. People are often attracted to those they consider to be like them. A probable explanation for this is that similar backgrounds, beliefs, attitudes, and values make it easier to understand one another—and all people like to feel that they are understood.

Complementarity

In reading the previous section on similarity, some of you probably shook your heads and said to yourselves, "No, that's not the way it is at all. My best friend and I are about as similar as an orchid and a fire hydrant!" No generalization is entirely true, and so it is with the principle of similarity. While there is some truth to the statement that birds of a feather flock together, it is also true that opposites attract. Thibaut and Kelley suggest that some interpersonal relationships are based primarily on similarity, while others are based on **complementarity**.[6] At times people may be attracted to others who exhibit qualities that they do not have but that they admire. While the principle of similarity seems to be the more pervasive phenomenon, everyone can cite instances of complementarity. For at least a partial explanation of attraction through complementarity, consider Schutz's theory of interpersonal needs, discussed earlier in this chapter. According to Schutz's theory, a person who has a high need to control would be most compatible with a person who has a high need to be controlled. The same would be true of needs to express and to receive inclusion and affection. These are complementary needs rather than similar needs.

Proximity/Contact/Interaction

You tend to be attracted to people who are physically close to you, who live and work with you, and whom you see and talk with often. If you know that you have to live or work close to another person, you may ignore that person's less desirable traits in order to minimize potential conflict. Furthermore, proximity, contact, and interaction breed familiarity, and familiarity has a positive influence on interpersonal attraction.[7] Interaction with another person helps you get to know that other person, and through this process the two of you may uncover similarities and discover ways in which you can satisfy each other's interpersonal needs. The actual physical distance between people, then, does not influence attraction, but the interpersonal possibilities illuminated by proximity, contact, and interaction do.

Physical Attractiveness

At least in the initial stages of interpersonal attraction, physical attractiveness influences people. If a person is physically beautiful, others tend to want to affiliate with that person.[8] However, evidence indicates that this factor diminishes in importance over time and that physical beauty is more important to males than to females.[9]

In sum, people seem to be attracted to others who are likely to understand them, who can fulfill their needs, who may complement their personalities, and who are physically appealing. Those individuals constitute a powerful influence on people's selection of groups.

"*Tom Willoughby, meet Howard Sylvester—one of us.*"

Drawing by Bernard Schoenbaum; © 1977 The New Yorker Magazine, Inc.

GROUP ATTRACTION

While individuals may be attracted to a group because they are attracted to the members who compose it, they may also be attracted to the group itself. Such attraction usually focuses on the group's activities, goals, or simply on the desirability of group membership.

Group Activities

Although research is not extensive in this area, it seems fairly clear that people who are interested in the same activities tend to form groups.[10] People who enjoy intellectual pursuits may join literary discussion groups. Bridge players may join bridge clubs. Beyond these obvious examples, people may be attracted to the activities of a group in a more general sense. Some may join groups simply because they enjoy going to regular meetings and joining in group discussions, regardless of the group's specific aims or goals. The structure and human contact provided by groups are potentially rewarding in and of themselves.

Group Goals

Another factor that may attract people to a group is the goal it meets for. If, for example, people believe that the spread of nuclear power must be curtailed, they may join a group dedicated to such curtailment. If they are committed to preserving and protecting the natural environment, they may join Friends of the Earth, the Sierra Club, the Audubon Society, or any organization that professes a goal similar to their own.

Group attraction includes elements of attraction which have already been mentioned: similarity in interpersonal attraction and the relationship between individual and group goals.

Group Membership

Sometimes it is not the members, activities, or goals of a group that attract people but membership itself. Potential members may perceive that membership in an exclusive club or honor society will bring them prestige, acceptance, or professional benefits outside of the group. For example, his or her superiors may expect a young executive to belong to some civic group because such memberships provide good public relations for the firm.

The need for affiliation—Maslow's belongingness need and Schutz's inclusion need—can make group membership attractive. You probably know of professional committee members who move from group to group because their lives seem incomplete without some type of group membership. The need for affiliation is basic to human nature. Group membership can help satisfy that need.

GROUP FORMATION: PUTTING PRINCIPLE INTO PRACTICE

While interpersonal needs, individual goals, group goals, interpersonal attraction, and group attraction have been treated separately, this book has really been examining an arena where all of these factors come together—the small group. You may have noticed some continuity and intrinsic relationships among the variables described. For example, there is a clear relationship between an individual's need for affiliation and the attractiveness of group membership, just as there is between similarity in interpersonal attraction and the attractiveness of a shared group.

The dynamic interrelatedness of all of the variables that affect small group processes makes the study of small group communication challenging and exciting. As you move through the rest of this book, it is important that you retain what you have previously learned. Only when you've fit all of the puzzle pieces together can you see a clear picture of small group communication.

This chapter has zoomed in on one part of the puzzle: those needs and goals that motivate people to join groups and that influence their behavior within those groups. In the formative, initial stages of group development, uncertainty is at its peak—uncertainty about the group, about its goals, and about people's place in it. How you communicate at this sensitive stage of group development provides the basis for future interaction. As you join new groups, keep in mind the following:

REVIEW BOX

Factors in Interpersonal Attraction

Factors	Definition	Notes/Comments
Similarity	The degree to which two persons are alike.	You tend to like people who resemble you in their thinking and experiences; it's reinforcing, and they are more likely than most to understand you.
Complementarity	The degree to which two persons are compatibly different from each other.	You tend to be attracted to people who possess qualities that you admire but do not yourself possess.
Proximity, contact, and interaction	The actual, physical availability of other people.	Talking with others reveals their similar and complementary traits and, thus, their attractiveness to you.
Physical Attraction	Interpersonal attraction based on perceptions of physical beauty or handsomeness.	Especially important in the early stages of a relationship; less important after you get to know someone.

Factors in Group Attraction

Factors	Definition	Notes/Comments
Group Activities	People interested in the same activities tend to group together.	The mere structure and human contact of group activities may provide rewards.
Group Goals	Attraction based on mutually shared goals.	Civic groups, the PTA, and environmental groups are examples.
Group Membership	Attraction based on the rewards of membership per se.	Membership is often seen as having prestige or status.

- At the first meeting of any new group, individuals feel anxious. Members are often uncertain who the others are, what each person's role is to be, and what to say to whom. At this stage it can be helpful if people share a little information about themselves and encourage others to do the same. Many group leaders will ask the members to say a few words about themselves. This strategy breaks the ice and provides some familiarity on which to base further discussion. In short, it reduces people's uncertainty and helps them relax.

- Sometimes you do not choose the groups you belong to, but are assigned to them, perhaps by a teacher, a supervisor, or an employer. When being assigned to a group damages morale, you need to overcome your resentment, your feeling of being stuck with the group, and the lack of commitment that such situations may foster. To overcome these feelings, your attitude toward the group is critical. The following advice is sound and helpful: When they throw a roadblock in your way, take the obstacle, embrace it, and make it your own; find a way to turn it into a strength. When you are assigned to a group, look carefully at the group's goal. Then assess the resources that you can bring to accomplishing that goal. Evaluate the benefits that you can derive from the experience. Decide what your level of commitment is to the goal and the group. Talk about it with the group, and begin establishing mutuality of concern.

- As people join new groups the question of what brings them to a particular place is one that they often ignore, frequently to the detriment of the group. Individual agendas, hidden or otherwise, can confound the group's progress, unless the agendas are examined openly. The section in this chapter on establishing mutuality of concern is important. Never assume that everyone in your group shares your level of commitment to the group and its task. This area of potential uncertainty needs to be clarified. Failure to do so can lead to the frequent complaint that "a couple of us are doing all the work while others just sit back." One way to overcome this problem, as Patton and Giffin suggested, is to tell the group openly and honesty how you feel about the group and its task, with the clear expectation that others will do the same.

  Of course, you need to ask some questions yourself: "Why am *I* a part of this group? What do *I* want to accomplish here? What are *my* goals? What do I want from these people . . . and what can I give to them?"

- If you ask and answer the questions listed above, you may find that you are attracted to a group because you are attracted to its members. If that is your only attraction, think twice before you join. When a group is dedicated to a common purpose, its members will probably resent someone there for purely social reasons.

In sum, people are attracted to groups for different reasons and join groups to satisfy a variety of needs. An understanding of these factors in group formation should guide your communicative behavior in groups.

PRACTICE

1. Make a list of the groups you are affiliated with. For each one, identify its members, its activities, and its goals. Then note your individual goals in regard to each group. Examine the results. What is your primary attraction to each

group? Are your individual goals compatible with the group's goals? Do you have any hidden agendas? Do your answers to these questions explain any of your attitudes about or behaviors within these groups?

2. Use the First Church case study and play the roles of the committee members. Observe the relationships between individual and group goals.

3. Observe a videotaped group discussion. Periodically stop the tape and identify the phase of the group's cycle (inclusion, control, affection) the group is operating in. What are the verbal and nonverbal cues that lead you to this conclusion? Continue the tape and note the group's strategies for passing from one phase into the next. As the group repeats the cycle can you observe any differences in the members' communicative behavior?

4. This chapter suggests one strategy for establishing mutuality of concern. What are some other strategies that groups could use in order to establish mutuality of concern?

Notes

1. Abraham Maslow, *Toward a Psychology of Being* (Princeton, New Jersey: D. Van Nostrand Company, 1968).

2. William Schutz, *The Interpersonal Underworld* (Palo Alto, California: Science & Behavior Books, 1958).

3. Frank E. X. Dance, "A Helical Model of Communication," in *Human Communication Theory* (New York: Holt, Rinehart & Winston, 1967), pp. 294–298.

4. Bobby Patton and Kim Giffin, *Decision-Making Group Interaction* (New York: Harper & Row, Publishers, 1978), pp. 118–119.

5. Charles S. Palazzo, "The Social Group: Definitions," in Robert S. Cathcart and Larry A. Samovar (eds.), *Small Group Communication: A Reader* (Dubuque, Iowa: Wm. C. Brown, 1988), pp. 11–12.

6. John Thibaut and Harold Kelley, *The Social Psychology of Groups* (New York: John Wiley & Sons, 1959).

7. Robert Zajonc, "Attitudinal Effects of Mere Exposure," *Journal of Personality and Social Psychology* 9 (1968): 1–29.

8. Marvin Shaw, *Group Dynamics: The Psychology of Small Group Behavior* (New York: McGraw-Hill Book Company, 1981), p. 93.

9. D. Krebs and A. A. Adinolf, "Physical Attractiveness, Social Relations, and Personality Style," *Journal of Personality and Social Psychology* 31 (1975): 245–253.

10. Marvin Shaw, *Group Dynamics: The Psychology of Small Group Behavior* (New York: McGraw-Hill Book Company, 1981), p. 85.

Chapter Four

Relating to Others in Small Groups

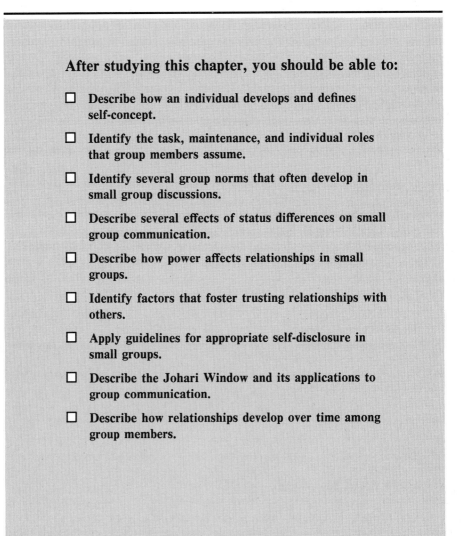

After studying this chapter, you should be able to:

☐ Describe how an individual develops and defines self-concept.

☐ Identify the task, maintenance, and individual roles that group members assume.

☐ Identify several group norms that often develop in small group discussions.

☐ Describe several effects of status differences on small group communication.

☐ Describe how power affects relationships in small groups.

☐ Identify factors that foster trusting relationships with others.

☐ Apply guidelines for appropriate self-disclosure in small groups.

☐ Describe the Johari Window and its applications to group communication.

☐ Describe how relationships develop over time among group members.

$\mathbf{D}$o you consider yourself to be a leader or a follower in small group meetings? Do you usually talk a lot or a little when you serve on a committee? Do you think you are a good or mediocre group member? Perhaps your answers depend on the quality of your relationships with others in the group.

Relationships refer to the feelings, roles, norms, status, and trust that both affect and reflect the quality of communication between you and others. If the members of your group are old friends, your relationships with them will obviously be different than if you have just met for the first time. Have you served on a committee with three or four other people that you felt were much better qualified than you were to contribute to the discussion? Your feeling of inferiority undoubtedly affected your relationship with the other group members.

In small groups, and in other communication contexts as well, the quality of interpersonal relationships often determines what people say to one another.

Relational communication theorists assert that every message people communicate to one another has both a content dimension and a relationship dimension. The content dimension of a message includes the specific information, thoughts, and ideas that are conveyed to someone. The relationship dimension refers to message cues that provide hints about whether you like or dislike the person you are communicating with. For example, the formality of their language and nonverbal cues provide important information about the relationship between two individuals having a conversation. Whether you are giving a public speech, talking with your spouse, or communicating with another member of a small group, you are providing information about the feelings you have toward your listener as well as about ideas and thoughts.

This chapter will emphasize the communication elements that affect the quality of the relationships you establish with other group members. Specifically, it will concentrate on five variables that have an important effect upon the relationships you establish with others in small groups. First, the chapter will discuss how **roles** are formed and how the roles you assume during a group discussion affect your relationships with others. Second, it will discuss the development of group **norms**, or standards, and how they influence your relationships with others in small groups. Third, it will describe how **status** differences in a group can affect interpersonal relationships and have an impact on the quality and productivity of the group's discussion. Fourth, it will consider the **power** some group members have to influence others. Finally, the chapter will discuss trust—how trusting relationships develop and how varying degrees of trust affect group members.

ROLES

Stop reading this chapter for just a moment, and reflect upon this question: Who are you? A simple question, you probably think. Perhaps you took little time to answer it. Maybe you responded by saying your name. Maybe you said you are a student—a label that summarizes your current status. Ask yourself the question again. Get a pencil and write ten different responses.

Who Are You?

1. I am _____
2. I am _____
3. I am _____
4. I am _____
5. I am _____
6. I am _____
7. I am _____
8. I am _____
9. I am _____
10. I am _____

Some of you may not have had trouble coming up with a profile of who you think you are. Others, however, may have more difficulty labeling multiple aspects of **self-concept**. As you relate to others in small groups, your concept of self—who you think you are—affects your communication and relationships with other group members. In addition, your self-perception will have an impact on how others relate to you.

   In trying to reduce the uncertainty that occurs when they communicate in groups, people quickly label the behaviors of others. They assign others roles, or sets of expectations. For example, Gloria seems like a leader; she usually takes charge and delegates responsibility. On the other hand, Hank doesn't talk much. He will probably just follow the recommendations of others rather than initiate ideas of his own—or at least this is the way others may label him. In a small group, roles result from (1) people's expectations about their own behavior—their *self-concepts,* (2) the perceptions others have about individuals' positions in the group, and (3) people's actual behavior as they interact with others. Since their self-concepts largely determine the roles people assume in small groups, it is important to understand how self-concepts develop—how people come to learn who they think they are.

Self-Concept Development: Role Formation

How do you know who you are? Why did you respond as you did when you were asked to consider the question "Who are you?" A number of factors influence your self-concept. First, other people influence who you think you are. Your parents gave you your name. Perhaps a teacher once told you that you were good in art, and consequently you think of yourself as artistic. Maybe your music teacher or your brother or sister told you that you cannot sing very well. Because you believed that person, you may now view yourself as not very musically inclined. Thus, you listen to others, especially those whose opinions you respect, to help shape your self-concept.

The various reference groups you affiliate with also help you define your self-concept. If you are attending college now, you may describe yourself as a student. If you are a member of a fraternity or sorority, you may consider that association a characteristic that sets you apart from others. Your religious affiliation, your political party, and your membership in civic and social organizations all contribute to the way you perceive yourself.

You also learn who you are by simply observing and interpreting your own behavior. Just before you leave your dorm, house, or apartment, you may look in the mirror to see if your hair is OK and if your clothes are wrinkle-free. You try to see yourself as others will see you. You stand back and look at yourself, almost as if you were looking at someone else, evaluating what you see and forming an impression of who you are. Of course, as both the observer and the observed, your impressions are subject to bias. You may be too critical in evaluating who you are. Your high expectations for your own behavior, when compared with your perceptions of your actions, may give you a distorted view. For example, you may want to be a great opera singer; yet your only opportunity to sing comes in the shower. Even though you may have an excellent voice, your expectations have not been fulfilled, so you tell others that you are not a very good singer. The contradiction between your expectations and your actual experiences affects your self-concept and self-worth.

Diversity of Roles in Small Groups

As a member of a small group, you bring with you the perceptions, expectations, and experiences you have had with other people. Your self-expectations thus provide a foundation for the roles you will assume in a group. Yet your role is also worked out between you and the other group members. As noted by Brown and Keller, "At the heart of every relationship lie the self-images of the persons involved, each created by interaction with the other."[1] As you interact with others, they form impressions of you and your abilities. As they reward you for your actions in the group, you learn what abilities and behaviors they will reinforce. These abilities and behaviors may, in turn, become part of your self-concept. Consider the following example:

Ken has long had an interest in physics and nuclear energy. When his small group in the group communication class considers a discussion of peaceful uses of nuclear energy, Ken is enthusiastically supportive. Other group members soon recognize Ken's knowledge and interest in the subject. Ken enjoys providing resources and information for the group. He soon emerges as the group member who provides most of the information and coordinates the group's research efforts. It is a role he enjoys, and the rest of the group appreciates his contributions.

Ken's role as an initiator of ideas, a contributor of information, and a coordinator resulted from his interest and ability (which were reflected in his self-concept). The group's need and desire to have him serve as a leader also helped determine his role.

People assume roles because of their interests and abilities and because of the needs and expectations of the rest of the group. At times, however, some roles are formally assigned to group members. When police officers arrive on the scene of an accident, bystanders do not generally question their leadership roles. In a task-oriented small group, a member may be assigned the role of secretary, which includes specific duties and responsibilities. A chairperson may be elected to coordinate the meeting and delegate responsibilities. Assigning responsibilities and specific roles reduces uncertainty. A group can sometimes get on with its task more efficiently if some roles are assigned. Of course, even if a person has been elected or assigned the role of chairperson, the group may reject his or her leadership in favor of that of another member who may better meet the needs of the group.

The kinds of roles discussed so far are **task roles**—they help accomplish a group's task. There are also two other kinds of roles. **Maintenance roles** define a group's social atmosphere. A member who tries to maintain a peaceful, harmonious group climate by mediating disagreements and resolving conflicts performs a maintenance function. **Individual roles**, the third general role type, call attention to individual contributions and tend to detract from overall group effort. These individual roles are often counterproductive to the group. Someone who is more interested in seeking recognition than in promoting the general benefit of the group is adopting an individual role.

A comprehensive list of possible roles that individual group members can assume has been compiled by Benne and Sheats.[2] Perhaps you can identify the various roles you have assumed while participating in small group discussions.

Group Task Roles

Initiator-contributor	Proposes new ideas or approaches to group problem solving; a person who occupies this role may suggest a different approach to procedure or organizing the problem-solving task.
Information seeker	Asks for clarification of suggestions; an information seeker also asks for facts or other information that may help the group deal with the issues at hand.
Opinion seeker	Asks for a clarification of the values and opinions expressed by other group members.

Information giver	Provides facts, examples, statistics, and other evidence that pertain to the problem the group is attempting to solve.
Opinion giver	Offers beliefs or opinions about the ideas under discussion.
Elaborator	Provides examples based upon his or her experience or the experience of others that help to show how an idea or suggestion would work if the group accepted a particular course of action.
Coordinator	Tries to clarify and note relationships among the ideas and suggestions that have been provided by others.
Orienter	Attempts to summarize what has occurred and tries to keep the group focused on the task at hand.
Evaluator-critic	Makes an effort to judge the evidence and conclusions that the group suggests.
Energizer	Tries to spur the group to action and attempts to motivate and stimulate the group to greater production.
Procedural technician	Helps the group achieve its goal by performing tasks such as distributing papers, rearranging the seating, or running errands for the group.
Recorder	Writes down suggestions and ideas of others; makes a record of the group's progress.

Group Building and Maintenance Roles

Encourager	Offers praise, understanding, and acceptance of others' ideas and suggestions.
Harmonizer	Mediates disagreements among group members.
Compromiser	Attempts to resolve conflicts by trying to find an acceptable solution to disagreements among group members.
Gatekeeper and expediter	Encourages less talkative group members to participate and tries to limit lengthy contributions of other group members.
Standard setter	Helps to set standards and goals for the group.
Group observer	Keeps records of the group's process and uses the information that is gathered to evaluate the group's procedures.
Follower	Basically goes along with the suggestions and ideas of other group members; serves as an audience in group discussions and decision making.

Individual Roles

| Aggressor | Destroys or deflates the status of other group members; may try to take credit for someone else's contribution. |
| Blocker | Is generally negative, stubborn, and disagreeable without apparent reason. |

Recognition-seeker	Seeks the spotlight by boasting and reporting on his or her personal achievements.
Self-confessor	Uses the group as an audience to report personal feelings, insights, and observations to.
Playboy	Lacks involvement in the group's process; lack of interest may result in cynicism, nonchalance, or other behaviors that indicate lack of enthusiasm for the group.
Dominator	Makes an effort to assert authority by manipulating group members or attempting to take over the entire group; may use flattery or assertive behavior to dominate the discussion.
Help-seeker	Tries to evoke a sympathetic response from others; often expresses insecurity or feelings of low self-worth.
Special interest pleader	Speaks for a special group or organization that best fits his or her own biases, to serve an individual need.

In looking at the preceding list of roles, you might be tempted to label group members according to these classifications. You may have easily recognized yourself as a harmonizer or a follower and said, "Yes, that's me. That's the role I usually take." You may also have tried to classify other group members into these categories. While identifying the characteristics of roles may help you understand the nature and function of roles in small group communication, stereotyping and labeling others can lock them into roles. Bormann and his colleagues have extensively studied role behavior in groups and note that participants, when asked to analyze group roles, often categorize members into roles corresponding to the category labels.[3] As you identify the roles adopted by group members, be flexible in your classifications. Realize that you and other members can assume several roles during a group discussion. In fact, a group member rarely serves only as an "encourager," "opinion seeker," or "follower." Roles are dynamic; they change as perceptions, experiences, and expectations change. An individual can assume leadership responsibilities at one meeting and play a supporting role at other meetings.

Since a role is worked out jointly between you and the group, you will no doubt find yourself assuming different roles in different groups. Perhaps a committee you belong to needs someone to serve as a procedural leader to keep the meeting in order. Because you recognize this need and no one else keeps the group organized, you may find yourself steering the group back on to the topic, making sure all members have a chance to participate. In another committee, where others serve as procedural leaders, you may be the person who comes up with good ideas. Whether consciously or not, you develop a role unique to your talents and the needs of the group. Your role, then, changes from group to group.

If you understand how group roles form and how various roles function, you should be better able to help a group achieve its purpose. For example, groups need members to perform both maintenance and task functions. Task functions help the group get the job done, and maintenance functions help the group run smoothly. If no one is performing maintenance functions, you could point this out to the

While in one group you may present ideas, in other groups you might assume the roles of encourager, evaluator, or observer.

group. You could assume some responsibility for maintenance functions. If you notice individuals hindering the group's progress because they have adopted individual roles (blocker, aggressor, recognition seeker, etc.), you could bring this to the group's attention or to the attention of the offending group member. Explain that individual group roles can make the group less efficient and can lead to conflict among members. While you cannot assume complete responsibility for distributing roles within your group, your insights can help solve some of the group's potential problems.

NORMS

You have undoubtedly seen a movie or television show about the Old West in which townspeople feared villains who had no respect for the law. According to the way movies depict history, people like Wyatt Earp were among the first to enforce the law and restore peace and order. In small groups as well as in the Old West, standards of acceptable behavior are necessary to keep peace and order. While a small group of people does not need Wyatt Earp to enforce order, it probably does need certain norms to help its members feel comfortable with their roles and their relationships.

Identifying Group Norms

Norms are rules or standards that determine what is appropriate and inappropriate behavior in a group. They establish expectations of how group members should behave. Norms reduce some of the uncertainty that occurs when people congregate. People's speech, the clothes they wear, the clothes they don't wear, and how and where they sit are all determined by group norms. Group norms also affect group member relationships.

If you recently joined a group, how do you know what the group's norms are? Do most groups draft a formal list of them? Should you just ask someone in the group, "Excuse me, but could you tell me what the norms are for this group? I don't want to say or do anything stupid." No, most groups do not formally state their norms, but, when given an opportunity, many group members can identify certain standards of acceptable behavior in their group. One way to identify norms is to observe any repeated behavior patterns. Note, for example, any consistencies in the way people talk or dress. In identifying normative behavior in a group, consider the following questions:

1. How do group members dress?
2. What are members' attitudes toward time (e.g., do group meetings begin and end on time? are members often late to meetings?)?
3. What type of language is used by most group members (e.g., is swearing acceptable? is the language formal?)?
4. Do group members use humor to relieve tension?
5. Do group members formally address the group leader?
6. Is it proper to address group members by their first names?

Answers to these questions will help you pinpoint a group's norms. Some groups even develop norms for developing norms. For example, members may discuss the type of clothing that will be worn to meetings or talk about what should be done with absent or tardy members.

Noting when someone breaks a rule can also reveal group norms. If a member arrives late and other members frown or grimace at that person, they probably don't approve of the violation of the norm. If, after a member uses obscene words, another member says, "I wish you wouldn't use words like that," you can be certain that for at least one person a norm has been broken. Thus, punishable offenses indicate violated norms. Often the severity of the punishment corresponds to the significance of the norm.[4] Punishment can range from subtle nonverbal expressions of disapproval (which may not even be noticed by the person expressing them) to death. The hangman's noose was commonly the ultimate punishment for those who violated the norms or laws of the Old West.

How Do Norms Develop?

Have you noticed that in some classes it's OK to say something without raising your hand but in others the instructor has to recognize you before you speak? Raising your hand is a norm. How did different norms develop for two similar activities?

At least two key reasons account for this: (1) People develop norms in new groups based on those of previous groups they have belonged to, and (2) norms develop based on what happens early in a group's existence.

Poole suggests that a group organizes itself based, in part, on norms members encountered in previous groups.[5] Poole calls this process *structurization*. Groups do things based on the ways those things were done in other groups. People bring norms with them. If many of your classmates previously had classes in which they had to raise their hands before speaking, then they will probably introduce that behavior into other groups. If enough people accept it, a norm is born—or, more accurately, a norm is reborn.

Norms also develop from the kinds of behavior that occur early in a group's development. Because of member uncertainty about how to behave when a group first meets, members are eager to learn what is acceptable behavior. If, for example, on the first day of class, a fellow student raises his or her hand to respond to something the instructor asked, and another student does the same, that norm is likely to stick. If, on the other hand, several students respond to the professor without a hand held high, chances are that raising hands will not be a necessary signal to initiate talk with others in the class.

Conforming to Group Norms

What influences how quickly and rigidly people conform to the rules and standards of the group? According to Reitan and Shaw, at least five factors affect conformity to group norms.[6]

The Personality Characteristics of the Group Members. In summarizing the research, Shaw notes:

> . . . more intelligent persons are less likely to conform than less intelligent persons; women usually conform more than men, at least on traditional tasks; there is a curvilinear relationship between age and conformity; persons who generally blame themselves for what happens to them conform more than those low on self-blame; and authoritarians conform more than nonauthoritarians.[7]

Thus, group members' past experiences and unique personality characteristics influence how they conform to established norms.

The Clarity of the Norm and the Certainty of Punishment for Breaking It. The more ambiguous a group norm, the less likely it is that members will conform to it. The military spells out behavior rules clearly so that little if any ambiguity remains. A new recruit is drilled on how to talk, march, salute, and eat. Failure to abide by the rules results in swift and sure corrective sanctions. Thus, the recruit quickly learns to conform. In some small group discussions, particularly when groups first meet, members have a great deal of uncertainty about how to act. Yet as soon as rules become clear and norms (particularly those that suggest how the group should proceed) are established, members will usually conform. The clearer the norms, the more likely group members will conform.

The Number of People Who Have Already Conformed to the Norm. Imagine walking into a room with five or six other people. Three lines have been drawn on a blackboard. One line is clearly shorter than the other two. One by one, each person is asked which line is shortest, and each says that all the lines are the same length. Finally, it is your turn to judge which of the lines is shortest. You are perplexed because your eyes tell you that one line is definitely shorter. Yet can the other members of your group be wrong? You answer that all of the lines are the same length. You conform. You do not want to appear odd to the other group members. Factors such as the size of a group, the number of people who agree with a certain policy, and the status of those who conform contribute to the pressure for conformity in a group.

The Quality of the Interpersonal Relationships that Have Developed in the Group. A group whose members like one another and respect one another's opinions is more likely to support conformity than is a less cohesive group. Employees who like their jobs, bosses, and coworkers and take pride in their work are more likely to support group norms than those who have negative or frustrating relationships with their employers or colleagues.

The Greater the Sense of Group Identification, the Greater the Likelihood of Group Conformity. If group members can readily identify with the goals of the group, they are more likely to conform to standards of behavior. For example, church members who support the doctrine of a church are probably going to conform to the wishes of those in leadership positions. In addition, group members who feel they will be a part of a group for some time are more likely to conform to group norms.

Although violating a group norm usually results in group disapproval and, perhaps, chastisement, such a violation can occasionally be beneficial to a group. Some norms may be detrimental to a group. Just because members conform unanimously to a rule does not mean that the rule is beneficial. For example, if a norm of low productivity were to develop in a group, work output would be adversely affected.

STATUS

> "My dad can run faster than your dad."
> "Oh, yeah? Well, my dad is smarter than your dad."
> "No, he's not!"
> "Oh, yes he is!"

"Says who?"

"Says me. Wanna make something of it?"

Even as children people are concerned about status—who is better, brighter, and more beautiful. *Status* refers to an individuals' importance. People with higher social status generally have more prestige and command more respect than do people of lower status. People want to talk to and talk about, see and be seen with those with high status. They are interested in the lives of high-status individuals. Fan magazines and weekly newspapers available at supermarket checkout counters are filled with features about the famous and near famous—status achievers and status seekers. The President of the United States, television personalities, authors, and athletes often provide the names that make name dropping the pastime of status seekers.

Privileges Accorded to High-Status Group Members

In television's long-running situation comedy "All in the Family," Archie Bunker's territorial claim to his chair suggests that within his family he enjoys certain high-status privileges. He removes lower-status individuals from his seat. Similarly, most people would probably like to be perceived as enjoying some status within a group. Because occupying a position of status fulfills a need for attention, it also builds self-respect and self-esteem. Bormann suggests that high-status positions are pleasant because:

> The group makes a high-status person feel important and influential. They show him deference, listen to him, ask his advice, and often reward him with a greater share of the group's goods. He gets a bigger office, more secretaries, better furniture, more salary, a bigger car, and so forth. Even in communication-class discussion groups, the high-status members receive considerable gratification of their social and esteem needs. One of the most powerful forces drawing people into groups is the attraction of high status.[8]

Perhaps you have participated in small groups in which the status of an individual afforded him or her certain privileges that were not available to the rest of the group. The chairperson of the board may have a private dining room or a private executive washroom while other members must eat in the company cafeteria and use public washrooms. Faculty members may have certain privileges, such as discounts at the university bookstore, that are not available to students. Status differences in the military are strictly observed. The numbers of stripes and stars on a uniform serve as not-so-subtle status markers.

Effects of Status Differences

In small groups, the status or social rank of group members exerts a significant effect on interpersonal relationships. Status affects with whom and how much a member talks. The status or reputation an individual has before joining a group

REVIEW BOX

Effects of Status Differences in Groups

Group members with high status:

talk more

communicate more often with other high-status members

have more influence

generally abide by group norms

are less likely to be ignored

are less likely to complain about their responsibilities

talk to the entire group

are likely to serve in leadership roles

Group members with low status:

direct conversation to high-status rather than low-status members

communicate more positive messages to high-status members

are more likely to have their comments ignored

communicate more irrelevant information

talk to high-status members as a substitute for climbing the social hierarchy in the group

---

certainly affects the role he or she assumes. In addition, norms that help groups determine how they will deal with status differences and what privileges they should allow those with greater prestige readily develop. Several researchers have observed how status differences affect the relationships among members of a small group. Consider the following research conclusions:

1. High-status group members talk more than low-status members.[9]
2. High-status group members communicate more with other high-status members than they do with those of lower status.[10]
3. Low-status group members tend to direct their conversation to high-status group members rather than to those of lower or equal status.[11]
4. Low-status group members communicate more positive messages to high-status members than they do to those of equal or lower status.[12]
5. High-status group members are likely to have more influence on the group's decision making than low-status members.[13]
6. High-status group members usually abide by the norms of the group more than do low-status group members. (The exception to this research finding occurs when high-status members realize that they can violate group norms and receive less punishment than low-status group members would receive; thus, depending on the situation, they may violate certain group norms.)[14]

7. Group members are more likely to ignore the comments and suggestions made by low-status members than those made by high-status members.[15]

8. Low-status group members communicate more irrelevant information than do high-status members.[16]

9. High-status members are less likely to complain about their jobs or their responsibilities.[17]

10. Communication with high-status group members can replace the need for the upward movement of low-status members in the group's status hierarchy.[18]

11. High-status group members tend to talk to the entire group more than members of lower status do.[19]

12. In small group communication and discussion courses, the leader of the small group is usually the member with the highest status. (The exception to this conclusion occurs when the leader emerges because of his or her capability and competence and not necessarily because of popularity. That kind of leader holds a lower status than does a more popular and well-liked group member.)[20]

Observing Status Differences to Predict Group Dynamics

Knowing how status affects the relationships among group members helps you predict who will talk with whom. If you can perceive status differences, you can also predict the type of messages communicated in a small group discussion. These research conclusions suggest that the social hierarchy of a group affects group cohesiveness, group satisfaction, and even the quality of a group's solution.

POWER

Sociologist Robert Bierstedt once observed that "In the entire lexicon of sociological concepts, none is more troublesome than the concept of **power**. We may say about it in general only what St. Augustine said about time, that we all know perfectly well what it is—until someone asks us."[21] While scholars debate definitions of power as well as its relationship to other variables such as status and authority, they generally agree that power, at its core, involves the ability of one person to control or influence some other person.[22] Power in a small group, then, is reflected in an individual's ability to get other members to conform to his or her wishes.

Certain group members may have more power in the group than will others. Sometimes the sources of their power are clear to members, such as in groups with large status differences, but in other cases the sources of power are not so clear. In order to map out the territory of social power in small groups, you need to look at power bases and the effects of power on group processes.

Power Bases

Your power base in a group is the sum of the resources that you can use to control or influence others. Because no two group members have exactly the same resources, each member operates from a different power base. What are some of these power bases? French and Raven identified five power bases in their study of small groups: legitimate power, referent power, expert power, reward power, and coercive power.[23]

Legitimate power stems from a group member's ability to influence others because of being elected, appointed, or selected to exert control over a group. Legitimate power comes from occupying a position of responsibility. The principal of a school has the legitimate power to control school policy. The senators from your state have legitimate power to represent their constituents. Many of the benefits reported in the previous section for high-status group members reflect this kind of power base. A small group member who has been elected chairperson or leader is given legitimate power to influence the group's procedures.

Referent power is the power of interpersonal attraction. Recall from Chapter Three that people are attracted to others whom they admire and want to be like. Put simply, people whom we like have more power over us than those people we do not like.

Expert power stems from a group member's ability to influence others, based upon the knowledge and information that the member possesses. As the saying goes, knowledge is power. Suppose you are a member of a group studying ways to improve the environment of the river in your community. If one of your group members has a Ph.D. in aquatic plant life, that person's knowledge and access to information gives him or her expert power. More than likely, that person can influence the group. However, just because a group member has knowledge does not mean that he or she will exert more influence in the group. The group must find the knowledge credible and useful.

Reward power is based on a person's ability to provide rewards for behaviors. If you are in a position to help another member gain money, status, power, acceptance, and so forth, this position gives you power over that person. Of course, group members are motivated by different needs and goals. What is rewarding to one may not be rewarding to others. Reward power is effective only if a person finds the reward satisfying or valuable. Others must also believe that a person actually has the power and resources to bestow the reward.

Coercive power, the negative side of reward power, is based on the perception that another can punish you for acting or not acting in a certain way. A person's ability to demote others, reduce their salaries or benefits, force them to work overtime hours, or fire them are examples of resources that can make up this power base. Even though coercive power may achieve a desired effect, group members usually resent threats and punishment intended to make them conform. Punished group members often try to win the next round or escape from heavy-handed efforts to accomplish a group goal.

Effects of Power on Group Process

Members who have power influence the group process. Whether their influence will be positive or negative depends on how wisely the members use their influence. The following principles summarize the impact of power on group deliberations.

- The struggle for power among group members can result in poor group decisions and less group cohesion.
- Members who overtly seek dominance and control over a group often focus attention on themselves rather than on achieving group goals. They typically serve as aggressors, blockers, recognition seekers, dominators, or special-interest pleaders (these individual roles were discussed earlier in this chapter). Individuals who seek power make the group less cohesive, and power struggles emphasize individual rather than group agendas.
- Group members with little power often talk less frequently in a group.
- Charles Berger observed that "persons who talk most frequently and for the longest periods of time are assumed to be the most dominant group members. In addition, persons receiving the most communication are assumed to be most powerful."[24] While not all powerful members dominate group conversations, a relationship exists between verbal contributions to the group and influence. The exceptions to this principle are members who talk so frequently that they are ignored by the group.
- Group members can lose power if other members think they use power for personal gain or keep a group from achieving its goals.
- Group members usually expect individuals with greater power to have high-status privileges. However, if members believe powerful members are having a detrimental effect on the group, their credibility and influence could be diminished. Too many perks and privileges given to some members sap a group's ability to do its job and can result in challenges to the influential group members.
- Too much power in one individual can lead to less group decision making and more autocratic decision making.
- Autocratic decision making occurs when one person with several power bases (for example, one who can reward and punish, has needed information, is well liked, and has been appointed to lead) makes a decision alone rather than with the group as a whole. Group members may not speak their minds for fear of reprisals.
- Increasing your level of activity in a group can increase your power and influence.

If you are participating in a group and sense that your influence is diminishing, try to participate more and to take an active role in helping the group achieve its goal. Volunteering to help with tasks and increasing your knowledge about group

---

REVIEW BOX

Power Bases

Legitimate Power	Influence based on being elected, appointed, or selected to lead the group.
Referent Power	Influence based on being well liked.
Expert Power	Influence based on the knowledge and information that a member has.
Reward Power	Influence based on providing rewards for desired behavior.
Coercive Power	Influence based on the ability to punish another.

---

problems, issues, or decisions can also enhance your influence. If you see other group members losing influence, you can give them specific tasks that will bring them back into the group's mainstream (assuming that they are willing to accept the responsibility).

TRUST

What do used-car salespeople, politicians, and insurance agents have in common? They are often stereotyped as people whose credibility is suspect. The untrustworthy images such people evoke are not always justified, but when people want something from you, whether it is money or a vote, you are often suspicious of the promises they make. When you trust people, you have faith that they will not try to take advantage of you and that they will be mindful of your best interests. In developing interpersonal relationships in small groups, the degree of trust you have in others affects your relationships with them.

"Sure, I can be at next Tuesday's group meeting," says Carl, a member of the social committee. You know about Carl's poor attendance record at previous group meetings, so you aren't too confident that he'll be there. On the other hand, Julie says she will try to get the entertainment for the annual picnic. Julie follows through with her promises; if she says she will do something for the group, it will be done. What qualities foster more trust in some people than in others? Why do you take greater risks with some group members than with others? The following sections will consider how trust in relationships affects group members and will suggest how you can elicit more trust as you interact with others.

Have you ever participated in a group in which you felt you couldn't trust the other members? If you have, you probably did not enjoy working in the group and would avoid working in it again. A study by Leathers gives some idea of what may happen if group members don't trust one another.[25] Leathers arranged for a person to work in a group and instructed this person to earn the other members' trust. Once a trusting relationship was established, the group member started to disagree with and criticize the "trusting friends" (the subject of Leathers' study). The subjects' nonverbal behaviors suggested they were uncomfortable and tense. The subjects became more defensive and began to respond to the criticism with insulting remarks. In short, the new lack of trust produced increased anxiety within the entire group. Thus, if group members do not trust one another, they may have less satisfactory discussions.

Developing Trusting Relationships

Why do you trust some people more than others? What is it about your closest friend that enables you to confide your most private feelings? How can group members develop trusting relationships? First, developing trusting relationships in a group takes time. Just as assuming a role in a group discussion requires time, so does developing confidence in others. Second, you base trust on the previous experiences you have had with others. You probably would not walk up to a stranger and give that person your bank account number. You would, however, more than likely trust this number to your spouse or to a friend you have known for several years. As you communicate with other people, you gradually learn whether you can trust them. Trust builds on past experiences. First you observe how an individual completes various tasks and responsibilities. Then you decide whether you can rely on that individual to get things done. Perhaps you have a friend you can always count on to help you. Your friend has helped you in the past so you trust that that help will be extended to you in the future. Trust, then, develops when you can predict how another person will behave under certain circumstances. Put another way, trust helps you reduce uncertainty as you form expectations of others. You trust people who offer you support and who you believe will continue to do so in the future. As you participate in a group, you trust those who, because of their actions and support in the past, have given you every reason to believe that they will support you in the future. Group members establish trusting relationships as they develop mutual respect for one another and as the group becomes more cohesive.

However, even time and experience cannot guarantee trust. A certain amount of risk is always involved whenever you trust another person. As Reichert suggests, "Trust is always a risk, a kind of leap in the dark. It is not based on any solid proof that the other person will not hurt you . . . trust is always a gamble."[26] Sometimes the gamble does not prove profitable. For example, if you have recently worked in a small group with several people in whom you placed little confidence, you may be reluctant to trust others in future groups. If you have developed a close relationship with a friend only to have that friend betray your trust, you may be reluctant to develop a close relationship with someone else. Thus, your good and bad experiences in past groups affect the way in which you relate to people in future groups.

Self-Disclosure

One of the most important ways to establish and maintain trusting relationships with others is through **self-disclosure**—the deliberate communication of information about yourself to others. Establishing trust in interpersonal relationships requires both time and a certain degree of risk. Time and risk are also involved in self-disclosure. When you reveal personal, private information, you open yourself to the possibility that others might reject you. John Powell, author of the book *why am i afraid to tell you who i am?*, says that people hesitate to disclose much about themselves because, "if I tell you who I am, you may not like who I am, and it's all that I have."[27]

Self-disclosure should be timed to suit the occasion and the expectations of the individuals involved. Telling all too soon may violate what the other person expects. It would not be appropriate to talk about the intimate aspects of your life (for example, your financial net worth or your romantic endeavors) when you first introduce yourself to someone. The other person may feel uncomfortable and want to terminate the relationship. Thus, when you first meet someone, you usually reveal information that is not too threatening or personal. As you establish a trusting relationship with an individual, you may feel more comfortable about discussing private feelings and concerns. Powell notes that the information you reveal about yourself often progresses through several predictable levels:

Level five: *Cliché communication.* You first establish verbal contact with others by saying something that lets them know that you acknowledge their presence. Standard phrases like *Hi, how are you?, Nice to see you, Beautiful weather, isn't it?,* and *How's it going?* signal the desire to initiate a relationship. Recall a recent group meeting during which members met for the first time. Chances are that the first words you spoke or heard could be labeled cliché communication.

Level four: *Facts and biographical information.* After using cliché phrases and responses to establish contact, you reveal nonthreatening information about yourself, such as your name, hometown, or occupation. Many groups have each member deliver a brief introduction to the rest of the group as the first item on the agenda.

Level three: *Personal attitudes and ideas.* After introducing yourself and getting down to business, you then respond to various ideas and issues, noting where you agree and disagree with others. When you share ideas, attitudes, and values, you open yourself to rejection by other group members. Sharing personal attitudes and ideas, then, involves more risk.

Level two: *Personal feeling.* Talking about your personal feelings makes you even more vulnerable than discussing emotions and ideas, particularly when you talk about feelings regarding yourself or others.

Level one: *Peak communication.* According to Powell, this is the ultimate level of self-disclosure. People seldom reach this level. Only with your closest friends or people you have known for some time will you share personal insights that may result in being rejected by others. Task-oriented small group discussions rarely achieve peak communication. The highest level of self-disclosure may take much time and trust to develop.[28]

By intentionally communicating information about themselves to others in the group, these students are disclosing themselves and establishing trust within the group.

These five levels of self-disclosure are merely a means of describing the self-disclosure process, so do not try to classify all of your personal communication with others into one of these categories. You should not concern yourself with analyses like "I'm now talking to someone in level four and maybe next week I'll reach level two." Such thinking may detract from an otherwise spontaneous conversation. While self-disclosure should not be used as a tool to manipulate others into trusting relationships, you should develop greater awareness of the self-disclosure process to help evaluate your relationships with others in small groups.

One researcher has described five characteristics of appropriate self-disclosure.[29] First, *self-disclosure is a function of the ongoing relationship.* This means that self-disclosure is not something you do just once; you continually share information about yourself with others.

Second, *self-disclosure is reciprocal* (i.e., when you disclose something to another person, that person will probably disclose something to you). This reciprocal nature of self-disclosure is known as the dyadic effect. When you reveal information about yourself to others, they will probably share information about themselves with you—at least, they probably will if you give them an opportunity. If you are talking constantly about yourself and rarely give others a chance to talk, they probably will not respond to you. If you want to create a climate of trust in your group, you must be willing to share with others.

Third, *self-disclosure is timed to what is happening in your group.* For example, if your group is discussing where a new highway should be located, it would not be appropriate for you to talk about how much you enjoy taking automobile trips with your family through the country. In other words, don't disclose just for the sake of disclosing. Your comments should be relevant to the discussion at hand.

Fourth, *self-disclosure should deal with what is happening among the people present.* Not only should your self-disclosure be appropriate to an occasion, but it should also be appropriate for the people in your group. You need not talk about a troubled relationship if it clearly is of no concern to the others present. You may find someone who will listen to you, but if the others present have no interest in your confessions, keep them to yourself.

Finally, *self-disclosure usually moves by small increments* (i.e., it takes time). Establishing trusting relationships with others cannot be rushed. If a group of people will be meeting for only two or three sessions, don't feel compelled to enter into a self-disclosure session and expect others to follow suit during the opening moments of your first session. While you may feel that really getting to know one another would be healthy for group members, don't try to rush genuine self-disclosure. If you do, you may inflict more harm than good. Group members may interpret your efforts to establish trust as prying into their personal lives. While you should not disclose too much too soon, you should persevere in trying to get to know other group members. Self-disclosure is a useful way to improve relationships.

The Johari Window

The **Johari Window** is a model that nicely summarizes the discussion of how self-disclosure affects and reflects your relationships with others. The model can apply to relationships between two people but was originally intended to describe relationships among several people. The Johari Window, shown in Figure 4-1, includes four types of information about you.[30]

Imagine that the model represents you as you communicate with others in a small group. At first glance, all four quadrants in the diagram seem to be the same size. That may not be the case (in fact, it probably isn't). Quadrant one, called the *open area,* contains information that others know about you and that you are also aware of. The more information that you reveal about yourself, the larger quadrant one will be. Put another way, the more risks you take by self-disclosing, the larger the open area will be. The open area might include such information as your age, your occupation, and other things you mention about yourself.

The *blind area* in the second quadrant consists of information that other people know about you but that you do not know. Do you remember when, in grade school, someone may have put a sign on your back that said, "Hit me"? Everyone was aware of it but you. The blind area of the Johari Window works in much the same way. For example, you may see yourself as generous, but others may see you as tight. Perhaps you've been in a group with members who thought they were group leaders but weren't aware that they did not command respect and approval. As you learn how others see you, the blind area of the Johari Window gets smaller. In order for it to shrink, others must tell you how they perceive you. Generally, the more you know about yourself and about how others see you, the better are your chances of establishing open and honest relationships. Still, you must remember that learning about how others see you should follow the same

Figure 4-1   The Johari Window

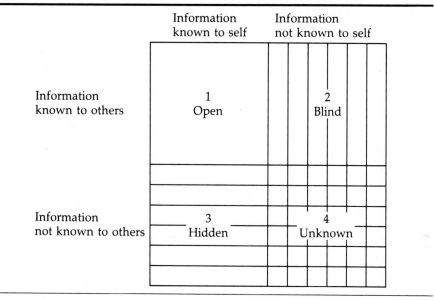

guidelines suggested for self-disclosure. Don't, for example, expect lots of verbal feedback about your performance in a group until you get to know the members well and they get to know you. In other words, don't expect too much feedback too soon. Certainly, feedback would be useful to you at times, but many people may want to know more about you first. As suggested earlier, self-disclosure should be timed to fit what is happening in the group and should be appropriate for the people who are present.

The *hidden area,* the third quadrant of the Johari Window, consists of information that you know about yourself but that others do not know about you. You can probably think of many things that you would not want anyone else to know. They may be feelings you have about yourself or feelings about other group members. Most advocates of self-disclosure do not claim that you should share everything with others. Once again, appropriate self-disclosure is timed to the situation and the people involved. It is selective. On the other hand, hidden agendas occasionally can hinder small group discussions. However, you should not reveal *all* of your secrets to another person to foster trust. No guidelines can tell you what you should and should not reveal. The important principle to remember, however, is that *self-disclosure can foster trust.* The other person, though, must be able to accept what you have selected to reveal. Otherwise, the revelation may decrease, rather than increase, communication.

The fourth quadrant in the Johari Window, the *unknown area,* consists of information that is unknown both to you and to others. Perhaps you do not know how you will react under certain stressful situations. Maybe you are not sure what stand you will take on an issue next year. Other people may also not be aware of how you would respond under certain conditions. Your potential, your untapped resources, are unknown. This area exists because eventually some of these things become known to you, to others, or to both you and others.

The Johari Window illustrates how self-disclosure can affect small group work. The model provides a deeper understanding of the relationships between what others know about you and what you know about yourself. People trust you only when they perceive you as being trustworthy. Both your self-concept and the perceptions others have of you determine your role in a group. Norms in small groups sometimes develop in response to the expectations people have about others in a group. Certainly the status that group members enjoy is a direct result of the perceptions others have about them.

THE DEVELOPMENT OF GROUP RELATIONSHIPS OVER TIME

One theme has consistently predominated this chapter's discussion of developing relationships: It takes time for relationships to develop. You experience some tension and anxiety the first time you participate in a small group. You are uncertain what your role in the group will be. The group has not met long enough for norms to develop. True, certain standards of behavior already exist because of the common culture that group members share, but these expectations provide only skeletal guidance for behavior. Status differences among group members can also create tension. Bormann has defined this initial uneasiness as **primary tension**, which is

> the social unease and stiffness that accompanies getting acquainted. Students placed in a discussion group with strangers will experience these tensions most strongly during the opening minutes of their first meetings. The earmarks of primary tensions are extreme politeness, apparent boredom or tiredness, and considerable sighing or yawning. When members show primary tension, they speak softly and tentatively. Frequently they can think of nothing to say, and many long pauses result.[31]

Thus, you should expect to find some primary tension during initial meetings. It is a normal part of group development. A group leader can minimize this tension, however, by helping members get to know one another. Get-acquainted exercises and brief statements of introduction can ease primary tension. While members of groups that meet only once might deem getting to know one another as impractical, using a few minutes to break the ice and manage some of the primary tension can help create more satisfying relationships among group members.

After a group resolves primary tension and develops norms, and its members become more comfortable with their roles (that is, they have fairly realistic expectations about how other members will react to them), another type of tension devel-

---

Group Tension

Primary Tension:	Uneasiness and uncomfortableness in getting aquainted and managing initial group uncertainty about the group task and group relationships.
Secondary Tension:	Tension that occurs as group members struggle for influence, develop roles, and explore differences in approaching the group task.

---

ops. **Secondary tension**, according to Bormann, occurs as conflicts arise and as differences of opinion emerge. Whether recognized as a personality conflict or simply as a disagreement, secondary tension surfaces when group members try to solve the problem, accomplish the task, or resolve specific issues facing the group. Secondary tension also is the result of power struggles and jockeying for positions of leadership and influence. Secondary tension usually establishes group norms. Joking or laughing often helps manage secondary tension. Regardless of how cohesive a group may be, some conflict over procedure will normally develop as relationships among members form. Chapter Seven will discuss the phases of a group's growth and development in more detail, and Chapter Nine will consider some suggestions for managing the conflict and controversy that result from secondary tension.

RELATING TO OTHERS IN SMALL GROUPS: PUTTING PRINCIPLE INTO PRACTICE

Four variables affect and reflect individuals' relationships with others in small groups: roles, norms, status, and trust. An understanding of how these concepts affect your performance and the performance of other group members will help you explain and predict the types and quality of relationships that form in small groups. As you attempt to apply the information presented in this chapter, consider these suggestions:

Roles

- Having a clearer understanding of your own self-concept and self-worth will help you understand your role as you work with others in small groups.
- Group roles can be classified as task roles, maintenance roles, and individual roles.
- An effective group includes members who perform task role functions and others who perform maintenance role functions. Most group members perform both task and maintenance role functions.

- If no one performs group maintenance functions, point this out to the group or assume the responsibility for performing them yourself.
- If you observe one or more group members hindering the progress of your group because they are adopting an individual group role (blocker, aggressor, recognition-seeker, etc.), bring this to the attention of the group or the offending group member.
- Don't try to fit yourself or other group members into just one or two group roles. You and other group members can assume several roles during the course of a discussion.

Norms

- Norms develop based on the norms that are derived from other groups and behavior that is reinforced as a norm early in a group's history.
- You can identify group norms by noting repeated patterns of behavior.
- Another way to identify group norms is by noting what kind of offenses group members punish.
- The personalities of the group members, the clarity of norms and the certainty of punishment for breaking them, the number of people who have broken norms, the quality of relationships among group members, and the sense of group identification all help determine whether members will conform to the group norms.

Status

- You can identify the status of group members by the privileges high-status group members receive.
- If you can spot status differences in small groups, you will be able to predict who talks to whom.
- By becoming aware of the status differences among group members, you can predict the content of the messages communicated.
- If you are aware of status differences, you can predict the quality of interpersonal relationships in a small group.

Power

- A group member with power is one who can influence the behavior of other group members.
- People develop power in a group because they can provide information, expertise, rewards, and punishment; because they have been elected or appointed; or because they are well liked or have status in the group.

- People who talk often and for long periods of time in group discussions are assumed to be powerful, influential group members.
- Too much power concentrated in one person can result in autocratic decision making.

Trust

- In most groups, don't expect trusting relationships to form too soon—it takes time for trust to develop.
- Self-disclosure is an important factor in developing trusting relationships with others.

Self-Disclosure

- Don't think that self-disclosure just happens once when the group first gets together; it is a function of ongoing group relationships.
- Don't talk solely about yourself without giving other people a chance to talk about themselves.
- Don't disclose merely for the sake of disclosing. Your revelations should be relevant to the discussion at hand.
- Appropriate self-disclosure should deal with what is happening among the persons present.
- Don't rush self-disclosure; appropriate self-disclosure moves by small increments.
- Familiarizing yourself with the Johari Window should give you a deeper understanding of the relationship between what others know about you and what you know about yourself as you interact with others.
- Get-acquainted exercises and brief statements of introduction during the first group meeting can help manage primary tension.

PRACTICE

Johari Window Exercise

The purpose of this exercise is to help you understand the Johari Window as presented in this chapter. In essence, you are to construct a Johari Window for a group in which you participate. Of course, you should realize that the impressions you have of the others and the impressions they have of you may be based only on a very brief opportunity to meet with one another. Your instructor will give you additional suggestions for completing this activity.

1. Form groups of three to five people.
2. Check five or six adjectives from the list below that best describe your personality as you see it.
3. Select three or four adjectives that describe the personality of each person in your group and write them on separate sheets of paper. Distribute these lists to the appropriate group members.
4. Fill in square number one ("known to self and known to others") with adjectives from the list that both you and at least one other member of your group have selected to describe your personality.
5. Fill in square number two ("not known to self but known to others") with those adjectives others in your group used to describe you but you did not use to describe yourself.
6. Fill in square number three ("known to self but not to others") with adjectives you have used to describe yourself but no one else used to describe you.

able	dependable	intelligent	patient	sensible
accepting	dignified	introverted	powerful	sentimental
adaptable	energetic	kind	proud	shy
bold	extroverted	knowledgeable	quiet	silly
brave	friendly	logical	reflective	spontaneous
calm	giving	loving	relaxed	sympathetic
caring	happy	mature	religious	tense
cheerful	helpful	modest	responsive	trustworthy
clever	idealistic	nervous	searching	warm
complex	independent	observant	self-assertive	wise
confident	ingenious	organized	self-conscious	witty

	known to self	not known to self
known to others	1	2
not known to others	3	unknown

Norm Exercise

Several behaviors are listed below. For each one indicate how appropriate or inappropriate you think it would be as a norm for your group. Write the number that shows your best estimate of how the group would feel—5 if the behavior is definitely appropriate as a norm, 4 if the behavior is somewhat appropriate, 3 if the behavior is questionable, 2 if it is somewhat inappropriate, and 1 if it is definitely inappropriate.[32]

————   1.   Said little or nothing in most meetings.

————   2.   Talked about the details of her sex life.

————   3.   Brought up problems he had with others who weren't in the group.

————   4.   Kissed another group member.

————   5.   Asked for reactions or feedback ("How do you see me in this group?").

————   6.   Talked mostly about what was going on in the group.

————   7.   Frequently joked.

————   8.   Pleaded for help.

————   9.   Challenged other members' remarks.

————   10.   Said she was not getting anything out of being in the group.

————   11.   Described his reactions to what was taking place in the group.

————   12.   Highlighted opposition among ideas.

————   13.   Formed a contract with another member about the use of each other's resources in meeting both their needs and goals.

————   14.   Refused to be bound by a group decision.

————   15.   Asked for the goal to be clarified.

————   16.   Noted competition in the group and asked how it could be reduced.

————   17.   Gave advice to other group members about what to do.

————   18.   Interrupted a dialogue between two members.

————   19.   Told another member that she was unlikable.

————   20.   Was often absent.

————   21.   Shouted with anger at another member.

————   22.   With strong feelings, told another member how likable he was.

————   23.   Tried to manipulate the group to get her own way.

————   24.   Hit another group member.

————   25.   Acted indifferently to other members.

————   26.   Dominated the group's discussion for more than one session.

————   27.   Encouraged other group members to react to the topic which was being discussed.

————   28.   Tried to convince members of the rightness of a certain point of view.

————   29.   Talked a lot without showing his real feelings.

_____ 30. Told the group off, saying that it was worthless.

_____ 31. Showed she had no intention of changing her behavior.

_____ 32. Resisted the suggestions of other members about procedures.

_____ 33. Commented that the decision-making procedure was not appropriate to the nature of the decision.

_____ 34. Asked that the causes of a group problem be analyzed.

_____ 35. Expressed affection for several group members.

After reacting to these items the members of your group may think of other behavioral norms to include. Once all members have rated the group norms, the group should discuss them and decide how each affects the cohesion of the group.

"What Role Shall I Play?"

An understanding of the various roles you may play in the group communication process will enhance your chances of contributing more productively to any group you are part of. The purpose of this exercise is to allow you to actually assume a role in an informal group discussion, which will be given before the class. The following procedure will be used. Allow about ten minutes to complete the first three steps.[33]

1. The class will divide into groups of approximately six to eight members.

2. Your group will decide on a subject that can be easily discussed in front of the class with little preparation. (For example, your group may pretend to be planning a party for some school organization.)

3. After the group has decided on a subject, each member should choose a role from the lists on pages 64–66 that can be acted out in a group discussion on the topic your group has chosen. Make sure that you clearly understand the definition of the role you will assume.

4. Each group will participate in a four- to five-minute discussion. Each group member will make statements during the role-playing situation that will make clear to onlooking class members which role he or she is acting out. (An *encourager,* for example, may say things during the discussion such as, "That was a very good suggestion, Jane!" or "You are doing a great job, Frank.")

5. At the end of each group discussion, the class will try to guess which role each group member was playing. After each group finishes its role-playing, class members may discuss how they drew conclusions about what roles were being played and how certain roles enhanced or detracted from the group discussion.

Notes

1. Charles T. Brown and Paul W. Keller, *Monologue to Dialogue* (Englewood Cliffs, New Jersey: Prentice-Hall, 1973), p. 2.

2. Kenneth D. Benne and Paul Sheats, "Functional Roles of Group Members," *Journal of Social Issues* 4 (Spring 1948): 41–49.

3. Ernest G. Bormann, *Discussion and Group Methods: Theory and Practice,* 2nd ed. (New York: Harper & Row, Publishers, 1975), p. 209.

4. S. Schacter, "Deviation, Rejection, and Communication," *Journal of Abnormal and Social Psychology* 46 (1951): 190–207.

5. Marshall Scott Poole, "Group Communication and the Structuring Process," in Robert S. Cathcart and Larry A. Samovar, *Small Group Communication: A Reader,* 5th ed. (Dubuque, Iowa: Wm. C. Brown, 1988), pp. 275–287.

6. H. T. Reitan and Marvin E. Shaw, "Group Membership, Sex-Composition of the Group, and Conformity Behavior," *Journal of Social Psychology* 64 (1964): 45–51.

7. Marvin E. Shaw, *Group Dynamics: The Psychology of Small Group Behavior* (New York: McGraw-Hill Book Company, 1981), p. 281.

8. Bormann, p. 215.

9. J. I. Hurwitz, A. F. Zander, and B. Hymovitch, "Some Effects of Power on the Relations Among Group Members," in D. Cartwright and A. Zander (eds.), *Group Dynamics: Research and Theory* (New York: Harper & Row, Publishers, 1953), pp. 483–492.

10. *Ibid.*

11. *Ibid.*

12. D. C. Barnlund and C. Harland, "Propinquity and Prestige as Determinants of Communication Networks," *Sociometry* 26 (1963): 467–479.

13. Shaw, p. 246.

14. George C. Homans, *The Human Group* (New York: Harcourt Brace and World, 1950).

15. John K. Brilhart, *Effective Group Discussion* (Dubuque, Iowa: Wm. C. Brown, 1978), p. 36.

16. H. H. Kelly, "Communication in Experimentally Created Hierarchies," *Human Relations* 4 (1951): 36–56.

17. *Ibid.*

18. *Ibid.*

19. Bormann, p. 215.

20. *Ibid.*

21. Robert Bierstedt, "An Analysis of Social Power," *American Sociological Review* 6 (1950): 7–30.

22. Marvin E. Shaw, *Group Dynamics: The Psychology of Small Group Behavior* (New York: McGraw-Hill Book Company, 1981), p. 294.

23. J. R. P. French and B. H. Raven, "The Bases of Social Power," in D. Cartwright and A. Zander (eds.), *Group Dynamics* (Evanston, Illinois: Row, Peterson, 1962), pp. 607–623.

24. Charles R. Berger, "Power in the Family," in Michael Roloff and Gerald Miller (eds.), *Persuasion: New Direction in Theory and Research* (Beverly Hills, California: Sage Publications, 1980), p. 217.

25. Dale Leathers, "The Process Effects of Trust-Destroying Behavior," *Speech Monographs* 37 (1970): 180–187.

26. Richard Reichert, *Self-Awareness Through Group Dynamics* (Dayton, Ohio: Pflaum/Standard, 1970), p. 21.

27. John Powell, *why am i afraid to tell you who i am?* (Niles, Illinois: Argus Communications, 1969), p. 12.

28. *Ibid.,* pp. 54–58.

29. Joseph Luft, *Of Human Interaction* (Palo Alto, California: National Press, 1969), pp. 132–33.

30. Joseph Luft, *Group Processes: An Introduction to Group Dynamics* (Mountain View, California: Mayfield Publishing Company, 1970).

31. Bormann, pp. 181–182.

32. David W. Johnson and Frank P. Johnson, *Joining Together: Group Theory and Group Skills* (Englewood Cliffs, New Jersey: Prentice-Hall, 1987), p. 421.

33. Developed by Cathy Fleuriet, Southwest Texas State University.

Chapter Five

Improving Group Climate

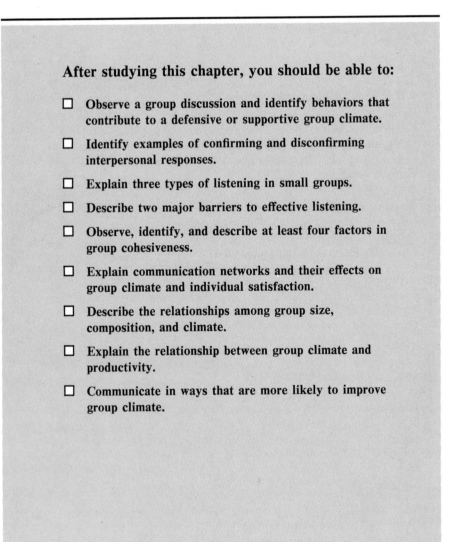

After studying this chapter, you should be able to:

☐ Observe a group discussion and identify behaviors that contribute to a defensive or supportive group climate.

☐ Identify examples of confirming and disconfirming interpersonal responses.

☐ Explain three types of listening in small groups.

☐ Describe two major barriers to effective listening.

☐ Observe, identify, and describe at least four factors in group cohesiveness.

☐ Explain communication networks and their effects on group climate and individual satisfaction.

☐ Describe the relationships among group size, composition, and climate.

☐ Explain the relationship between group climate and productivity.

☐ Communicate in ways that are more likely to improve group climate.

What does the word *climate* call to mind? If you've taken a course in geography or meteorology or have studied weather patterns, you may think of temperature gradients, barometric pressure, and how bodies of water, latitude, ocean currents, and mountains affect the weather of a particular region. Look out your window. What is the weather like? Does today's weather make you want to curl up with a book? Go to the beach? Go skiing? Would you say that climate affects your desire to engage in certain activities? How do you feel about a cold, snowy night spent in front of a roaring fire in a cozy room?

Group climate is roughly analogous to geographical climate. A variety of factors interact to create a group feeling or atmosphere. How group members communicate, to whom they communicate, and how often they communicate influence their satisfaction as well as productivity. You may have participated in groups where there was a genuine sense of warmth, trust, camaraderie, and accomplishment. The question this chapter asks is how can people communicate in ways that help the group establish such a climate? The chapter begins with a case study.

A CASE STUDY

Not long ago I received a telephone call from a good friend. The friend's message was rather mysterious. He said that he and his wife had a business proposition for me and my wife, which they would like to discuss as soon as they could. No, he really didn't want to discuss any details over the phone. When could we meet? Tuesday evening? At my place? They'd see us then.

Our curiosity piqued, we anxiously awaited the Tuesday evening rendezvous. What could our friends possibly have up their sleeves? The appointed hour arrived. The bottle of wine was being chilled. Right on time, the doorbell rang. ("Unusual," we thought, "they're usually a half hour late.") Our next surprise was that our friend George was dressed in a three-piece suit, his wife Margaret in a tailored dress. My wife and I looked at each other in our jeans, bare feet, and shirts, then returned our gaze to George and Margaret and asked whether they had just returned from a funeral. They laughed nervously (?) at the joke (?!), marched past us, and began to set up a small demonstration board on our dining room table.

Turning down our offer of wine, they asked if we could begin the meeting. This was becoming stranger by the moment. My wife Nancy and I were beginning to feel like we had invited insurance agents into our home even though we knew that wasn't the case. These were people with whom we have gone camping, hiking, canoeing, and with whom we've spent many an evening over many a beer. Something didn't fit, but our curiosity was aroused so we decided to play along.

It wasn't long before the experience began to get frustrating. George and Margaret asked us what we wanted out of life. We suggested that they probably ought to have some idea of that by now—that most of our goals were inward, state-of-being kinds of goals, like having a greater awareness of ourselves and others, peace of mind, and so forth. This answer agitated our guests, who responded by suggesting that it might be nice if we never again had to worry about money. We agreed that that would, indeed, be pleasant. At this, they seemed to breathe a little more easily and proceeded to haul out charts, graphs, and illustrations which, they claimed, proved that we could double our present income in a little over a year—in our spare time, of course.

After an hour, George and Margaret were still refusing to tell us what it was we would have to sell (we'd figured *that* much out) or to whom we'd have to sell it. ("Please bear with us until the end," they said.) Something was definitely wrong. Here I was sitting in my own dining room with my wife, my friends, and a glass of wine, yet I felt as if I were back in junior high being asked to please hold all my questions until the end. I've had the same experience with life insurance and encyclopedia salespeople. They were treating us not as people, but as faceless members of that great mass of consumers whom sales manuals target and who serve as the inspiration for countless commercials where housewives dance, sing, and extol the virtues of airtight plastic containers, soap powders, and kitchen floors that shine like new.

George and Margaret were still making their pitch. They had finally revealed the name of the company and its line of products and were now setting about the task of showing how rapidly the company had grown due to its unique marketing concepts, fine products which sell themselves (of course), and so forth. It didn't matter. I had already decided not to do it. I felt dehumanized, abused by my friends. Why hadn't they simply told us that they were involved with the company (which we had heard of long before) and that they'd like to explore the possibilities of our becoming involved as well? With friends, it would be a much more effective approach—certainly a more honest one.

The formal part of the presentation was over. They were asking for our comments and questions. I was ready and "loaded for bear." As a teacher of speech communication I am well versed in the art of critiquing oral presentations and visual aids. I proceeded to evaluate their entire presentation, emphasizing their failure to adequately analyze their audience and to adapt their communicative style accordingly. George and Margaret were shocked and hurt. They had not, they said, come into our home to be criticized. They had come in good faith with an honest proposal from which we all stood to benefit. If they had offended us, they were sorry. No, they still did not care for a glass of wine. We'd get together again sometime soon.

DEFENSIVE COMMUNICATION

This case study illustrates many of the principles discussed in this text. Clearly, some group norms were being violated, particularly the interpersonal expectations of openness and honesty. Likewise, group roles to which all of the participants had adjusted were altered dramatically as new roles of "salesperson" and "critic" were introduced. Messages, both verbal and nonverbal, were interpreted differently (e.g., their "professional" attire seemed "out of place" to the author). The scenario is a particularly good example of the type of communication which fosters a *defensive climate* in the small group.

A closer look at the case study above reveals that from the first telephone call, information was withheld—a pattern which repeated itself throughout the entire episode. When George and Margaret arrived they were dressed in a very business-like fashion, suggesting (once funeral attendance was ruled out) a change in what had become a typical pattern of interaction for the two couples. George and Margaret took *control* of the conversation. They maintained control of information and, to an extent, controlled others' choices (through limiting alternative responses). The response to George and Margaret was defensive, verbal aggression. The author gave an evaluative critique of the presentation that aroused further defensiveness, hurt, and anger in a cyclical process which left old questions unanswered and new ones unasked—a very uncomfortable and unproductive evening. The specific examples of **defensive communication** we find occurring here are *strategy, control,* and *evaluation.*

DEFENSIVE AND SUPPORTIVE CLIMATES

For several years Dr. Jack Gibb observed the communicative behavior of people in groups and identified the types of behaviors that contribute to defensive climates and those that develop supportive climates. Gibb suggests that a defensive climate is clearly counterproductive in any group.

> The person who behaves defensively, even though he also gives some attention to the common task, devotes an appreciable portion of his energy to defending himself. Besides talking about the topic, he thinks about how he appears to others, how he may be seen more favorably, how he may win, dominate, impress, or escape punishment, and/or how he may avoid or mitigate a perceived or an anticipated attack.[1]

The key to building a supportive climate in the group lies, of course, in communication, and in this case it is not so much *what* people communicate as *how* they communicate it. A message can be delivered in ways that evoke support or defense. Consider some examples based on Gibb's categories.

Evaluation *Versus* Description

Problem solving in small groups involves generating and evaluating ideas. Unfortunately, not all ideas are perfect, and the group needs to discover this if it is to reach the most effective decision. When someone puts forth a less-than-perfect idea, you can respond in one of two ways: You can say, "Listen, you cretin, that's the most ridiculous and outlandish idea I've heard in a decade," or you can say, "As I think through that idea and apply it to our problem, I run up against some other problems. Am I missing something?" Imagine yourself on the receiving end of the first comment. Imagine that your supervisor (whom you are trying to impress) says it to you. Think of all the others in the group who are looking at you, waiting for a response. How do you feel? Not very good? You have just been put down and are likely to be defensive. This is an example of evaluation (albeit an extreme one). The latter response, an example of description, is much more effective and support-ive. Your idea may, in fact, be terrible, but at least the second response is not an attack. Instead, it allows you to save face. It also keeps the door open for further discussion of your idea. Quite possibly, further investigation into your bad idea may lead to a better idea.

In a nutshell, *evaluation* is "you" language: It directs itself to the other person's worth or the worth of that person's ideas. As a result, it can provoke much defensiveness. *Description,* on the other hand, is "I" language: It describes the speaker's thoughts about the person or idea. This type of response leads to more trust and cohesiveness in groups.

Control *Versus* Problem Orientation

Communicative behavior that aims at controlling others can produce much defen-siveness in group members. This pattern characterizes many aggressive salespeople who, quite intentionally, manipulate you into answering trivial questions that lead up to the final question of whether or not you want to buy a product. Various persuasive tactics aim at controlling behavior (as any student of television commer-cials can observe). Implicit in attempts to control lies the assumption that the controller knows what is good for the controllee—the "I know what's good for you" assumption. When people become aware of this attitude, they frequently get defensive.

In a group, *problem orientation* is a more effective approach. If others perceive you as a person who genuinely strives for a solution that will benefit all concerned (rather than just yourself), this perception will contribute to a supportive climate, greater cohesiveness, and increased productivity.

Strategy *Versus* Spontaneity

Like controlling behavior, strategy suggests manipulation. The effects of strategy on the group's climate can be seen in the case study that began this chapter. Because we perceived George and Margaret to be acting with hidden motivations and withholding information, we became defensive. We felt used and manipulated. Again, this sort of behavior places the self before the group and does not lead to the most effective solutions to group problems.

On the other hand, if others perceive you as a person who acts *spontaneously* (that is, not from hidden motivations or agendas) and as a person who immediately

Defensive *Versus* Supportive Communication

Defensive Behaviors	Supportive Behaviors
Evaluation	Description
Control	Problem Orientation
Strategy	Spontaneity
Neutrality	Empathy
Superiority	Equality
Certainty	Provisionalism

and honestly responds to the present situation, you are likely to contribute to making a more supportive climate.

Neutrality *Versus* Empathy

If you behave in a detached, uncaring fashion, as if the people in your group and the outcome of the group's process don't concern you in the least, your behavior will probably arouse defensiveness. Involvement and concern for the group task and for other group members are perceived as supportive.

Superiority *Versus* Equality

If you feel superior, a small group meeting is not the place to show it. You probably know of people who approach you in class after tests have been returned and ask, "What'd ya get?" Frequently these students use this question merely as a preface to showing you their superior grade. Sound familiar? Most people think such behavior is obnoxious. It makes them feel defensive. In groups, some people preface their remarks with words such as "obviously" or point out their greater knowledge, their greater experience, or some such strategy to make themselves appear superior to other members. Most likely, their behavior will meet with some resistance. People create more supportive climates when they indicate a willingness to enter into participative planning with mutual trust and respect.

Certainty *Versus* Provisionalism

Do you know people who always have all the answers, whose ideas are truths to be defended, who are intolerant of those with the wrong (that is, different) attitudes? These highly dogmatic people are well-known for the defensiveness they produce in others. People's usual response is to want to prove them wrong. This behavior is counterproductive in groups. Individuals are likely to be more effective

A good group leader encourages a non-judgmental atmosphere by responding enthusiastically to each member's suggestions and by expressing confidence in the group as a whole.

if their attitudes appear to be held *provisionally:* that is, if they appear flexible and genuinely committed to solving problems rather than to simply take sides on issues. If people leave themselves open to new information and can admit that, from time to time, they may be wrong about something, they will be more effective group members and will help build more supportive group climates.

As a communicator, you control your own actions. Your knowledge of defensive and supportive behaviors will help you make your group work more effectively. Another area of research and application in group climate is interpersonal confirmation and disconfirmation. This research deals not with communicative behaviors that you initiate, but with the ways in which you respond to other group members.

A non-judgmental atmosphere is naturally fostered in informal gatherings where group members respond spontaneously to each other's ideas.

DISCONFIRMING AND CONFIRMING RESPONSES

Group process often seems to go nowhere. Questions are left unanswered and ideas remain ignored. One of the most frequent complaints among group members is that communication in the group seems disconnected and disjointed, fostering vague feelings of uneasiness, as if the members are being disregarded.[2] Unfortunately, this is a common phenomenon and one that does not satisfy task, process, or individual needs. While attending a series of committee meetings, one observer noted that hardly anyone directly acknowledged what anyone else said. Rather, the meetings proceeded as a series of soliloquies. Not surprisingly, most group members expressed dissatisfaction with the group's process and frustration with the its inability to reach decisions.

In an investigation of communication in effective and ineffective groups, Evelyn Sieburg examined the ways in which group members responded to the communicative acts of others. In this seminal study and in later work with Carl Larson, Sieburg identified several types of responses that she classified as *confirming* or *disconfirming*. Simply stated, **confirming responses** are those that cause people to value themselves more, while **disconfirming responses** are those that cause people to value themselves less.[3] Sieburg's identification of confirming and disconfirming responses has been one of the most salient contributions to the understanding of group climate.

Some interpersonal responses are obvious examples of confirmation and disconfirmation, such as when a person responds to another with overt praise or sharp criticism. However, group members confirm and disconfirm one another in more subtle ways. Sieburg and Larson identify some of those behaviors as follows:

Disconfirming Responses

1. *Impervious response.* When one speaker fails to acknowledge, even minimally, the other speaker's communicative attempt, or when one ignores or disregards the other by not giving any ostensible acknowledgment of the other's communication, this response may be called impervious.

2. *Interrupting response.* When one speaker cuts the other speaker short or begins while the other is still speaking, the response may be called interrupting.

3. *Irrelevant response.* When one speaker responds in a way that seems unrelated to what the other has been saying, or when one speaker introduces a new topic without warning or returns to his or her earlier topic, apparently disregarding the intervening conversation, the response may be called irrelevant.

4. *Tangential response.* When one speaker acknowledges the other person's communication but immediately takes the conversation in another direction, the response may be called tangential. Occasionally, individuals exhibit what may appear to be direct responses to the other, such as "Yes, but . . ." or "Well, you may be right, but . . . ," and then respond with communicative content very different from what preceded. Responses such as these may still be called tangential.

5. *Impersonal response.* When a speaker conducts a monologue, when his or her speech communication behavior appears intellectualized and impersonal, contains few first-person statements and many generalized "you" or "one" statements, and is heavily loaded with euphemisms or clichés, the response may be called impersonal.

6. *Incoherent response.* When the speaker responds with sentences that are incomplete, or with rambling statements difficult to follow, or with sentences containing much retracing or rephrasing, or interjections such as "you know" or "I mean," the response may be called incoherent.

7. *Incongruous response.* When the speaker engages in nonvocal behavior that seems inconsistent with the vocal content, the response may be called incongruous. For example, "Who's angry? I'm not angry!" (said in a tone and volume that strongly suggest anger). Or, "I'm really concerned about you" (said in a tone that suggests lack of interest or disdain).

Confirming Responses

1. *Direct acknowledgment.* One speaker acknowledges the other's communication and reacts to it directly and verbally.
2. *Agreement about content.* One speaker reinforces information expressed by the other.
3. *Supportive response.* One speaker expresses understanding of the other, reassures the other, or tries to make the other feel better.
4. *Clarifying response.* One speaker tries to clarify the content of the other's message or attempts to clarify the other's feelings. The usual form of a clarifying response is to elicit more information, to encourage the other to say more, or to repeat in an inquiring way what was understood.
5. *Expression of positive feeling.* One speaker describes his or her own positive feelings related to prior utterances of the other, for example, "Okay, now I understand what you are saying."[4]

The implication of this research for improving communicative effectiveness and thus the effectiveness of groups is this: By using confirming responses rather than disconfirming responses when communicating with other group members, people contribute toward a supportive, trustful climate and therefore promote greater group effectiveness and individual satisfaction.

DEFENSIVENESS AND UNCERTAINTY

Take a moment and imagine yourself alone at night in a strange city. You step off a bus and, as it roars off into the night, you realize that you got off at the wrong stop. The street is unfamiliar to you. A couple of sinister characters eye you from a doorway. Your senses sharpen. You can trust nothing in this environment. You don't want to let down your guard. Anything could happen to you.

This is probably not a time when you'll ponder what to buy your mother for her birthday or how to approach your boss for that raise you think you deserve. You're too busy trying to figure out how to preserve yourself in this alien environment. What will you do if one of those sinister characters follows you? You are expecting the unexpected.

Now imagine yourself in your hometown on the street where you live. Again, it is nighttime, and you're walking alone. Now, however, the sensation is different. You are familiar with your surroundings. You know what to expect. If you live in a rough neighborhood, even the danger is familiar, and you know what you will do if you feel threatened. Here you may find your mind wandering from your immediate surroundings.

The point is this: When your surroundings are unfamiliar—that is, unfamiliar and potentially dangerous—you become preoccupied with those immediate surroundings. When you can't trust the environment, you become more self-centered. You relate to your interpersonal environment in much the same way. When you attend a party where you know virtually no one, you are likely to be a bit self-conscious for a while. At home with your family, you are more relaxed. You have no need to be defensive when your surroundings are familiar, when they cause little uncertainty, and when there is trust. You tend to trust what is familiar and predictable.

When you perceive others' behavior as threatening to your emotional security or position in a group, your uncertainty about your role in the group increases. Individual needs are elevated to a place equal to or even greater than the group's task and process needs. If you respond defensively you are likely to evoke further defensiveness from the rest of the group. People do not trust one another in a defensive, disconfirming climate. The realization that you cannot trust another suggests that that person's behavior is unpredictable—that you don't know for sure how he or she will respond. It's like being in that unfamiliar neighborhood. You're simply not sure what's going to happen so you guard against all contingencies. This uncertainty is counterproductive in a problem-solving group. On the other hand, in a supportive, confirming climate where mutual respect and trust prevail, you are more certain of your own well-being. This security, in turn, allows you to increase your concentration on the task and the process needs of the group.

LISTENING

Poor listening habits are one of the most common sources of defensiveness and disconfirmation. If you do not actively attend to what another person says, your responses will be perfunctory at best, and apathetic, impervious, or tangential at worst. It is even easier to be a poor listener in groups than it is in interpersonal situations because you do not have to respond to the speaker. All of those others can pick up the conversation. However, groups cannot reach their maximum effectiveness unless members listen actively to one another.

Listening is a skill that can be improved with practice. It is an active process through which people select, attend, understand, and remember. Listening takes effort. To listen effectively, people must actively select and attend to the messages they receive. This involves filtering out the other stimuli that compete for their attention: the hunger pangs they're starting to feel, the groceries they need to pick up on the way home, the attractive person nearby. Improving any skill takes knowledge and practice. This section will provide some knowledge. The practice is up to you. Are you listening?

Types of Listening

Glatthorn and Adams suggest that the three types of listening are hearing, analyzing, and empathizing.[5]

Hearing is the fundamental type of listening on which the other two types are built. "Hearing is receiving the message as sent."[6] Glatthorn and Adams point out that in order to achieve this seemingly simple objective, you must perform several complex operations. You must:

receive the sounds as transmitted;

translate these sounds into the words and meanings that were intended;

understand the relationship of those words in the sentences spoken;

note the relevant nonverbal cues that reinforce the message; comprehend the entire message as intended.[7]

Viewed in this way, hearing becomes a great deal more than a physiological response to stimuli. To say "I hear you" takes on new meaning.

Analyzing is "discerning the purpose of the speaker and using critical or creative judgment." Analyzing involves hearing but goes far beyond; it includes making judgments about unspoken messages, as well as the broader context in which messages were received. For example, many messages in small groups are aimed at persuading other group members. Often these messages contain emotional appeals, such as "Our group's failure to stand up in support of antiabortion laws is tantamount to murder!" Hearing this message is not difficult, particularly if the speaker's nonverbal behavior reinforces it. Analyzing it is a bit trickier. An appropriate response requires that you analyze the content of the message, the intent of the speaker, and the context within which the transaction takes place. You need to consider the persuasive strategy the speaker is employing, his or her degree of commitment to the issue, the nature and objectives of the group, and the probable positions other group members hold on the issue. In short, to respond with maximum effectiveness, you need to consider multiple factors instantaneously. Glatthorn and Adams claim that analyzing involves the following steps:

hearing the message accurately;

identifying the stated purpose;

inferring the unstated purpose;

determining if a critical or creative judgment is required;

responding accordingly.[8]

Empathizing is the most complex and difficult type of listening. It requires concentration, a sensitivity to the emotional content of messages, an ability to see the world from the speaker's viewpoint, and a willingness to suspend judgment.

Empathizing involves hearing and analyzing but again moves beyond them. It involves these steps:

hearing the message accurately;

listening to the unstated purpose;

withholding judgment;

seeing the world from the perspective of the speaker;

sensing the unspoken words;

responding with acceptance.[9]

Often problems that affect a group are expressed obliquely—not in the words themselves, but in the feelings behind the words.

Cindy: You all can do whatever you want to do. I'll go along with anything.

Toni: You sound as if you're not all here tonight. Is it something you can talk about?

Cindy: Oh, I'm having some problems at home. It'll all work out, but I can't get it out of my mind. I'm sorry if I'm a little distant tonight.

Floyd: That's OK. We understand.

Cindy has a problem that she brought with her to the group. While her problem does not affect the group directly, it can be a potential source of misunderstanding and conflict. Her seeming lack of interest in the group may be a cause for unwarranted anger:

Cindy: You all can do whatever you want. I'll go along with anything.

Lou: Dammit Cindy, I'm not going to let you get away with that. This group needs your ideas as much as anyone's and you just can't sit back and let us do all the work.

This insensitive response reflects Lou's failure to empathize, which results in a disconfirming response to Cindy. Toni's empathizing response in the first dialogue, however, was accepting and supporting. It promoted the group's understanding of the situation, which led to a more positive group climate.

Barriers to Effective Listening

As explained earlier, listening is the process of selecting, attending, understanding, and remembering. The previous discussion suggests that this process can take place at a number of levels. To fully attend to, understand, and remember what another is saying at any of these levels requires that you overcome the common obstacles

Effective listening skills—attending to, understanding, and remembering what others say—are essential for moving smoothly through a decision-making process.

to effective listening. There are many such barriers—outside distractions, an uncomfortable chair, a headache—but the focus here will be on two prevalent and serious barriers: prejudging and rehearsing.

Prejudging the Communicator or the Communication. Sometimes you simply don't like some people, or always disagree with them. You anticipate that what these people will say will be offensive, and you begin to tune them out. An example of this is many people's tendency not to listen carefully to the speeches of politicians who hold political beliefs different from their own. In a group you must overcome the temptation to ignore those you think are boring, pedantic, or offensive. Good ideas can come from anyone, even from people you don't like. Likewise, you should not prejudge certain topics as being too complex, boring, or controversial. This can be difficult, especially when a cherished belief is criticized or when others say things about you that you might not want to hear. These are precisely the times when communication needs to be clear, open, honest, and confirming. To communicate in that way, you need to listen.

Rehearsing a Response. This barrier is perhaps the most difficult to overcome. It is the tendency people have to rehearse in their minds what they will say when the other person is finished. One of the reasons for this barrier is the difference between speech rate and thought rate. Most people speak at a rate of about 100 to 125 words per minute, but they have the capacity to think or listen at a rate of 400 or more words per minute! This gives them the mental time and space to wander off while keeping one ear on the speaker. The thought/speech differential is better used, though, to attend fully to what the speaker is saying—and not saying. When people learn to do this, their responses can be more spontaneous, accurate, appropriate, confirming, and supportive.

A Guide to Active Listening

Supportive, confirming communication focuses not only on verbal messages but on the emotional content of nonverbal behaviors as well. Learning to quiet one's own thoughts and to avoid prejudging others is a first step. Fully understanding others, though, involves considerable effort.

Active listening is an attempt to clarify and understand another's thoughts and feelings. To listen actively involves several steps. You need to: (1) stop, (2) look, (3) listen, (4) question, (5) paraphrase content, and (6) paraphrase feelings.

Stop. Before you can effectively tune in to what someone else may be feeling, you need to stop what you are doing, eliminate as many distractions as possible, and focus fully on the other person.

Look. Now look for nonverbal clues that will help you identify how the other person is feeling. Most communication of emotion comes through nonverbal cues. The face provides important information about how a person is feeling, as do that person's voice quality, pitch, rate, volume, and use of silence. Body movement and posture clearly indicate the intensity of a person's feelings.

Listen. Listen for what another person is telling you. Even though that person may not say exactly how he or she feels, look for cues. Match verbal with nonverbal cues to decipher both the content and the emotion of the person's message. In addition, ask yourself, "How would I feel if I were in that person's position?" Try to interpret the message according to the sender's code system, rather than your own.

Ask Questions. As you try to understand another person, you may need to ask some questions. Most of these will serve one of four purposes: (1) to obtain additional information ("How soon will you be ready to give your part of our presentation?"), (2) to find out how someone feels ("Are you feeling overwhelmed by this assignment?"), (3) to ask for clarification of a word or phrase ("What do you mean when you say you didn't realize what you were getting into?"), and (4) to verify your conclusion about your partner's meaning or feeling ("Are you saying that you can't complete the project without some additional staff assistance?").

Paraphrase the Content. Paraphrasing is restating in your own words what you think another person is saying. Paraphrasing is different from parroting back everything that person has said. After all, you can repeat something perfectly without understanding what it means. Rather, from time to time, quickly summarize the message another person has given you so far.

> Emily: I think this job is too much for me; I'm not qualified to do it.
> Howard: You think you lack the necessary skills.

Note that at this point Howard is dealing only with the content of Emily's message. The goal of active listening, though, is to understand both the feelings and the content of another person's message.

Paraphrase Feelings. In the example above, Howard could follow his paraphrase of the content of the message with a question such as, "You're probably feeling pretty frustrated right now, aren't you?" Such a paraphrase would allow Emily either to agree with Howard's assessment or to clarify how she's feeling. For instance, she might respond, "No, I'm not frustrated. I'm just disappointed that the job's not working out."

Effective listening skills can contribute a great deal to building a supportive, cohesive group. Cohesiveness is an important factor in the life of a group and is the subject of the next section.

VERBAL DYNAMICS IN THE SMALL GROUP

The most obvious yet elusive component of small group communication is the spoken word. Words lie at the very heart of who and what people are. Their ability to represent the world symbolically gives humans the capacity to foresee events, to reflect on past experiences, to plan, to make decisions, and to consciously control their own behavior. Words are the tools with which people make sense of the world and share that sense with others.

Words As Barriers to Communication

While words can empower people to create new realities and to influence attitudes and behaviors, they can also impede the process that they facilitate. While speech communication gives individuals access to the ideas and inner worlds of other group members, it can also—intentionally or unintentionally—set up barriers to effective communication. Words affect group climate.

If you grew up in the United States you can probably remember chanting, defensively, "Sticks and stones can break my bones but names can never hurt me." Even as you uttered these lines you knew you were using a lie to protect yourself. You often unwittingly communicate in ways that threaten and make others feel defensive. When group members feel a need to protect themselves, they shift their attention from the group's goal to their own personal goal of self-protection, thus creating a barrier to effective group process. Some more subtle but pervasive word barriers are bypassing, allness, and fact-inference confusion.

Bypassing. The meanings of the words you use seem so obvious to you that you assume those words suggest the same meanings to others. Nothing could be further from the truth. Bypassing takes place when two people assign different meanings to the same word. Many words are open to an almost limitless number of interpretations. Consider, for example, the words *love, respect,* and *communication.* You may know precisely what you mean when you say that the department's account is "seriously overdrawn," but how are others to interpret that? How serious is "seriously"?

According to some estimates, the 500 most frequently used words in the English language have over 14,000 dictionary definitions. Considering that a dictionary definition reflects only a tiny percentage of all possible meanings for a word and that people from different cultures and with different experiences interpret words differently, it's amazing that people can understand one another at all.

In groups, the problem of bypassing is compounded by the number of people involved; the possibility for multiple misunderstandings is always present. This points to the importance of good feedback among group members. Feedback is any response by listeners that let speakers know whether they have been understood accurately. To overcome word barriers, people must understand that words are subjective. They need to check that what they understand from others is really what those others intend.

Allness. Allness statements are simple but untrue generalizations. You've probably heard such allness statements as "Women are smarter than men," "Men can run faster than women," and "Football players are stupid." These statements are convenient, but they simply aren't accurate. The danger of allness statements is that you may begin to believe them and to prejudge other people unfairly based on them. Therefore, be careful not to overgeneralize; remember that each individual is unique.

Fact-Inference Confusion. This problem occurs when people respond to something as if it were something they have actually observed when, in reality, it is merely a conclusion they have drawn. While statements of fact can be made only after direct observation, inferences can be made before, during, or after an occurrence—no observation is necessary. The key distinction is that in statements of inference people can speculate about and interpret what they *think* occurred. Suppose, for example, that you heard someone comment, "Men are better than women at math." If this statement were true, it would mean that *all* men and

REVIEW BOX

A Summary of Word Barriers and Their Solutions

Barrier	Description	Solution
Bypassing	Occurs when the same word is used to mean two different things.	Use specific language; be aware of multiple interpretations of what you say; clarify.
Allness Statements	Simple but untrue generalizations.	Don't overgeneralize; remember that all individuals are unique.
Fact-Inference Confusion	Mistaking a conclusion you have drawn for an observation.	Clarify and analyze; learn to recognize the difference between fact and inference, and communicate the difference clearly.

women were tested and that the results indicated that men are better in math than women. The statement is, in reality, an inference. If the speaker is summarizing research that has investigated the issue, he or she should say "Some studies have found that . . ." rather than "It's a fact that . . . ." The first statement more accurately describes reality than does the second. Like bypassing and allness statements, fact-inference confusion can lead to inaccuracy and misunderstanding.

GROUP COHESIVENESS

If this were a textbook in Introductory Physics, it would define *cohesion* as the mutual attraction that holds together the elements of a body. This, of course, is a small group communication textbook, but it offers a very similar definition of **group cohesiveness**. Cohesiveness is the degree of attraction that members feel toward one another and the group. It is a feeling of deep loyalty, of "groupness," of esprit de corps and the degree to which each individual has made the group's goal his or her own. Cohesiveness results from the interaction of a number of variables, including group composition, individual benefits derived from the group, task effectiveness, and, first and foremost, communication.

Composition and Cohesiveness

As noted in Chapter Three, people often join groups because they feel an attraction toward the people in that group. Factors discussed earlier, such as the similarity of group members or the degree to which group members' needs complement one another, are influential in the development of group cohesiveness. If people choose their own groups instead of being assigned to them, a strong sense of cohesiveness will more likely develop in those groups. According to Hare:

Since individuals who desire to be close to people will choose others who prefer closeness, it is generally true that "birds of a feather flock together." However, individuals who like to initiate tend to choose those who like to receive, so that it is also true that "opposites attract."

Groups containing a larger number of mutual choices on either a "work" or "play" criterion are often said to be highly "cohesive" in that they will "stick together" longer than groups in which there are few mutual choices.[10]

Individual Benefits and Cohesiveness

If cohesiveness is a combination of forces that hold people in groups, clearly the membership that brings people personal satisfaction must be important. Depending on the nature of the group, its members can derive benefits of affiliation, power, affection, and prestige. People like to be with groups in which these needs are satisfied. Such groups can become important reference groups in that they allow people to validate their judgments about themselves and others.[11] An important determinant of group cohesiveness, then, is the degree to which a particular group is capable of meeting members' needs in comparison to the ability of any other group to meet those same needs. If people perceive that they derive benefits from a group that no other group could provide, their attraction toward that group will strengthen considerably. This factor partially accounts for the intense attraction most people feel toward their families or closest friends.

Task Effectiveness and Cohesiveness

The relation of personal and interpersonal variables to group cohesiveness has already been discussed. The performance of the group as a whole has considerable influence as well; success fosters cohesiveness. The mutuality of concern for the group's task, which provides the focal point for working toward that task, becomes socially rewarding when the task is completed successfully. Here is another example of the interrelatedness of the task and social dimensions: Reaching a particular goal provides a common, rewarding experience for all group members. This commonality, or shared experience, further sets a group apart from other groups.

Communication and Cohesiveness

None of the factors described so far is enough, in and of itself, to build a cohesive group. Rather, the interaction of these variables determines the degree of cohesiveness in a group. Communication is the vehicle through which this interaction takes place. Through communication, individual needs are met and tasks are accomplished. In other words, "the communication networks and the messages that flow through them ultimately determine the attractiveness of the group for its members."[12]

Most of this book is devoted to the study of how communication affects small group process. The earlier discussion of defensive and supportive communication, for example, suggests some ways in which people can adjust their communicative behavior to improve group cohesiveness. In addition to the *quality* of communication, the *amount* of communication in the group also affects cohesiveness. Homans suggests: "If the frequency of interaction between two or more persons increases, the degree of their liking for one another will increase, and vice versa."[13] Free and open communication characterizes highly cohesive groups. The more people interact with one another, the more they reveal themselves to others and the more others reveal themselves to them. Through communication, people negotiate group roles, establish goals, reveal similarities and differences, resolve conflict, and express affection. It makes sense, then, that as the frequency of communication increases, so does the group's cohesiveness. Communication is also the foundation for interpersonal trust within the group.

Suggestions for Building a Cohesive Team

"Go team!" can be heard at most group sports events. Whether at a kindergarten touch football game or at the Super Bowl, team members are encouraged and rewarded for working together. How do teams become cohesive? Their members can begin to understand this process by learning how to identify characteristics of cohesive groups. Following are several suggestions to help you develop a cohesive team.[14]

1.   *Take time to learn about the needs, hopes, and goals of other team members.* A team goal is based on the individual goals of group members. One of the first tasks for team members is to become better acquainted with one another. What are members' goals and dreams for the group? Early group meetings should include activities that allow members to learn about one another. Chapter Four noted the value of self-disclosure in establishing comfortable interpersonal relationships. Revealing your hopes and goals for a group is an important part of the team-building process.

2.   *Clarify the goal of the group.* After individuals make suggestions about what a group should accomplish, the group needs to develop a single goal or set of goals. Without a common goal it will be difficult for members to work together as a team. Group goals need to weave individual goals into a framework that all group members can support. A group is like a symphony orchestra in that each member must be playing the same music.

3.   *Identify barriers that may keep the team from achieving its goal.* Once a goal is clearly articulated, a group needs to identify what keeps it from achieving that goal. The group should identify the barriers that it can change or overcome and the barriers that are beyond its resources to change. It needs to gather information, review the issues under consideration, and analyze the current situation.

REVIEW BOX

Suggestions for Enhancing Group Cohesiveness

Effective Groups	Ineffective Groups
Talk about the group in terms of "we" rather than "I."	Only emphasize individual contributions of group members.
Reinforce good attendance at group meetings.	Make no effort to encourage group members to attend every meeting.
Establish and maintain group traditions (e.g., each meeting ends with refreshments).	Make little or no effort to develop group traditions.
Set clear short-term as well as long-term group goals.	Avoid setting goals or establishing deadlines.
Encourage everyone in the group to participate in the group task.	Only use the most talkative members to do most of the work.
Celebrate (e.g., order a pizza, have a party, go to a movie together) when the group acheives a short-term as well as a long-term goal.	Discourage group celebrations; group meetings should be all work.
Let the group reflect on its history.	Group members talk only about getting the job done.
Stress teamwork.	Stress individual achievement.
Encourage the development of group norms.	Discourage the group from establishing common norms.

Adapted from Ernest G. Bormann and Nancy C. Bormann, *Effective Small Group Communication* (Minneapolis: Burgess Publishing Company, 1980), pp. 70–72.

---

4.   *Develop a plan to accomplish the goal.* Just as most sports teams have a playbook, any team needs a plan to accomplish a goal. A plan should be designed to help the group overcome the obstacles that are keeping the group from achieving its goal. If the barrier is too little money in the treasury, then the group needs a plan to raise funds. If lack of information is the problem, the group needs a research plan. To foster maximum team spirit, the plan should involve all team members, who should feel that their roles are important to achieving the team goal.

5.   *Put the plan into action.* Now the group must get to work. The most efficient way is to divide the plan into smaller tasks, make assignments, and complete the work. While this approach is efficient, make sure group members feel that they're working together to achieve a goal. They need to report back to the group periodically to keep everyone informed and to let other members suggest ideas and approaches for completing the assignments.

Figure 5-1 Equal Distribution of Communication

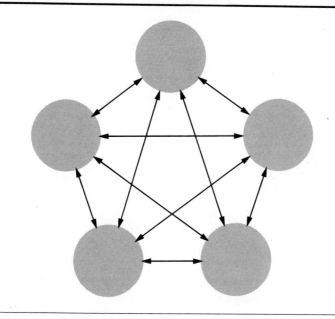

6. *Evaluate the plan and team procedures.* As the team works together, the group needs to evaluate how things are going periodically. Stop and assess whether the group's approach is achieving the desired results. Just like football coaches who look at films of last week's game, the group needs to replay its procedures and examine whether they're appropriate.

COMMUNICATION NETWORKS

Another influence on group climate is the **communication network**: Who talks to whom? If you think about the group meetings in which you participate, it may seem that while some people talk more than others, most of their communication is addressed to the group as a whole. Next time you're in a group, note who is talking to whom. You will find that people address relatively few comments to the group as a whole and that they direct most of what they say in groups toward specific persons. In some groups, people find that communication tends to be distributed equally among group members. Figure 5-1 represents such a distribution.

In some groups members address most comments to one central person, perhaps the designated leader or chairperson. Figure 5-2 represents this type of communicative pattern.

Other patterns may emerge, such as circular patterns, in which people talk primarily to those sitting next to them, or linear patterns, in which people communicate in a kind of chain reaction. These patterns may be built into the group from

Figure 5-2   Leader-Addressed Communication

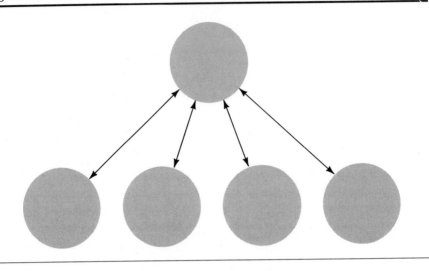

the outset, or they may emerge spontaneously. Either way, networks tend to stabilize over time. Once people establish channels of communication, they continue to use these same channels. This network of channels influences group climate as well as group productivity.

A review of research suggests that, in general, "groups in which free communication is maximized are generally more accurate in their judgments, although they may take longer to reach a decision."[15] People tend to feel more satisfied in groups in which they participate actively. When interaction is stifled or discouraged, people have less opportunity to satisfy their needs through communication. Groups with centralized communication networks (see Figure 5-2) are certainly more efficient. That efficiency enhances group cohesiveness, but considerable evidence suggests that free and open communication networks, which include everyone in the group (see Figure 5-1), are more likely to lead to more accurate group judgments as well as to more attractive group climates and to greater individual satisfaction.

ANOTHER FACTOR: GROUP SIZE

In a group, there is a positive relationship between the level of people's participation and the degree of their individual satisfaction. Obviously, as the size of a group increases, the opportunity to interact with other members decreases. What size should a group be in order to achieve maximum cohesiveness and productivity? Three heads are better than one, but are twenty heads better than three?

No one knows the precise number of people that will maximize the effectiveness of your group, but some observations may provide guidance. As a group's size increases, the principle of diminishing returns affects it. Imagine a long rope attached to a heavy weight. By yourself, using all of your strength, you may not be able to move that weight. As more people join you in your effort, the weight begins to move and the task becomes easier. But as the group size increases, individuals use smaller and smaller percentages of their total strength.[16] One study found that cohesiveness is positively related to the opportunity for interaction afforded by group size: As group size increases, the opportunity for interaction decreases.[17] Cohesiveness is also related to productivity. What, then, is the optimum size?

Herbert Thelen has suggested the principle of "least group size." Clearly people want groups small enough to encourage maximum participation yet large enough to generate the maximum number of ideas. Thelen says that "the group should be just large enough to include individuals with all the relevant skills for problem solution."[18] While this principle provides no firm rule about group size, it does at least provide a guideline. In small group communication, bigger is not necessarily better. Groups of five to seven members are just about right in size. Twelve is just about the right size for a small group—if five people don't show up.

GROUP CLIMATE AND PRODUCTIVITY

Thus far this chapter has discussed many variables that affect group climate—defensive behavior, confirming and disconfirming responses, group cohesiveness, group size—and has made some suggestions about how to improve the climate of groups. As already suggested, when communication is free and open and when everyone participates, people tend to feel more attraction toward the group and consequently receive more personal satisfaction. Another reason for developing and maintaining a positive group climate is that climate affects productivity.

When a group has a trusting, open atmosphere and a high level of cohesiveness, members "do not fear the effects that disagreement and conflict in the task dimension can have on their social fabric. *Cohesive groups have strong enough social bonds to tolerate conflict.*"[19] Chapters Seven and Nine explore the function of conflict in groups. Here it is enough to say that through constructive conflict, groups deal with the difficult issues confronting them. When there is no conflict, it is usually because people do not trust one another enough to assert their individuality. Avoiding the issues does not lead to clarity concerning those issues. An absence of clarity does not help the group reach the most effective solutions.

It is a mistake to view positive group climate or group cohesiveness as a condition in which everyone is nice all the time. Quite the contrary. In a highly cohesive group, members know that they will not be rejected for their views and are therefore more willing to express them—even though expressing them may provoke disagreement.

> At a point where someone in a cohesive group would say, "You're wrong!" or "I disagree!" an individual in a less cohesive group will say, "I don't understand," or "I'm confused." Members of groups with little cohesion have yet to create much of a common social reality.[20]

This common "social reality," which includes group roles and group norms, gives people the freedom to assert their individuality within a predictable context. In a cohesive group people already know that they are accepted in the group.

Another aspect of this social reality is the degree to which group members make the group's goal their own. In highly cohesive groups, individuals personally commit themselves to the group's well-being and to accomplishing the group's task. In part, this personal commitment can be attributed to the feeling that this particular group meets people's needs better than any other group. When this is the case, as it often is in a cohesive group, people have a degree of *dependence* on the group. This dependence increases the *power* the group has over individuals. To put this in a less intimidating way, "There can be little doubt that members of a more cohesive group more readily exert influence on one another and are more readily influenced by one another."[21] These factors—personal commitment to the group, personal dependence on the group, group power over individuals within the group—come together in a positive group climate. The result is that cohesive groups work harder than those groups with little cohesiveness, regardless of outside supervision.[22]

With few exceptions, building a group climate in which cohesiveness can grow results not only in greater individual satisfaction but in greater group productivity as well.

IMPROVING GROUP CLIMATE: PUTTING PRINCIPLE INTO PRACTICE

This chapter has taken a foray into some of the dynamics that contribute to group climate, examining variables that can make the group experience either stimulating and rewarding or stifling and frustrating. Material presented ranged from case studies to discussions of scholarly research:

- Jack Gibb found that people often communicate in ways that arouse *defensive* responses in others. When people are busy defending themselves, they cannot give much of themselves to the group effort. Conversely, people can communicate in ways that others perceive as *supportive.* To the extent that you engage in supportive communication, you will foster a positive group climate in which people are free to focus their attention on the group and its task.
- Sieberg identified patterns of communicating with responses that are either *confirming* (causing the others to value themselves more) or *disconfirming* (causing the others to value themselves less). If you can develop a sensitivity to your own confirming and disconfirming behaviors, you can become more

confirming in your group behavior, thus contributing to a more positive group climate.

- *Listening* is an active process of selecting, attending, understanding, and remembering. Effective listening is crucial to maintaining a positive group climate. Only by listening attentively can people gain the understanding necessary to respond accurately, appropriately, and supportively to others. To do this they need to overcome the barriers of prejudging and inner rehearsal. Listen actively. Remember to stop, look, listen, ask questions, and paraphrase.

- *Group cohesiveness* is measured by the degree of attraction that group members feel toward one another and the group. Cohesiveness is the result of the interaction of a number of variables, including the group's composition, individual benefits derived from the group, and task effectiveness and communication. Being aware of these factors can help foster group cohesiveness.

- Communication networks—patterns of interaction within a group—tend to stabilize over time. Keeping open the channels of communication among all group members improves group cohesiveness and the quality of group decision making. While such a network is usually desirable, it is less efficient (in terms of time alone) than communication networks in which all communication passes through one centralized person, such as a chairperson.

- People tend to have more positive feelings toward a group when they participate actively in it. Therefore, a point of diminishing returns affects group size. If you are forming a group, include just enough people to ensure the presence of all of the relevant skills for problem solving—and no more.

- A positive group climate is essential if you are to reach your maximum potential as a working group. A trusting and open climate allows all members the freedom of being themselves: to agree or disagree, or to engage in conflict without fear of rejection. The ability of a group not only to withstand but to benefit from constructive conflict is crucial to a group's productivity.

Perhaps you can use this information in ways that will contribute positively to the climate in *your* group.

PRACTICE

Confirmation/Disconfirmation

In your discussion group, stage a discussion in which group members attempt to use all of the disconfirming responses listed in this chapter. Choose a familiar topic about which everyone has something to say. Have observers keep a record of the number and type of disconfirming responses and the reactions (especially nonverbal) to them. Now repeat the discussion, covering as many of the same topics as possible, but this time concentrate on using only confirming responses. Again, have observers keep records. When you have completed both rounds of discussion, have group members discuss their reactions and have observers report their findings.

Group Climate Self-Assessment

How does your behavior affect group climate? The following questions may provide some insight. Circle the number of the response that most accurately describes your behavior in groups.[23]

1. I try to clarify the ideas of others.

7	6	5	4	3	2	1
Always	Usually	Frequently	50% yes 50% no	Occasionally	Seldom	Never

2. I plan what I am going to say while others are speaking.

1	2	3	4	5	6	7
Always	U	F	50/50	O	S	N

3. I tend to tell others when their ideas are irrelevant or inappropriate.

1	2	3	4	5	6	7
A	U	F	50/50	O	S	N

4. It is extremely important to me for the group to adopt my point of view.

1	2	3	4	5	6	7
A	U	F	50/50	O	S	N

5. My responses to others' comments are direct and supportive.

7	6	5	4	3	2	1
A	U	F	50/50	O	S	N

6. I express my ideas without concern for others' previous comments and personal feelings.

1	2	3	4	5	6	7
A	U	F	50/50	O	S	N

7. I make frequent contributions to a group discussion.

7	6	5	4	3	2	1
A	U	F	50/50	O	S	N

8. In a group I feel free to share my feelings about the group's task and other group members.

7	6	5	4	3	2	1
A	U	F	50/50	O	S	N

9. I encourage my group to confront problems as they arise.

7	6	5	4	3	2	1
A	U	F	50/50	O	S	N

10. I praise others for their good ideas.

7	6	5	4	3	2	1
A	U	F	50/50	O	S	N

Add up the circled numbers to determine your score. Compare your score with other group members. Discuss the results.

Variation: Complete this exercise as you believe other group members would respond. To what degree do your perceptions and theirs coincide? Why are there differences?

Fact or Inference?

Read the following three stories. Assume that all the information presented is accurate. You can refer back to the stories whenever you wish. Next, read the statements following each story. If the statements following the story are true (verified by information in the story as factual) circle *T* for true. If the statements are false (contrary to the information in the story) circle *F* for false. If you are unable to determine whether the statements are true or false (an inference) circle the *?*

 After you have completed these three exercises individually, meet in a small group and reach consensus as a group on the correct answer. Your instructor will supply the correct answers to help you sort out fact from inference.[24]

Story A: As you step onto your front porch from your living room you observe a delivery truck approaching along the street. You see that your next-door neighbor is backing her car from her garage into the street in the path of the approaching truck. You see the truck swerve, climb over the curbing, and come to a stop against a tree, which crumples one of its front fenders.

Statements About Story A

1. Your next-door neighbor was backing her car into the street in the path of an approaching truck.   T   F   ?
2. The delivery truck was traveling at a reasonable speed.   T   F   ?
3. The only damage resulting from the incident was to the truck's fender.   T   F   ?
4. You saw the truck swerve and climb over the curbing.   T   F   ?
5. Your neighbor across the street was backing her car out of the garage.   T   F   ?
6. The truck suffered no damage.   T   F   ?
7. You saw the truck approaching as you stepped onto your front porch from your living room.   T   F   ?
8. The man who drove the delivery truck swerved and ran his truck up over a curbing.   T   F   ?

9. The delivery truck driver swerved in order to miss a child play-
    ing in the street.   T F ?

Story B: A man, his wife, and his sons, aged 11 and 14, drove across the country
on a vacation trip in their three-year-old automobile. They started the trip on a
Friday, the thirteenth of the month. The wife said she did not like the idea of
leaving on that day, and the man laughed at her statement. In the course of the
trip the following mishaps occurred:

> The automobile radiator sprang a leak.
> The 11-year-old boy became carsick for the first time in his life.
> The wife was badly sunburned.
> The man lost his fishing rod.

Statements About Story B

1. There were fewer than two children in the family.   T F ?
2. The sedan's radiator sprang a leak.   T F ?
3. The wife really didn't mind leaving on Friday the thirteenth. T F ?
4. A fishing reel was lost.   T F ?
5. The family's trip began on Friday the thirteenth.   T F ?
6. The 11-year-old boy lost his fishing rod.   T F ?
7. The story mentions the name of the family taking the trip.   T F ?
8. The make of the automobile in which the family made the trip
    was not mentioned in the story.   T F ?
9. The man laughed at his wife's fears of Friday the 13th.   T F ?

Story C: John and Betty Smith are awakened in the middle of the night by a noise
coming from the direction of their living room. John Smith investigates and finds
that the door opening into the garden, which he thought he had locked before going
to bed, is standing wide open. Books and papers are scattered all over the floor,
around the desk in one corner of the room.

Statements About Story C

1. Betty Smith was awakened in the middle of the night.   T F ?
2. John Smith locked the door from his living room to his garden
    before going to bed.   T F ?
3. The books and papers were scattered between the time John
    Smith went to bed and the time he was awakened.   T F ?
4. John Smith found that the door opening into the garden
    was shut.   T F ?

5. John Smith did not lock the garden door.   T   F   ?
6. John Smith was not awakened by a noise.   T   F   ?
7. Nothing was missing from the room.   T   F   ?
8. Betty Smith was sleeping when she and her husband
    were awakened.   T   F   ?
9. The noise did not come from their garden.   T   F   ?
10. John Smith saw no burglar in the living room.   T   F   ?
11. John and Betty Smith were awakened in the middle of the night
    by a noise.   T   F   ?

Notes

1. Jack R. Gibb, "Defensive Communication," *Journal of Communication* 11 (September 1961): 141.

2. Alvin Goldberg and Carl Larson, *Group Communication: Discussion Processes and Applications* (Englewood Cliffs, New Jersey: Prentice-Hall, 1975), p. 105.

3. Evelyn Sieburg and Carl Larson, "Dimensions of Interpersonal Response," (paper delivered at the annual conference of the International Communication Association, Phoenix, April 1971): 1.

4. Goldberg and Larson, pp. 103–104.

5. Allan A. Glatthorn and Herbert R. Adams, *Listening Your Way to Management Success* (Glenview, Illinois: Scott, Foresman and Company, 1984).

6. *Ibid.,* p. 1.

7. *Ibid.,* p. 2.

8. *Ibid.,* p. 2.

9. *Ibid.,* p. 3.

10. A. Paul Hare, *Handbook of Small Group Research,* 2nd ed. (New York: Free Press, 1976), p. 10.

11. *Ibid.,* p. 171.

12. Ernest G. Bormann, *Discussion and Group Methods: Theory and Practice,* 2nd ed. (New York: Harper & Row, Publishers, 1975), pp. 162–163.

13. George C. Homans, *The Human Group* (New York: Harcourt Brace, 1950), p. 112.

14. Adapted from David W. Johnson and Frank P. Johnson, *Joining Together: Group Theory and Group Skills* (Englewood Cliffs, New Jersey: Prentice-Hall, 1975), p. 304.

15. Hare, p. 343.

16. W. Moede, "Guidelines for a Psychology of Achievement," *Industrielle Psychotechnik* 4: 193–209.

17. Stanley Seashore, *Group Cohesiveness in the Industrial Work Group* (Ann Arbor: University of Michigan Press, 1954).

18. Herbert A. Thelan, "Group Dynamics in Instruction: Principle of Least Group Size," *School Review* 57 (1949): 139–148.

19. Bormann, p. 145.

20. *Ibid.,* pp. 144–145.

21. Dorwin Cartwright and Alvin Zander, *Group Dynamics: Research and Theory,* 3rd ed. (New York: Harper & Row, Publishers, 1968), p. 104.

22. Hare, p. 340.

23. We extend our gratitude to our colleague Norman H. Watson for his assistance in developing this questionnaire.

24. This exercise was developed by T. Richard Cheatham and Robert Shermer for Oral Communication Handbook (Warrensburg, Missouri: Central Missouri State University, 1972).

Chapter Six

Nonverbal Group Dynamics

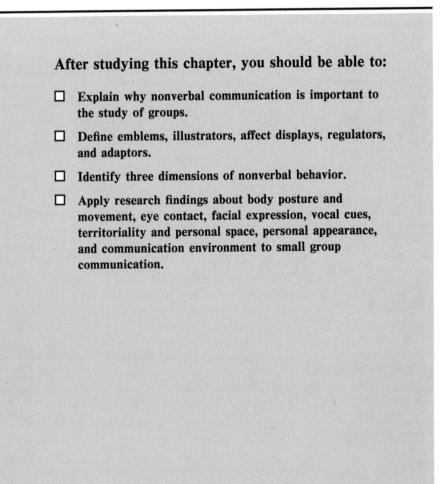

After studying this chapter, you should be able to:

☐ Explain why nonverbal communication is important to the study of groups.

☐ Define emblems, illustrators, affect displays, regulators, and adaptors.

☐ Identify three dimensions of nonverbal behavior.

☐ Apply research findings about body posture and movement, eye contact, facial expression, vocal cues, territoriality and personal space, personal appearance, and communication environment to small group communication.

The scene is Paris, 1968. As the world holds its breath, delegates from the United States, South Vietnam, North Vietnam, and the National Liberation Front gather to negotiate an end to the long Vietnam conflict. All sides seem willing to compromise, but the talks come close to ending before they begin when bitter disagreement erupts over the seemingly trivial matter of seating arrangement. Newspaper headlines announce: "NEGOTIATORS DISAGREE OVER SEATING ARRANGEMENT—PEACE TALKS POSTPONED." Who sat where would have reflected the status of the conferees, and on that issue they were not prepared to compromise. It took eight months for negotiators to agree on a round table, *a la* King Arthur, so that all representatives could be at an equal distance from one another. The initial squabble over seating arrangement had an unproductive effect on the talks. In this case, the individuals involved represented governments; however, similar nonverbal dynamics come into play in corporate boardrooms, conferences, and other groups.

What is nonverbal communication? Just what is involved in nonverbal group dynamics? Scholars have yet to arrive at a consensus regarding these questions. The following definition of **nonverbal communication** is useful: Nonverbal communication is communication behavior other than written or spoken language that creates meaning for someone. In the context of a small group, this definition includes such behaviors as body posture and movement, eye contact, facial expression, seating arrangement, tone of voice, spatial relationship, and personal appearance.

Much of the research about nonverbal group behavior summarized in this chapter is not based on studies that have specifically examined nonverbal communication in small groups; relatively few studies of this nature have been conducted. Researchers have found it difficult to observe and classify nonverbal cues in a group where each person emits a myriad of nonverbal cues simultaneously. Despite the lack of research on nonverbal dynamics in small groups, understanding how you display and respond to nonverbal cues should help you become more sensitive to the effects of nonverbal behaviors in groups. As already noted, communicating with several people in a small group can result in anxiety and uncertainty. You may not know how to solve the problem confronting the group, what role to assume, and how to maintain group cohesiveness so that all members will be satisfied with the outcome. Learning about what types of nonverbal behavior occur in small group discussions and some effective methods for sending and processing nonverbal information can reduce much of the uncertainty that frequently surfaces during problem-solving group discussions.

Every message contains both content and information about relationships. Nonverbal messages, particularly facial expression and vocal cues, are often the prime source of information about interpersonal relationships. They thus play important **metacommunication** functions. Metacommunication literally means communication about communication. The nonverbal aspects of a message communicate information about verbal aspects of a message.

The purposes of this chapter are (1) to identify the importance of nonverbal communication to the study of small groups, (2) to identify two frameworks for describing nonverbal communication, and (3) to discuss the application of research in nonverbal communication to small groups.

THE IMPORTANCE OF NONVERBAL COMMUNICATION TO GROUP COMMUNICATION

Have you been involved with a small group student project or served on a committee in which you felt uncomfortable or out of place? While you couldn't identify why you felt odd, you knew something was wrong. You felt uneasy, not because of what was being said, but perhaps because of something unspoken. Maybe the apathetic facial expressions or the unenthusiastic vocal qualities exhibited by other group members bothered you. Maybe it was the room in which your meeting was held. (Was it hot and stuffy or unattractively decorated?) You may not have realized it at the time, but the nonverbal dynamics of that unexciting, uncomfortable meeting probably helped create an unproductive group climate. On the other hand, you can probably remember some small group discussions that were positive experiences because other members were sensitive to both verbal and nonverbal processes. Members' body posture and eye contact may have suggested that they were involved in the discussion. Perhaps you met in a comfortable room. In short, the group meeting seemed interesting, exciting, and productive. Although not all unexciting group discussions result from poor nonverbal communication, nonverbal variables dramatically affect a group's climate and members' attitudes toward the group.

Nonverbal communication variables are important to small group communication for at least three reasons. First, group participants spend more time communicating nonverbally than they do verbally. Second, people believe nonverbal communication cues more than verbal messages. Third, people communicate emotions primarily by nonverbal cues.

1. *In groups people spend more time communicating nonverbally than they do verbally.* In a small group discussion, usually only one person speaks at a time. The rest of the members can, however, emit a host of nonverbal cues that influence group deliberations. Eye contact, facial expression, body posture and movement (some cues are controlled consciously, others are emitted less intentionally) occur

even when only one person is speaking. Since group members are usually within just a few feet of one another, they can easily observe most nonverbal cues. Viewing nonverbal communication from the broadest perspective, it is safe to say that "you cannot *not* communicate."

2. *People believe nonverbal messages more than verbal messages.* Nonverbal communication affects how others interpret our messages. Nonverbal cues are so important to communication that when a verbal message (either spoken or written) contradicts a nonverbal message, people are more inclined to believe the nonverbal message. The group member who sighs and, with a sarcastic edge, says, "Oh, what a great group this is going to be," communicates just the opposite meaning of that verbal message. One researcher estimates that people communicate 65 percent of the social meaning of messages nonverbally.[1]

Perhaps people often have more faith in the validity of the nonverbal message than they do in the verbal message because nonverbal messages are more difficult to fake. People can easily monitor their speech—they hear what they are saying. However, they are not always aware of what they are doing nonverbally. As you read this page, are you constantly aware of your posture? Are you moving your hands or your feet? Are you aware of your facial expression? Sigmund Freud, in noting the validity of nonverbal messages, wrote, "He that has eyes to see and ears to hear may convince himself that no mortal can keep a secret. If his lips are silent, he chatters with his fingertips; betrayal oozes out of him at every pore."[2] Actions do speak louder than words.

3. *People communicate emotions and feelings primarily by nonverbal cues.* If a group member is frustrated with the group or disenchanted with the discussion, more than likely you will detect those feelings by observing that person's nonverbal behavior—even before the member verbalizes his or her frustration. If a member seems genuinely interested in the discussion and pleased with the group's progress, this, too, can be observed through nonverbal behavior. Albert Mehrabian and some of his colleagues devised a formula that suggests how much of the total emotional meaning of a message is based on verbal components and how much on nonverbal components.[3] According to his research, only 7 percent of the emotional meaning of a message is communicated through its verbal content. About 38 percent of the impact of the emotional content is derived from the voice (from such things as the rate, pitch, quality, and volume). The largest source of emotional meaning, 55 percent, is a speaker's facial expression. Generalizing from this formula, approximately 93 percent of emotions are communicated nonverbally. Although these percentages cannot be applied to all situations, Mehrabian's research suggests that when inconsistencies exist between people's verbalized emotional states and their true emotions, expressed nonverbally, nonverbal cues carry more clout in determining how receivers interpret speakers' emotions.

An understanding of nonverbal communication, then, is vital to even a cursory understanding of communication in general and of group communication in particular. As you become a more skillful observer of nonverbal behavior, you will understand more thoroughly the way people interact in small groups.

FRAMEWORKS FOR DESCRIBING AND ANALYZING NONVERBAL CUES

To better observe nonverbal behavior in small groups, you need a basic vocabulary to help you describe the behavior you see. Researchers have developed various systems for classifying nonverbal behavior. While these approaches have not been devised specifically for small groups, two of these systems should help you analyze nonverbal behavior and interpret the meanings of nonverbal messages.

A system devised by Ekman and Friesen will help you describe nonverbal messages in small groups.[4] A framework developed by Mehrabian will help you assess the meaning of nonverbal messages.[5]

Categories of Nonverbal Communication

Ekman and Friesen identified five major types of nonverbal behavior: (1) **emblems**, (2) **illustrators**, (3) **affect displays**, (4) **regulators**, and (5) **adaptors**.

Emblems. Emblems are nonverbal cues that have specific verbal counterparts and are shared by all group members. Emblems often take the place of spoken words, letters, or numbers. Group leaders who want groups to quiet down and place index fingers vertically in front of their lips use a nonverbal emblem to take the place of the words, "Shhhh, let's be quiet now." A hitchhiker's raised thumb and a soldier's salute are other examples of emblems. Group members who point to their watches to indicate that the group should get on with it because time is running out and group members who use their index fingers and thumbs to signify all is OK also depend on nonverbal emblems to communicate their messages.

Illustrators. Illustrators are nonverbal behaviors that add meaning to accompanying verbal messages. In a group you may see a gesture illustrating emphasis. Several researchers have observed that people synchronize many of their body movements to their speech.[6] A blink of the eyes, a nod of the head, and a shift in body posture accent spoken messages. A nonverbal illustrator might contradict what someone is saying. A group member who stares out the window with an apathetic facial expression and says, "Sure, I'm interested in working in this group," nonverbally illustrates boredom and apathy. A group member who emphasizes a point by shaking a fist in the face of another member illustrates conviction and determination.

Affect Displays. An affect display is a nonverbal cue that communicates emotion. As mentioned before, the face is the primary source of emotional display. Research suggests that the body indicates the intensity of the emotion, or affect, that is being

Categories of Nonverbal Communication

Category	Description	Example
Emblems	Movements and gestures that replace spoken messages.	Group members shake their heads to communicate no.
Illustrators	Nonverbal behaviors that add meaning to accompany verbal communication.	Group members say "it was this long," holding their hands three feet apart.
Affect Displays	Expressions of feeling and emotions.	Frowning, smiling, grimacing, smirking.
Regulators	Behaviors that control the flow of communication between people.	Eye contact, raising a hand or a finger to signal you want to talk.
Adaptors	Movements that satisfy personal needs and help you adapt to your environment.	Scratching, yawning, adjusting your glasses.

expressed. For example, the faces of group members may indicate that they are bored with a meeting. If they are also slouched in their chairs, they are probably more than just moderately apathetic about the discussion. If you've seen a television game show in which a young woman has just won a new sports car, you've noticed that her face tells you she's happy and that her jumping up and down and hugging and kissing the MC tells you the intensity of her ecstasy.

Regulators. Regulators help control the flow of communication. They are very important to small group discussions because people rely on them to know when they should talk and when they should listen. Regulators also provide cues to when other group members want to contribute to the discussion. Eye contact, posture, gestures, facial expression, and body position all help regulate communication in a group discussion. Generally, large groups operate with a rather formal set of regulators; participants raise their hands so that the chairperson will recognize them before they speak. In a less formal discussion, group members rely on direct eye contact (to indicate that a communication channel is open), facial expression (raised eyebrows often signify a desire to talk), and gestures (such as a raised index finger) as cues to regulate the flow of communication.

Adaptors. This final category includes nonverbal acts that satisfy personal needs and help people adapt to their immediate environment. Adaptors are also important for learning to get along with others and for responding to certain situa-

Nonverbal cues, such as a body posture that indicates boredom at the stockholders' meeting shown here, are important indicators of how well a group is performing.

tions. Generally, people are not aware of most of their adaptive nonverbal behavior. Self-adaptors, for example, refer to things people do to their own bodies, like scratching, rubbing, or touching themselves. Researchers have noted that when people become nervous, anxious, or upset, they frequently display more self-adaptive behaviors.[7]

Dimensions of Nonverbal Meaning

Ekman and Friesen's five-category framework helps describe more accurately the nonverbal behavior people observe in groups and in other situations that involve interpersonal communication. Mehrabian, another researcher interested in nonverbal communication, has developed a three-dimensional model that identifies how people respond to nonverbal messages. Again, even though Mehrabian's approach was not designed exclusively for small groups, his framework can be usefully applied to nonverbal group dynamics. By identifying the kinds of information people receive from nonverbal messages, Mehrabian's framework helps assign meaning to specific nonverbal behaviors. His research suggests that people ascribe meaning to nonverbal behavior based on (1) **immediacy**, (2) **potency**, and (3) **responsiveness**.

Immediacy. As defined by Mehrabian, immediacy refers to whether individuals like or dislike others. The immediacy principle states, "People are drawn toward persons and things they like, evaluate highly, and prefer; and they avoid or move away from things they dislike, evaluate negatively, or do not prefer."[8] According to Mehrabian's research, such nonverbal behaviors as touching, leaning forward, reducing distance and personal space, and maintaining direct eye contact can communicate liking or positive feelings. Based on the immediacy principle, group members who consistently sit closer to you, establish more eye contact with you,

REVIEW BOX

Dimensions of Nonverbal Meaning

Dimension	Definition	Nonverbal Cues
Immediacy	Behaviors that signal liking, attraction, and interest.	Touch, forward lean, close personal space, eye contact.
Potency	Behaviors that communicate power, status, and influence.	Protected space, increased distance, relaxed posture.
Responsiveness	Behaviors that communicate active interactions and attention.	Eye contact, varied vocal cues, animated facial expression.

and, in general, are drawn to you probably like you more than group members who generally don't look at you and who regularly select seats away from you.

Potency. Mehrabian's second dimension of meaning refers to the communication of status or power. People of higher status generally determine the degree of closeness permitted in their interactions. A person of higher status, for example, generally has a more relaxed body posture when interacting with a person of lower status.[9] During weekly sales meetings, the sales manager may feel quite comfortable leaning back in a chair with feet propped on the desk, while salespeople with considerably less status probably maintain more formal postures in the presence of their boss.

Responsiveness. Responsiveness refers to whether you perceive others as active or passive, energetic or dull, fast or slow. Body movement, facial expression, and variation of vocal cues (such as the pitch, rate, volume, and quality of the voice) all contribute to your perceptions of others as responsive or unresponsive. A group leader who communicates energy and enthusiasm would be rated highly responsive.

APPLICATIONS OF NONVERBAL COMMUNICATION RESEARCH

Nonverbal cues do not create meaning independently of other communication cues (e.g., message content, language style, and message organization). Also keep in mind that at this point in the development of nonverbal communication theory, there is much we do *not* know about nonverbal communication. After reading the research conclusions reported here you may be tempted to interpret someone else's body language, but you should remember several principles when ascribing meaning to the posture and movement of others.

1.   *Nonverbal behavior must be interpreted in the context in which it occurs.* Just as you can misunderstand the meaning of a sentence taken out of context, so can you make an inaccurate inference about a nonverbal behavior when it is interpreted out of context. Simply because a group member sits with crossed legs and folded arms does not necessarily mean that that person doesn't want to communicate with others. Other variables in the communication system may be affecting the member's posture and position.

2.   *People respond differently to different stimuli.* Not all people express emotions in the same manner. It may take considerable time before you can understand the unique, idiosyncratic meaning underlying specific nonverbal behaviors that another person exhibits.

3.   *People respond nonverbally in a manner appropriate for the culture from which they learned the behavior.* Several researchers have documented cultural differences in the ways people use posture, movement, personal space, territory, facial expression, and time.[10] The groups you belong to may adopt certain normative nonverbal behaviors. They may develop behaviors acceptable in their specific groups that may not be appropriate in other groups. For example, a group of students may find it acceptable for members to sit on the floor with their legs crossed. A group that includes faculty and administrators might expect a more formal seating posture.

4.   *The longer you associate with your group, the more likely it becomes that you can accurately assess members' nonverbal messages.* As you spend time working with group members, chances are that you will gain insight in how to interpret their nonverbal cues. For example, when you first met Lee you weren't sure why he seemed so distant and aloof. His lack of eye contact suggested that he wasn't interested in being a productive member of the group. After you'd spent several meetings getting to know him better, you realized that Lee is simply shy. He has good ideas but needs to be drawn out. Working with him convinces you that you shouldn't make snap judgments of other group members. First impressions are not always accurate.

5.   *If you are unsure about how to interpret someone's nonverbal behavior, seek more information; ask others if your interpretation is accurate.* You draw conclusions about others based on their behavior rather than their intent. The only way to determine what others intend is to ask them. Since nonverbal cues can be misleading, if you want to interpret someone's nonverbal behavior correctly, simply ask that person what he or she intended.

As chairperson of a committee to raise money for a new library, you suggest a door-to-door campaign to bring in additional revenue. As you suggest this, group members look at you in silence. You could infer that they think your idea is stupid, and you might quickly say, "Oh, forget it. I guess it really wasn't a good idea."

Group members may like your suggestion, but they could just be thinking about how to implement it. If you're not sure what their silence means, ask them. You could say, "Does your silence mean that you're not really in favor of the idea?" Check your perception of members' response. Don't just assume you are accurately reading them by their nonverbal clues alone.

These principles point to a key conclusion: Nonverbal messages are considerably more ambiguous than verbal messages. No dictionary has definitive meanings for nonverbal behaviors. Exert caution, then, when you attempt to interpret the nonverbal behavior of other group members.

The following sections describe some research so that you can become more sensitive to your own nonverbal behavior and to the role nonverbal communication plays in small group discussions. Specifically, the sections will discuss the following aspects of research in nonverbal communication in small groups: (1) body posture and movement, (2) eye contact, (3) facial expression, (4) vocal cues, (5) territory and personal space, (6) personal appearance, and (7) communication environment.

Body Posture and Movement

On the cover of Julius Fast's best-selling book *Body Language,* a female model with a black miniskirt, legs crossed at the knee, and a cigarette poised between the fingers of her right hand looks seductive while she flashes a faint Mona Lisa smile. The caption on the book cover reads, "Does her body say that she's a loose woman? Does her body say that she's a manipulator? . . . is she a phony? . . . is she lonely?"[11] You are meant to infer that by "reading" another person's body language (and by reading Fast's book, of course), you will be able to answer those questions. Unfortunately, the sophistication of nonverbal communication theory does not permit you to make conclusive statements about an individual's personality and habits based solely on nonverbal information. You do know, however, that body posture and movement provide information about status, intensity of attitudes, warmth, and search for approval. Thus, a group member who is sensitive to the body postures and movements of other group members is probably in a better position to evaluate the overall mood and climate of the group.

Mehrabian has done extensive testing to identify what types of nonverbal postures and movements contribute to other people's positive perceptions of you. As noted in the discussion of Mehrabian's immediacy principle, an open body and arm position, a forward lean, a relaxed posture, and touching may increase perceived liking.[12] People may often exhibit greater immediacy behaviors (e.g., more eye contact, more direct body orientation, more of a forward lean, and closer distance to others) when attempting to persuade others.[13] They may also be more successful at changing attitudes if they elicit more nonverbal immediacy cues.[14] During your next small group discussion, when one member tries to persuade another, see if you can detect increased immediacy displayed on the part of the group member advocating a point.

Mehrabian also associates body posture and movement with status. In summarizing the results of Mehrabian's research on status, Knapp concludes that:

> [High-status individuals] are associated with less eye gaze; postural relaxation; greater voice loudness; more frequent use of arms akimbo; dress ornamentation with power symbols; greater territorial access; more expansive movements and postures; greater height; and more distance.[15]

If status differences exist among members of groups to which you belong, try to identify the nonverbal behaviors that enhance high-status positions in the group.

Do you think you can tell whether someone is lying by observing that person's nonverbal cues? Several researchers have investigated how nonverbal behaviors betray people's efforts to conceal their thoughts. Ekman and Friesen found that feet and legs often reveal people's true feelings.[16] The researchers theorize that while people consciously manipulate their facial expressions to hide deception, they are not so likely to monitor their feet. You may more readily detect anxiety, then, by observing nervous movement of people's feet and legs than by looking for clues in their faces or other areas of the body that they are likely to control consciously. Consider the following description of nonverbal behaviors that could indicate lying or deception:

> ... liars will have a higher pitch, less gaze duration and longer adaptor duration, fewer illustrators (less enthusiastic), more hand-shrug emblems (uncertainty), more adaptors—particularly face play adaptors; and less nodding, more speech errors, slower speaking rate and less-immediate positions relative to their partners.[17]

Simply because group members may exhibit one or more of these nonverbal behaviors does not mean that they are attempting to deceive other members. While an individual attempting to conceal something or to lie may exhibit the cues listed above, not everyone who displays such behavior is deceptive. The ambiguity of nonverbal cues prevents you from drawing such definitive conclusions about the motives of other people based on nonverbal cues alone.

Still other researchers have attempted to identify which nonverbal cues are correlated with leadership. O'Connor discovered that frequent gesturing was highly correlated with individuals who were perceived by other members to be leaders in small groups.[18] In a follow-up study, Baird found that group members who were thought by other members to be group leaders used shoulder and arm gestures more often.[19] While leaders may gesture more frequently than followers, it does not mean that frequent gesturing causes a person to emerge as a leader. The evidence does not suggest a cause-and-effect relationship.

Do individuals in small groups use certain nonverbal cues during their attempts to persuade others? Mehrabian and Williams found that persuasive communicators exhibit more animated facial expressions, use more gestures to emphasize their points, and nod their heads more than do those who are less persuasive.[20] Another team of researchers found that people trying to project warm, friendly images will be more likely to smile, be less likely to fidget with their hands, and be more likely to shift their postures toward others.[21]

A final interesting line of research into body posture and movement suggests that in social situations you synchronize your movements and posture to the movements, postures, and speech of others. For example, at the end or beginning of a sentence spoken by another, you may nod your head or display a facial expression to agree or disagree with the comment. Condon and others, using slow-motion films, documented a distinct relationship between facial expressions and head movements and speech.[22] Kendon observed that people may shift their body positions in response to verbal messages.[23] Navarre and Emihovich report similar evidence that group members may respond in synchrony to the movements and postures of others.[24] These authors suggest that people, during group interactions, may adapt poses similar to those of others they like or agree with. Thus, coalitions of group members may be identified not only by their verbal agreement but also by their synchronized nonverbal behavior. It is probably more than just coincidence that group members consistently fold their arms and cross their legs in the same way. Just as religious services use singing and group litanies to establish unity and a commonality of purpose, small groups may unwittingly utilize common nonverbal behaviors to foster cohesiveness. Counselors report that they can help clients self-disclose by adopting body postures similar to those of their clients. By synchronizing body position, counselors believe they can better empathize and establish rapport with their clients. In your small group discussions, observe the similarity and dissimilarity of members' postures, positions, and gestures. Such cues may reveal interesting insights about group climate, leadership, and cohesiveness.

Collectively, the studies of body posture and movement suggest how you will be perceived by other group members in terms of status, deception, leadership, and persuasiveness.

Eye Contact

Have you ever felt uncomfortable because the person you were talking with seemed reluctant to establish eye contact? Maybe you've wondered, "Why doesn't she look at me when she's talking to me?" Perhaps you've had just the opposite experience—the person you were talking with seemed to stare constantly at you. You become uneasy in these situations because they violate norms of eye-contact. While you may think that you do a pretty good job of establishing eye contact with others, researchers estimate that most people look at others only between 30 and 60 percent of the time.[25] Eye contact usually lasts less than 10 seconds.

Several factors determine when eye contact occurs. Based on a summary of the literature, Knapp provides a good review of the factors that generally encourage and discourage eye contact in interpersonal situations.[26] You are *more* likely to engage in eye contact with others when:

you are physically distant from your partner
you are discussing easy, impersonal topics

there is nothing else to look at

you are interested in your partner's reactions—that is, you are interpersonally involved

you are interested in your partner—that is, like or love the partner

you are trying to dominate or influence your partner

you are from a culture that emphasizes visual contact in interaction

you are an extrovert

you have high affiliative or inclusion needs

you are dependent on your partner (and the partner has been unresponsive)

you are listening rather than talking

you are female

You are *less* likely to look at others when:

you are physically close

you are discussing difficult, intimate topics

you have other relevant objects, people, or backgrounds to look at

you are not interested in your partner's reactions

you are talking rather than listening

you are not interested in your partner—that is, dislike the partner

you are from a culture that imposes sanctions on visual contact during interaction

you are an introvert

you are low on affiliative or inclusion needs

you have a mental disorder like autism, schizophrenia, and the like

you are embarrassed, ashamed, sorrowful, sad, submissive, or trying to hide something

When eye contact does occur in a small group setting, it may serve one or more important functions: (1) cognitive function, (2) monitoring function, (3) regulatory function, and (4) expressive function.[27]

Cognitive Function. This function of eye contact operates when eyes indicate thought processes. For example, some people look away when they are thinking of just the right words to say. Others look away just before they speak so that they will not be distracted by the person they are talking to.

Monitoring Function. Monitoring is the way you seek feedback from others when communicating with them. While addressing a small group, you determine how effectively or ineffectively you are expressing yourself by looking at group members and monitoring their feedback. If you say something that other members disagree with, you may observe a change in facial expressions, body postures, or movements.

Eye contact not only provides other people with cues about your thoughts and attitudes but tells them how involved or how uninvolved you are in the discussion.

You may then decide that you need to spend more time developing and explaining your point.

Regulatory Function. Eye contact plays a vital role in regulating the back-and-forth flow of communication. You can invite interaction simply by looking at others. For example, assume the chairperson of a committee asks for volunteers for an assignment. If you don't want to be volunteered for the task, you probably will not establish eye contact with the chairperson, just as you do not establish eye contact when a teacher asks a question and you don't know the answer. Direct eye contact may be interpreted as an open communication channel, meaning that you would not mind being called on for the answer.

Expressive Function. While eyes generally do not provide clues about specific emotions, the immediate area around the eyes provides quite a bit of information about feelings and emotions.

Functions of Eye Contact

Cognitive Function	Provides cues about thought processes.
Monitoring Function	Seeks feedback from others.
Regulatory Function	Signals when the communication channel is open and closed.
Expressive Function	Provides information about feelings, emotions, and attitudes.

Eye contact, then, reveals information about thought processes, provides feedback, regulates communication channels, and expresses emotions. In addition to these functions, eye contact may provide clues about status and leadership roles in small groups. In the next small group meeting you attend, determine who receives the most eye contact in the group. Where do group members look for information and guidance? They probably look at the group leader. If, as in many groups, several group members share leadership, participants may look toward any of those leaders, depending on the specific problem or level of uncertainty facing the group. For example, Alex may function as procedural leader. When the group needs help in how to proceed or wonders what the next step in the discussion is, they look to Alex for assistance. Phyllis may be the group leader most knowledgeable on the discussion topic. When group members need information, they look at Phyllis. When members need someone to relieve tension, they look at Carolyn. Thus, eye contact can indicate leadership and other roles within the group. Watch for it.

Facial Expression

As discussed before, the face is the most important revealer of emotions. Sometimes you can cleverly mask your emotional expressions, but the face is usually the first place you look to determine someone else's emotional state. Facial expressions are particularly significant in interpersonal and small group communication because of the close proximity of communicators to one another. You can readily detect emotions displayed on a person's face. Even though some researchers estimate that the face can produce over twenty thousand different expressions, Ekman and Friesen have identified six primary emotions displayed on it: happiness, anger, surprise, sadness, disgust, and fear.[28]

Ekman has also developed a method of identifying which areas of the face play the most important roles in communicating emotions.[29] According to his research, people communicate happiness with the area around their eyes and with smiles and raised cheeks. They reveal disgust with raised upper lips, wrinkled noses, lowered eyelids, and lowered brows. They communicate fear with the area around their eyes, but their mouths are also usually open when they are fearful. When they are angry, people are likely to lower their eyebrows and stare intensely. They communicate surprise with raised eyebrows, wide-open eyes, and often open mouths. They communicate sadness in the area around the eyes and mouth.

Facial expressions are important sources of information about a group's emotional climate, particularly if several members express similar emotions. Their faces might suggest that they are bored with the discussion or that they are interested and pleased. Remember that group members may attempt to mask their facial expressions in an effort to conceal their true feelings.

Vocal Cues

"John," remarked a group discussion member, obviously upset, "it's not that I object to what you said; it's just the way you said it." The pitch, rate, volume, and quality of your voice (also called **paralanguage** cues) play important parts in determining the meanings of your messages. As mentioned earlier in this chapter, Mehrabian estimates that as much as 38 percent of the emotional meaning of a message is derived from vocal cues.

You can, then, make inferences about how a speaker feels about you from that individual's paralanguage cues. You may also base inferences about a person's competence and personality on vocal cues. A speaker who mispronounces words and uses uhs and ums is probably going to be perceived as less credible than a speaker who is more articulate.[30] In addition to determining how speech affects a speaker's credibility, researchers have also been concerned with the communication of emotion via vocal cues.[31]

At times you can detect emotional states from vocal cues, but as a group discussion member you should beware of improperly drawing inferences and derogatorily labeling someone just because of vocal cues. As this chapter has emphasized, nonverbal cues do not operate in isolation. They should be evaluated in the context of other communication behaviors.

Territoriality and Personal Space

The next time you're sitting in class, note the seat you select. Even though no one instructed you to sit in the same place, chances are that you tend to sit in about the same general area, if not in the same seat, during each class. Perhaps in your family each person sits at a certain place at the table. If someone sits in your chair, you feel that your territory has been invaded and you may try to reclaim your seat.

Territoriality is a term used in the study of animal behavior to note how animals stake out and defend given areas. Humans, too, stake out and defend areas.

Understanding territoriality may help you understand certain group behaviors. For example, the readiness of group members to defend personal territory may provide insights about their attitudes toward the group and toward individual members. At the next meeting you attend, observe how members attempt to stake out territories. If the group is seated around a table, do members place objects in front of and around them to signify that they are claiming territory? Higher-status individuals generally attempt to claim more territory.[32] Notice how group members manipulate their posture and gestures should their space be invaded. Lower-status individuals generally permit greater territorial invasion. Note too how individuals claim their territory by leaving markers, such as books, papers, or a pencil, when they have to leave the group but expect to return shortly.

Several researchers have studied **small group ecology**—the consistent way in which people arrange themselves in small groups. As you interact with others in a small group, see if you can detect relationships between participants' seating arrangements and their status, their leadership roles, and the amount of communication they direct toward others. Stenzor found that when group members are seated in a circle, they are more likely to talk to those across from them than to those on either side.[33] Other researchers suggest that more dominant group members select seats at the heads of rectangular tables or select seats that maximize their opportunity to communicate with others.[34] On the other hand, people who sit at the corners of tables generally contribute the least to a discussion. Armed with this information, if you find yourself in a position to prepare the seating for a discussion or conference, you should be able to make choices to maximize group interaction. If, for example, you know that Sue, who always dominates the discussion, will be attending the next meeting, you may suggest that she sit in a corner seat rather than at the head of the table.

Did you know that an individual's position relative to other group members in a small group discussion can influence that person's chances of becoming the leader of the group? In a study by Howells and Becker, five people sat around a table, three on one side and two on the other. The researchers discovered that the participants had a greater probability of becoming leaders if they sat on the side of the table facing the three discussion members.[35] More direct eye contact with numerous group members, which can subsequently result in a greater control of the verbal communication, may explain why the two individuals who faced the other three emerged as leaders.

Additional research suggests that where you sit in a group may determine whether you initiate or receive information during deliberations. One team of researchers who observed groups of three people in snack bars, restaurants, and lounges found that more visible group members tended to receive communication while more centrally located members usually initiated communication.[36] Another research team came to a similar conclusion: Group members who were visually central to other group members spoke most often.[37] As noted previously, eye contact seems to be an important factor in determining who speaks, who listens, and who has the greatest opportunity to emerge as group leader.

Other researchers have discovered that such variables as stress, gender, and personality also affect how people arrange themselves in small groups. Some people prefer greater personal space when they are under stress.[38] If you know that an upcoming discussion will probably produce anxiety, hold the meeting in a room that would permit members to have more freedom of movement. This would help them find their preferred personal distance from fellow group members.

Sommer found that women tend to sit closer to others (whether those others are men or women) than men tend to sit to other men (i.e., men generally prefer greater personal space when sitting next to other men).[39] In a study to find out whether personality characteristics affect seating arrangements, Cook discovered that extroverts tend to sit across from another person more than do introverts.[40] Introverts generally prefer distance between themselves and others. Collectively, these studies suggest that people arrange themselves in small group discussions with some consistency. A discussion leader who understands seating preferences should provide a comfortable climate for small group discussions.

Personal Appearance

How long does it take to determine whether or not you like someone? Some researchers claim that within seconds after meeting another person you complete your initial judgment of whether you should continue to communicate with someone or try to excuse yourself politely from the conversation. You base many of your initial impressions of others primarily on personal appearance. The way people dress, their hair styles, weight, and height affect your communication with them.

Imagine that you are serving on a committee for a local civic organization. You arrive for your first meeting and find a slightly overweight, unshaven, and generally unkempt man; an attractive woman, dressed in the latest style; and an older gentleman, clad in overalls and a flannel shirt and wearing a straw hat. Would the personal appearances of these people affect your ability to work with them in a task-oriented, problem-solving group? Would you be tempted to form judgments about their personalities? According to recent research, you probably would.[41] Is it also possible that certain group members can be more persuasive and exert more influence on the group because of their personal appearance? The results of several studies suggest that the answers to these questions is yes.

Research suggests that women who are thought to be attractive are more effective in changing attitudes than are women thought to be less attractive.[42] In addition, more attractive individuals are often thought by others to be more credible than less attractive people. They are also perceived to be happier, more popular, more sociable, and more successful than are those rated as being less attractive. Even people's general shape and body size affects how they are perceived by others.[43] People with fat, round silhouettes are consistently rated as older, more old-fashioned, less good-looking, more talkative, and more good-natured. Athletic, muscular people are rated as more mature, better looking, taller, and more adventurous. Tall and thin people are rated as more ambitious, more suspicious of others, more tense and nervous, more pessimistic, and quieter. Even though the research reported here was not conducted in small groups, it is reasonable to conclude that perceived attractiveness and body type can affect how group members perceive one another. Such perceptions may have an impact on interaction, decision making, problem solving, overall group climate, and member satisfaction.

Research supports the assumption that personal appearance can affect the social influence you exert on others. As a participant in small group discussions, pay close attention to your personal appearance; the contribution you make to the group may depend on it.

Sources of Nonverbal Cues

Posture and Movement	Provide information regarding status, intensity of attitude, warmth, approval seeking, group climate, immediacy, deception.
Eye Contact	Provides cognitive, monitoring, regulatory, and expressive functions.
Facial Expression	Communicates emotion, especially happiness, anger, surprise, sadness, disgust, and fear.
Vocal Cues	The pitch, rate, volume, and quality of the voice that communicate emotion, credibility, and personality perceptions.
Personal Space	Use of individual space, which communicates power, status, and intimacy.
Territoriality	Staking out, claiming, and defending a given space.
Personal Appearance	Clothing, body shape, and general attractiveness influence others' perceptions and reactions.
Communication Environment	The general attractiveness or unattractiveness of a space that contributes to the group's productivity and overall group climate.

Communication Environment

Five students have been assigned to work together on a project for their group communication class. Their task is to formulate a policy question and solutions to it. Their first problem is finding a place to meet. Apparently, the only available place is a small, vacated office in Smythe Hall, the oldest building on campus. No one seems happy about holding meetings in the old office; but the students are relieved to have found a place to meet. When they arrive for their first meeting, they find a dirty, musty room with peeling paint and only three hardback wooden chairs and a gray metal desk. The ventilation is poor, and half of the light bulbs have burned out. Such a dismal environment will undoubtedly affect the group's ability to work.

In a classic study, Maslow and Mintz examined whether decor has an effect on the occupants of the room.[44] These researchers decorated three rooms. An "ugly room" was made to resemble a drab, cluttered, janitor's storeroom and was rated as "horrible" and "repulsive" by observers assigned to examine the room. The second room was decorated to look like an "average room," described as looking "similar to a professor's office." The third room was decorated with carpeting, drapes, tasteful furniture and decorations, and labeled a "beautiful room." After the rooms were decorated, subjects were assigned to one of the three rooms and were told to rate several facial photographs. The results indicated that the environment had a significant effect on how subjects rated the faces. Subjects in the "beautiful room" rated facial photographs as being more attractive than did those in the "ugly room." Subjects in the "ugly room" also reported that the task was more unpleasant and monotonous than did subjects in the "beautiful room." Finally, subjects assigned to the "ugly room" attempted to leave sooner than subjects assigned to the "beautiful room."

People can generally comprehend information and solve problems better in a more attractive environment. Research does not suggest, however, that one environmental condition is best for all group communication situations. The optimal environment for any group depends on its specific task as well as the needs and expectations of its members. Some students need absolute quiet while reading or studying while others can be productive while listening to music. Group members or leaders should attempt to find the best environments for their groups based on group needs and the types of tasks confronting their groups. Group leaders could ask members which type of environment they prefer. If groups must solve problems that require considerable thought, energy, and creativity, they might work best in quiet, comfortable rooms. If groups will meet over long periods of time, comfortable chairs and pleasant decor are essential.

Even the President of the United States knows the effects room arrangement and seating comfort can have on group problem solving. The following memo from President Richard Nixon illustrates his interest in group comfort.

April 6, 1970

TO: Haldeman

FROM: The President

I would like a quiet check made with regard to the chairs in the Cabinet Room, without saying anything to anybody else. I have a distinct feeling that these chairs, probably because of their style, are pretty uncomfortable. For one thing they do not leave enough leg room beneath the table and, as I told you before, at least insofar as my chair is concerned, it is stiff and hard and pretty uncomfortable after a meeting goes as long as an hour or more.

I realize that they represent a substantial investment, but a lot of important decisions will be made around that table, and if my reaction is shared by others who have tried the chairs, perhaps we ought to meet the problem immediately and have them quietly rebuilt or exchanged for a different model. I emphasize "quietly" because we don't want to give the press a chance to have another "police hat" incident.[45]

NONVERBAL GROUP DYNAMICS: PUTTING PRINCIPLE INTO PRACTICE

This chapter has noted that nonverbal communication variables have a profound impact on small group dynamics. Group members send more messages nonverbally than they do verbally—people cannot *not* communicate. Nonverbal cues

"Just a few more pages, Hansen, and we'll take a short break."

Drawing by C. Barsotti; © 1989 The New Yorker Magazine, Inc.

affect the meanings of messages; individuals generally believe these cues more than they believe verbal messages. Nonverbal cues are particularly important in communicating emotions.

Several applications of nonverbal communication research to small groups have been discussed. Consider the following suggestions.

Interpreting Nonverbal Behavior

- Observe nonverbal behavior, but beware of trying to read a group member's behavior like a book. Remember to consider that (1) the context of a nonverbal cue is important, (2) people respond differently to different situations, and (3) differences in culture affect how people react to others' nonverbal cues.

Body Posture and Movement

- You may be more effective in persuading others when you use eye contact, maintain a direct body orientation, and remain physically close to others.
- You can often identify high-status group members (or at least those who perceive themselves as having high status) by such nonverbal cues as relaxed postures, loud speaking voices, territorial dominance, expansive movements, and sometimes, their keeping themselves at a distance from others.
- Someone lying often speaks with a higher pitched voice, uses less eye contact, shows less enthusiasm, shrugs his or her hands more often, nods less, speaks more slowly and with more errors, and adopts a less-immediate posture.
- Group leaders may gesture more than followers.

- Observing the similarity of group members' posture and gestures can reveal insights about group climate, leadership, and cohesiveness.

Eye Contact

- People sometimes interrupt eye contact with others not because they are not interested but because they are trying to think of the right words to say.
- When talking with others in a small group, be sure to look at all members so that you can respond to the feedback they provide.
- You can sometimes draw a person into the conversation just by establishing direct eye contact.
- Because eye contact signals whether a communication channel is open or closed, you may be able to quiet an extremely talkative member by avoiding eye contact.
- By noting who looks at whom in a small group, you can get a good idea of who is the leader of the group. Group members usually look at their leader more than they look at any other member (assuming that they respect their leader's ideas and opinions).

Facial Expression

- Look at group members' facial expressions to find out the emotional climate in the group.

Vocal Cues

- You may find that you dislike a group member not because of what he or she says but because of that person's vocal quality, pitch, or rate of speech. People's vocal cues affect your perceptions of those people.

Territoriality and Personal Space

- Early on in the group gatherings, members will probably stake out their territory or personal space.
- When group members' territories are invaded, they will probably respond nonverbally (via posture or territorial markers) to defend their territories.
- Since most small group meetings take place in what one researcher calls the "social distance category" (four to twelve feet), a group leader should try to see that the distances between small group participants fall within this range.
- In a group, you are more likely to talk to someone across from you than to someone sitting next to you.
- If you know that a group member generally monopolizes the conversation, try to get that member to select a corner seat rather than a seat at the head of a conference table.

- You are more likely to emerge as a group leader if you sit so that you are able to establish eye contact and a direct body orientation with most of the group members.
- Since people prefer greater personal space when they are under stress, you should make sure that group members have plenty of territory if you know that a meeting is going to be stressful.

Personal Appearance

- Your personal appearance will affect the way other group members perceive you. Your appearance can also influence your ability to persuade others.

Communication Environment

- Make sure that the physical environment for a group meeting is as comfortable and attractive as possible; environment can affect a group's satisfaction and productivity.

PRACTICE

Receiving Nonverbal Reinforcement

Pair up with another student and take turns telling each other about an important idea, feeling, or experience. Your partner should give no nonverbal indications that he or she is paying attention while you speak: no smiles, nodding of the head, "um-hums," postural orientation, facial expressions. After each person talks for three to five minutes, your instructor will lead you in a discussion of what it felt like (a) to receive no nonverbal attention and (b) to give no nonverbal attention. After you discuss the importance of nonverbal communication, talk with your partner, this time providing genuine nonverbal feedback. Your instructor will lead you in a discussion of the differences between receiving and not receiving nonverbal reinforcement.

Nonverbal Group Observation

If you are working on a group project, videotape one of your group meetings or videotape your group attempting to solve a case study, such as "The Bomb Shelter" case in Chapter Eight. Replay the video recording with the sound turned off.

1. Notice group members' use of emblems, illustrators, affect displays, regulators, and adaptors.

2. Observe how nonverbal cues regulate the flow of communication.

3. How do body posture and movement communicate members' status and attitudes?

4. Try to identify the four functions of eye contact in your group.

5. Do group members communicate much emotion with their faces?

6. Note relationships between territoriality behavior, seating arrangement, and leadership, status, and verbal interaction in the group.

7. If your group had to meet in a special room to videotape the session, how did the change in environment affect the group?

Small Group Ecology

Five people have been assigned by their instructor to work on a small group project for their group communication class. All of their meetings will take place in a room approximately twenty feet by twenty feet. One large rectangular table stands in the center of the room. Several chairs are also in the room. A small circular table is shoved up into a corner.

Based on the small group ecology research, what do you think would be the ideal seating arrangement for this group? Justify your arrangement with the practices and principles presented in this chapter.

Consider these personality profiles of the five members:

Herbert: You worked with Herbert on a small group project last semester. You know that he likes to be the leader. However, he usually does not pull his weight when it comes to getting a job accomplished. He likes to feel that he is in control of the group. Most group members were not satisfied with his leadership ability last semester. Chances are he will try to assume leadership and control of this group if you give him the opportunity to do so.

Jane: Jane is very intelligent. She has made the Dean's List each semester, and others usually respect her opinions. However, she only participates in a discussion when she is encouraged to do so. She is very shy. She does not enjoy group projects.

Nell: Nell is very outgoing. When there is a party or celebration, she is the first to volunteer to help make the arrangements. She enjoys working with people, and people enjoy working with her. She is well liked by most students.

Bill: Bill has real leadership potential. He has a talent for organizing people and accomplishing jobs. Although he is a very hard worker, he usually does not like to be considered a leader. He doesn't want people to think that he is just after status and prestige. He can be a real asset to a small group, but sometimes he must be encouraged to participate.

Barbara: Most people don't enjoy working with Barbara because she is very pessimistic. She usually fears the worst will happen. She is not a very hard worker because she thinks that a group probably will not successfully complete a project. She is intelligent and is a good researcher, but she usually doesn't volunteer to work very hard unless she is encouraged by other group members.

Nonverbal Freeze

Before participating in the group discussion, set a kitchen timer to go off five to ten minutes into the discussion. No one should know the exact time the timer will sound. When it does sound, members should stop talking and freeze in position. They should not change their body orientation, facial expression, and so on. Discuss the possible meanings of the information revealed by body position and other nonverbal cues.

Nonverbal Photo Analysis

Have someone photograph your group during a deliberation. If possible use an instant camera. After the discussion distribute the photos for group members to analyze for the nonverbal information revealed in them. Make observations about immediacy, power, and responsiveness cues that you can identify from the photos.

Notes

1. R. L. Birdwhistell, *Kinesics and Context* (Philadelphia: University of Pennsylvania Press, 1970).
2. Sigmund Freud, "Fragment of an Analysis of a Case of Hysteria (1905)" *Collected Papers,* Vol. 3 (New York: Basic Books, 1959).
3. Albert Mehrabian, *Nonverbal Communication* (Chicago: AVC, 1972), p. 108.
4. P. Ekman and W. V. Friesen, "The Repertoire of Nonverbal Behavior: Categories, Origins, Usage, and Coding," *Semiotica* 1 (1969): 49–98.
5. Mehrabian, *Nonverbal Communication,* pp. 178–179.
6. W. S. Condon and W. D. Ogston, "Soundfilm Analysis of Normal and Pathological Behavior Patterns," *Journal of Nervous and Mental Disease* 143 (1966): 338–347.
7. P. Ekman and W. V. Friesen, "Hand Movements," *Journal of Communication* 22 (1972): 353–374.
8. Albert Mehrabian, *Silent Messages* (Belmont, California: Wadsworth Publishing Company, 1972), p. 108.
9. Mehrabian, *Nonverbal Communication,* p. 30.
10. E. T. Hall, *The Hidden Dimension* (Garden City, New York: Doubleday & Company, 1966); R. Shuter, "Proxemics and Tactility in Latin America," *Journal of Communication* 26 (1976): 46–52.
11. Julius Fast, *Body Language* (New York: M. Evans & Company, 1970).
12. Mehrabian, *Nonverbal Communication,* p. 30.
13. *Ibid.*
14. Albert Mehrabian and M. Williams, "Nonverbal Concomitants of Perceived and Intended Persuasiveness," *Journal of Personality and Social Psychology* 13 (1969): 37–58.

15. Mark L. Knapp, *Nonverbal Communication in Human Interaction* (New York: Holt, Rinehart & Winston, 1978), p. 228.

16. Paul Ekman and W. V. Friesen, "Nonverbal Leakage and Clues to Deception," *Psychiatry* 32 (1969): 88–106.

17. Knapp, *Nonverbal Communication,* p. 229.

18. J. O'Connor, "The Relationship of Kinesics and Verbal Communication to Leadership Perception in Small Group Discussion," unpublished Ph.D. dissertation, Indiana University, 1971.

19. John Baird, "Some Nonverbal Elements of Leadership Emergence," *Southern Speech Communication Journal* 40 (1977): 352–361; also see Laurence M. Childs et al., "Nonverbal and Verbal Communication of Leadership," paper presented at the Annual Meeting of the American Psychological Association, Los Angeles, 1981.

20. Albert Mehrabian and M. Williams, "Nonverbal Concomitants of Perceived and Intended Persuasiveness," *Journal of Personality and Social Psychology* 14 (1969): 37–58.

21. M. Reece and R. Whitman, "Expressive Movements, Warmth, and Verbal Reinforcement," *Journal of Abnormal and Social Psychology* 64 (1962): 234–236.

22. W. S. Condon and L. W. Sander, "Neonate Movement Is Synchronized with Adult Speech: Interactional Participation and Language Acquisition," *Science* I (January 1974): 99–101; W. S. Condon and W. D. Ogston, "Soundfilm Analysis of Normal and Pathological Behavior Patterns," *Journal of Nervous and Mental Disease* 143 (1966): 338–347.

23. A. Kendon, "Some Relationships Between Body Motion and Speech: An Analysis of an Example," in A. W. Siegman and B. Pope (eds.), *Studies in Dyadic Communication* (Elmsford, New York: Pergamon Press, 1972).

24. Davida Navarre and Catherine A. Emihovich, "Movement Synchrony and the Self-Analytic Group," paper presented at the Eastern Communication Association, Boston, 1978.

25. M. Argyle and A. Kendon, "The Experimental Analysis of Social Performance" in L. Berkowitz (ed.), *Advances in Experimental Social Psychology* 3 (New York: Academic Press, 1967), pp. 55–98.

26. Knapp, *Nonverbal Communication,* p. 313.

27. A. Kendon, "Some Functions of Gaze-Direction in Social Interaction," *Acta Psychologica* 26 (1967): 22–63.

28. P. Ekman and W. V. Friesen, *Unmasking the Face* (Englewood Cliffs, New Jersey: Prentice-Hall, 1975).

29. Paul Ekman, W. V. Friesen and S. S. Tomkins, "Facial Affect Scoring Technique: A First Validity Study," *Semiotica* 3 (1971): 37–58; P. Ekman and W. V. Friesen, *Unmasking the Face* (Englewood Cliffs, New Jersey: Prentice-Hall, 1975).

30. K. K. Sereno and G. J. Hawkins, "The Effect of Variations in Speakers' Nonfluency upon Audience Ratings of Attitude Toward the Speech Topic and Speakers' Credibility," *Speech Monographs* 34 (1967): 58–64; G. R. Miller and M. A. Hewgill, "The Effect of Variations in Nonfluency on Audience Ratings of Source Credibility," *Quarterly Journal of Speech* 50 (1964): 36–44.

31. J. R. Davitz, *The Communication of Emotional Meaning* (New York: McGraw-Hill Book Company, 1964).

32. Albert Mehrabian, "Significance of Posture and Position in the Communication of Attitude and Status Relationships," *Psychological Bulletin* 71 (1969): 363.

33. B. Stenzor, "The Spatial Factor in Face to Face Discussion Groups," *Journal of Abnormal and Social Psychology* 45 (1950): 552–555.

34. F. Strodtbeck and L. Hook, "The Social Dimensions of a Twelve Man Jury Table," *Sociometry* 36 (1973): 424–429; A. Hare and R. Bales, "Seating Position and Small Group Interaction," *Sociometry* 26 (1963): 480–486.

35. L. T. Howells and S. W. Becker, "Seating Arrangement and Leadership Emergence," *Journal of Abnormal and Social Psychology* 64 (1962): 148–150.

36. Ronald L. Michelini, Robert Passalacqua, and John Cusimano, "Effects of Seating Arrangement on Group Participation," *The Journal of Social Psychology* 99 (1976): 179–186.

37. C. Harris Silverstein and David J. Stang, "Seating Position and Interaction in Triads: A Field Study," *Sociometry* (1976): 166–170.

38. M. Dosey and M. Meisels, "Personal Space and Self Protection," *Journal of Personality and Social Psychology* 11 (1969): 93–97.

39. R. Sommer, "Studies in Personal Space," *Sociometry* 22 (1959): 247–260.

40. M. Cook, "Experiments on Orientation and Proxemics," *Human Relations* 23 (1970): 61–76.

41. J. Kelly, "Dress as Non-Verbal Communication," paper presented to the annual conference of the American Association for Public Opinion Research, May 1969; M. Lefkowitz, R. Blake, and J. Mouton, "Status Factors in Pedestrian Violation of Traffic Signals," *Journal of Abnormal and Social Psychology* 51 (1955): 704–706; J. Mills and E. Aronson, "Opinion Change as a Function of the Communicator's Attractiveness and Desire to Influence," *Journal of Social Psychology* 1 (1965): 73–77.

42. J. E. Singer, "The Use of Manipulative Strategies: Machiavellianism and Attractiveness," *Sociometry* 27 (1964): 128–151.

43. W. H. Sheldon, *Atlas of Man: A Guide for Somatyping the Adult Male at All Ages* (New York: Harper and Row, 1954).

44. A. H. Maslow and N. L. Mintz, "Effect of Esthetic Surroundings," *Journal of Psychology* 41 (1956): 247–254.

45. Bruce Oudes (ed.), *The President, Richard Nixon's Secret Files* (New York: Harper and Row, 1988).

Chapter Seven

Understanding Decision Making and Problem Solving in Small Groups

After studying this chapter, you should be able to:

- ☐ Differentiate between group problem solving and group decision making.

- ☐ Describe the steps of group decision making.

- ☐ Identify the characteristics of good group decision making.

- ☐ Formulate a question of fact, value, or policy for a problem-solving discussion.

- ☐ Identify three criteria for a well-phrased policy discussion question.

- ☐ Identify appropriate methods for researching group discussion questions.

- ☐ Compare and contrast descriptive and prescriptive approaches to problem solving in small groups.

- ☐ Identify the four phases of group process.

- ☐ Discuss the three types of group activity tracks.

$\mathbf{Y}$ou're either helping solve the problem or you're part of the problem. Whether or not you agree with this statement, you probably do spend quite a bit of time and energy trying to solve problems. When you think about problem solving, perhaps you first think about the many problems you face each day. "How can I finish my work by the deadline?" "How can I pay off my charge card bill?" You may also remember times when you were part of a group or committee responsible for deciding how to allocate more resources to a library or how a campaign platform should be drafted. While this chapter may suggest strategies for solving your personal, everyday problems or for making decisions, it will focus on understanding *group* decision making and problem solving.

DECISION MAKING VERSUS PROBLEM SOLVING

Although the two terms are sometimes used interchangeably, decision making and problem solving are different things. Decision making is really part of the problem-solving process. **Decision making** involves making a choice from among several alternatives. **Problem solving** requires a group to make many decisions as they identify a problem, determine how to solve it, and eliminate or manage obstacles. For many people, making a decision seems to be a problem. However, as part of a larger problem-solving process, group decision making is an effort to overcome an obstacle that keeps the group from achieving its goals. This chapter will examine both decision making and problem solving in greater detail and will note suggestions for improving group decision making and problem solving.

Group Decision Making

When you make a decision, you are choosing from several alternatives. For example, in deciding which college or university to attend, you probably considered several choices. According to Hirokawa and Scheerhorn, **group decision making** includes the following steps.[1]

1. *The group assesses the present situation.* A group analyzes a situation based on available information. The group determines that it needs to make a

decision. For example, the board of directors of an airline trying to decide whether to lower fares looks at competitions' fares and the number of passengers those competitors fly each day.

2. *The group either identifies alternatives or identifies group goals.* After assessing the current situation the group usually does one of two things. Based on its needs a group either identifies its goals and objectives or begins to identify alternative courses of action. A group uncertain about its task usually identifies objectives; if its goal is clear, a group begins to identify alternatives or choices.

3. *The group identifies positive and negative consequences of alternatives.* The greater the number of alternatives a group generates, the greater the likelihood that the group will make a good decision. Poor decisions usually occur when a group fails to generate enough good possible choices. A group must do more, however, than identify alternatives; it should also assess the positive and negative implications of each alternative before making a decision. What are the implications of lowering air fares by 10 percent? The number of passengers might increase. If a lower fare is not properly advertised and no additional passengers fly with the airline, profits could decrease 10 percent.

4. *The group selects the alternative (makes a decision).* The alternative selected should potentially have a maximum positive outcome with minimal negative consequences. A group is more likely to select the best alternative if it has carefully assessed the present situation, considered group goals, identified several choices and noted the positive and negative implications of each, and then selected the alternative with maximum potential to help the group achieve its goal.

Characteristics of Good Decisions

Based on this four-step process, Hirokawa and Scheerhorn have identified five factors that improve group decisions.[2] Knowing how to avoid the pitfalls of group decision making can help your group evaluate the decision-making process and make better decisions. Note the following suggestions for enhancing group decision making.

1. *Accurately assess the choice-making situation.* A group can make a poor decision because members analyze the present situation incorrectly or have inaccurate or inappropriate information. The best decisions result from group members who have done their homework and have gathered data to help them assess the current situation.

2. *Establish clear and appropriate group goals and objectives.* If a group does not know what it is trying to accomplish and attempts to make decisions or choices,

The Group Decision-Making Process

1. A group assesses the present situation.
2. A group identifies alternatives or group goals.
3. A group identifies the positive and negative consequences of alternatives.
4. A group selects the best alternative.

it will most likely make a poor decision. A group makes its best decisions when all members have an understanding of what the group (not just some individuals in the group) is trying to accomplish.

3.   *Identify accurate positive and negative consequences of alternatives.* A group that makes a poor choice has usually not thought about all of the negative consequences of a decision and may have misjudged the positive outcome of a choice. This suggestion can be summarized by the maxim "Look before you leap."

4.   *Have accurate information.* Hirakawa and Scheerhorn note that a major factor that leads to faulty decisions is a "flawed information base." If group members accept inaccurate information as accurate, they will be likely to make a poor decision.

5.   *Draw reasonable conclusions from available information.* Groups that make good decisions are groups that know how to draw conclusions from evidence. They don't accept an idea as valid just because others have done so; they make sure that the evidence supports the conclusion and that they have enough examples to support a conclusion. How to use evidence and draw valid conclusions will be discussed later in this chapter.

Methods of Group Decision Making

After a group identifies alternatives and the positive and negative consequences of a decision, it must make a choice—it must select one or more of the alternatives. Following are some methods groups use to make choices.[3]

Decisions by Experts in Groups. A group may have one person who seems the most informed about the issue, and members can turn to this person to make the choice. This expert may or may not be a group's designated leader. Deferring to an expert from within a group may be an efficient way to make a decision, but without adequate discussion, the group may not be satisfied with the outcome.

Comparing Effective and Ineffective Group Decision Making

Effective Group Decision Making	Ineffective Group Decision Making
Accurately assesses the present situation.	Improperly analyzes the present situation.
Establishes clear and appropriate group goals.	Does not establish clear and appropriate group goals.
Accurately identifies positive and negative consequences of decision alternatives.	Fails to identify enough positive and negative consequences of decision alternatives.
Has accurate information.	Works from too little information or information that is wrong.
Draws reasonable conclusions from available information.	Is unable to draw accurate conclusions from the information available.

Decisions by Experts Outside Groups. A group may decide that no one in it has the credibility, knowledge, or wisdom to make a decision and that the group is unable or unwilling to make a decision. Members can turn to someone outside the group, someone with authority to make a decision. While an outside expert may make a fine decision, a group that gives up its decision-making power to one loses the advantages of greater input and a variety of approaches.

Averaging Individual Rankings or Ratings. Group members are asked to rank or rate possible alternatives. After the group averages the rankings or ratings, it selects the alternative with the highest average. Although this method of making decisions can be useful to start discussions and to see where the group stands on an issue, it is not the best way to make a decision, since it does not take full advantage of the give-and-take of group discussion.

Random Choice. Sometimes groups become so frustrated that they make no decisions. They resort to coin tosses or other random approaches. These methods are not recommended for groups who take their decision making seriously. When groups resort to random methods, they usually are desperate.

Majority Vote. This is the method of group decision making most often used. Majority rule can be swift and efficient but can also leave an unsatisfied minority. Unless it allots time for discussing an issue, a group may sacrifice decision quality and group cohesiveness for efficiency.

Decision by Minority. Sometimes a minority of group members makes a decision. The minority may yell the loudest or threaten to create problems for the group

Decision making involves assessing a situation, identifying alternative solutions and their positive and negative consequences, and selecting the best alternative.

unless given its way. Members may ask, "Does anyone have any objections?" and, if no one answers immediately, consider the decision to be made. Minority members who get their decision adopted may temporarily rejoice, but over time the group will have difficulty implementing the decision if it is not widely accepted.

Decision by Consensus. Consensus occurs when all group members agree on a course of action. This method is time-consuming and difficult, but members are usually satisfied with a decision. If group members must also implement the solution, this method works well. To reach a decision by consensus, group members must listen and respond to individual viewpoints and manage conflict and disagreements that arise. Several suggestions for reaching consensus and managing group conflict are identified in Chapter Eight.

All of these methods of group decision making have one element in common: Group members select the best choice from available alternatives. Problem solving, on the other hand, involves making many decisions during the process of overcoming an obstacle. The group has a goal it wants to achieve, but it can't do so unless the obstacle is removed or managed.

Group Problem Solving

A board of directors of a multinational corporation, a PTA fund-raising committee, and a group of students doing a project for a group communication class all

---

REVIEW BOX

Three Elements of a Problem

Undesirable Present: Something is wrong with the way things are.
Obstacles: Something keeps a group from achieving its goal.
Goal: A group cannot accomplish its goal because of obstacles.

---

have something in common—they have problems to solve. Problem solving is the process of seeking a solution to a problem caused by an obstacle. Why does a group or committee usually form when a problem needs to be solved? Have you ever been involved in group problem solving and thought to yourself, "If I weren't working in this silly group, I could probably be more productive"? Despite the frustrations of group work, a small group of people has the potential of arriving at a better solution than do individuals working alone. People who work collectively have a larger pool of information to draw on.

According to Kepner and Tregoe, a problem consists of three elements: an undesirable existing situation, a goal someone wishes to achieve, and obstacles that keep that person from achieving his or her goal.[4] Group problem solving is a group's effort to eliminate or manage the obstacles that keep it from achieving its objective.

Like decision making, problem solving begins with assessing the present situation. What's wrong with what is happening now? Almost every problem can be phrased in terms of something you want more of or less of. Problems often can be boiled down to such things as lack of time, money, information, or agreement. For example, a school board that decides a district needs a new high school yet realizes it hasn't the money for one has a problem: The district has too many students for existing facilities. The board needs fewer students or more space. The goal the board wants to achieve is quality education for all district students. The board cannot achieve this goal with the existing undersirable situation. The obstacles that keep the board from reaching its goal include lack of classroom space and lack of money to build more space. Every problem can be identified by noting the three elements of a problem: the undesirable present, obstacles, and the group goal.

A group must first decide on its purpose. Sometimes a group forms for a specific task. For example, the president of the local Jaycees may appoint a committee to organize a Fourth of July celebration. Another group decides on its specific purpose only after the group is formed. Several neighbors may congregate because they are concerned about improving their neighborhood, but they decide what they want to do for their neighborhood only after they meet. Eventually, they may agree that they have a problem (such as a lack of security or lowered property values) that needs to be solved.

If a group decides that its function is to solve a specific problem, it must define the problem. For some groups, defining a problem is easy; for other groups, agreeing on the exact nature of a problem will take considerable time and debate.

After determining and defining a problem, a group continues to gather data and analyze the problem and then generates alternatives to try to solve it. In a group of four or five people, each of whom has different values, attitudes, and beliefs, problem solving can create uncertainty. Each person attempts to solve the problem based on his or her individual problem-solving strategy. No two group members may approach the problem from the same perspective. Sensing this disparity in approaches, each group member may become uncertain about his or her own strategy, while not really understanding anyone else's. It takes patience, understanding, and effective communication to help relieve this uncertainty.

Characteristics of Effective Group Problem Solvers

In problem-solving groups, some group members seem to have a knack for helping the group reach its goal. Regardless of the method used to structure a discussion, some individuals have skills that enable the group to resolve issues and solve problems. Several research studies confirm the importance of specific skills that can enhance a person's ability to be an effective group problem solver. The following paragraphs examine these skills.[5]

1. *An effective problem solver sees the problem from a variety of viewpoints.* You often look at a problem as it affects you. A skilled problem solver considers how the problem affects others, too, and is able to think about something from other people's vantage points. If you are a farmer in an area suffering from a drought, you certainly know how the problem affects you. In trying to solve the problem, however, you should also think about how the drought will affect consumers, agricultural businesses, and politicians.

2. *An effective problem solver gathers data and researches issues.* Good problem solvers do not rely on their own opinions. They spend time in the library or develop surveys to gather information and others' opinions about an issue. Appendix A includes suggestions for conducting research to enhance your problem-solving skills.

3. *An effective problem solver evaluates the opinions and assumptions of others.* Don't just accept another person's conclusion or opinion at face value. One study found that groups that reach better solutions include members who take the time to test the assumptions of others. While you should not attack another person's credibility, your opinions and assumptions need to be supported by evidence. A group that tactfully examines the basis for an opinion can determine whether the opinion is valid.

4. *An effective problem solver knows how to use evidence to reach a valid conclusion.* Besides just asking for evidence, a good problem solver needs to know how to use evidence to reach a conclusion. This chapter will discuss types and tests of evidence.

5. *An effective problem solver is concerned for both the group task and the feelings of others.* Being too task-oriented is not good for the overall group climate. As discussed in Chapter Five, sensitivity to the feelings of others can enhance the group climate and foster a supportive, rather than defensive, approach to achieving a group goal.

6. *An effective problem solver asks appropriate questions to keep the discussion on track.* One big problem groups have is keeping the discussion focused on the issues. Members often bounce from one idea or topic to the next. Good problem solvers know this and use questions to help keep the group moving toward its goal. Such questions as "Where are we now?" or "What's the next step in solving our problem?" or "Aren't we getting off the track here?" can help the group get back to the task. Remember, however, that groups need time for some socializing and for developing relationships.

7. *An effective problem solver searches for many alternatives or solutions to a problem.* One clear conclusion from the literature on problem solving stands out: The more alternatives generated, the greater the chances that one of them can help solve a problem. Some groups stop searching for solutions once someone suggests the first seemingly acceptable one. The next chapter discusses using brainstorming as a technique for generating ideas.

8. *An effective group problem solver listens to minority arguments and opinions.* It is always tempting to disregard the voice of a lone dissenter. That individual may, however, have a great idea or a legitimate complaint about the majority point of view. Assume that all ideas have merit; do not discount ideas because they come from members who aren't supporting the majority at the moment.

9. *An effective group problem solver tests solutions to see if they meet preestablished criteria.* Criteria are standards for acceptable solutions. Such criteria as, "It should be within the budget" and "It should be implemented within six months" are important to problem solving. If a group has generated criteria for a solution, a good problem solver reminds the group what the criteria are and evaluates possible solutions according to standards previously identified.

10. *An effective group problem solver takes a vacation from a problem if a group can't reach a solution.* If the group gets bogged down and can't reach agreement, postpone farther discussion. Sometimes you get a burst of creativity when you are not even thinking about a problem. Have you ever had an idea come to you while you were jogging, driving a car, or taking a shower? Give your mind a chance to work on the problem by giving yourself a break from agonizing over a solution.

Even though group problem solving has advantages, you must understand the problem-solving process to achieve these advantages. The remainder of this chapter

Effective and Ineffective Problem-Solving Skills

An effective group problem solver:	**An ineffective group problem solver:**
Sees the problem from a variety of viewpoints.	Sees the problem only from his or her own viewpoint.
Has gathered data and has researched the issues.	Does not research the problem or gather data.
Evaluates the opinions and assumptions of others.	Never examines or evaluates other opinions or assumptions.
Knows how to use evidence to reach a valid conclusion.	Does not know how to use evidence.
Is concerned for both the group task and the feelings of others.	Is not concerned about the feelings of others or only focuses on the task.
Asks appropriate questions to keep the discussion on track.	Does not help the group stay on target.
Searches for many alternatives or solutions to a problem.	Stops searching for a solution after one is identified.
Listens to minority arguments.	Does not listen to dissenting viewpoints.
Tests solutions to see if they meet preestablished criteria.	Does not match proposed solutions against established criteria.
Takes a vacation from a problem if the group can't reach a solution.	Consciously thinks about the problem all the time.

provides additional insight into this process. It will explain how formulating a discussion question will help you begin the problem-solving process; it will also discuss three different types of group discussion questions: questions of fact, value, and policy. The last part of this chapter will identify both descriptive and prescriptive approaches to problem solving, presenting the descriptive approach in some detail. Chapter Eight will elaborate on several prescriptive approaches to problem solving.

FORMULATING DISCUSSION QUESTIONS

Before most scientists begin an experiment or conduct scholarly research, they have some idea of what they are looking for. Some researchers start with a *hypothesis,* a guess based on previous theory and research about what they will find in their search for new knowledge. Other investigators formulate a *research question* that provides a direction for their research. Like scientific research, problem solving seeks answers to questions. It makes sense, then, for group members to formulate a question before searching for answers. By identifying a specific question that they

Problem-solving groups must formulate their research questions carefully so that members have a clear idea of how to go about answering them.

must answer, members can reduce some of the initial uncertainty that accompanies their discussion.

Phrasing a discussion question should be done with considerable care. It is an important part of initiating and organizing any group discussion, particularly problem-solving discussions, since the quality and specificity of a question usually determine the quality of the answer. The better a group does in preparing a discussion question, the greater are their chances of having a productive and orderly discussion.

In some group discussions and conference situations, the question has been predetermined. Government committees and juries exemplify such groups. But usually groups are faced with a problem or need and are responsible for formulating a specific question to guide their deliberations. There are basically three types of discussion questions: **questions of fact, questions of value**, and **questions of policy**. To help you determine which type would be most appropriate for your various group discussions, we'll discuss each.

Questions of Fact

In summarizing the responsibilities of the jury during a criminal court case, the judge provides a very specific question of fact to help guide the jury in their discussion. "Your job," instructs the judge, "is to decide whether the defendant is guilty or innocent of the charges against him." A question of fact asks whether something happened or did not happen; its answer determines what is true and what is false.

A question of fact can ultimately be answered by one of two responses—either "yes" or "no" (although, of course, a "yes" or "no" response can be qualified in terms of the probability of its accuracy). The question, "Did the Twins win the World Series in 1980?" is a question of fact; either they did or they did not. "Is the Soviet Union expanding military operations in South America?" Again, the answer is either "yes" or "no," depending on the evidence. But questions of fact often appear deceivingly simple. In trying to answer a question of fact, it is important to define the critical words or phrases in the question. In the preceding question, for example, what is meant by "expanding military operations"? Does this mean building new missile bases or does it mean sending a few military advisors to a Latin American country? By reducing the ambiguity of a question's meaning, a group can save considerable time in agreeing on a final answer.

Another important consideration is whether or not your group should try to investigate a question of fact. You must consider your group's objective. If the group wants to determine what is true and what is false, then formulate a question of fact and define the key words in the question to give it greater focus and clarity. If the group intends to make a less objective value judgment or to suggest solutions to a problem, choose one of the following types of questions.

Questions of Value

A question of value generally produces a lively discussion because it concerns attitudes, beliefs, and values about whether an issue is good or bad or right or wrong. Answering a question of value is more complicated than simply determining whether an event occurred or did not occur. "Are Democratic presidents better leaders than Republican presidents?" is an example of a question of value. Group members' responses to this question depend on their attitudes toward Democrats and Republicans.

A **value** is also often defined as an enduring conception of good and bad. Your values affect your perceptions of what is right and wrong. A value is more resistant to change than an attitude or a belief.

An **attitude** is a learned predisposition to respond to a person, object, or idea in a favorable, neutral, or unfavorable way. In essence, the attitudes you hold about your world determine whether you like or dislike what you experience and observe. A favorable attitude toward Democrats will affect your response to the value question, "Are Democratic presidents better leaders than Republican presidents?"

A **belief** is the way in which you structure what is true and false. Put another way, it is the way you structure reality. If you believe in God, you have structured your reality to assume that God exists. If you do not believe in God, you have structured your perception of what is true and false so that God is not part of your reality.

What are your values? Which of your values have the most influence on your behavior? Because values are so central to how you respond in the world, you may have trouble coming up with a tidy list of your most important values. You may be able to list things you like and do not like (attitudes) or what you believe is true and not true (beliefs), but your values are sometimes difficult to identify as the guiding forces affecting your behavior. Figure 8-1 shows values in the center of the diagram to indicate that they are *central* to your behavior; the next ring, *beliefs,* are influenced by your values. Finally, you hold the attitudes you do because of what you value and what you believe is true and false.

Understanding the differences between attitudes, beliefs, and values should help you better understand what happens when a group discusses a value question because, as noted previously, you base your response to a value question on your own attitudes, beliefs, and values. You can better understand the statements of other group members, as well as your own responses, if you can identify the underlying attitudes, beliefs, and values that influence the responses to a value question.

Questions of Policy

Most problem-solving discussions revolve around questions of policy. Policy questions help groups determine what course of action or policy change would enable them to solve a problem or reach a decision. "What should be done to improve the quality of education in colleges and universities in the United States?" and "What can Congress do to reduce America's trade deficit?" are examples of policy questions. These questions can be easily identified because answers to them require changes of policy or procedure. Discussion questions including phrases such as, "What should be done about . . . ?" or "What could be done to improve . . . ?" are policy questions. Most legislation in the U.S. Senate and House of Representatives is proposed in response to specific policy questions.

A well-worded policy question should imply that a specific problem must be solved. The question "What should be done about UFOs?" is not an appropriate policy question for a group to consider because it does not provide enough direction to a specific problem. Do not confuse a discussion topic with a discussion question. If your group is going to discuss UFOs it has a topic, but it is not trying to solve a problem. The group could rephrase the discussion question to make it more policy-oriented: "What could be done to improve the way the government handles and investigates UFO sightings in the United States?" The rephrased question more clearly implies that there is a problem in the way the government investigates sightings of UFOs. The latter question provides clearer direction for research and analysis.

Figure 7-1   Interrelationship of Values, Beliefs, and Attitudes

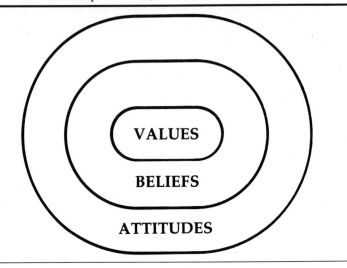

A good policy question is limited in scope. Don't try to tackle a complex problem unless your group has the time and resources to solve it. A group of students in a communication class was assigned the task of formulating a policy question, discussing it, and then reporting the results of the discussion to the class. The students had three weeks to analyze and suggest possible solutions to the problem they had chosen to investigate—"What should be done to deal with the federal debt?" While the question clearly implies a specific problem, its lack of focus frustrated the group. A more limited discussion question, such as, "What should be done to improve the tax base in our community?" would have been more manageable. You would do better to consider a simple, clearly worded question that can be analyzed in the time period allotted to your group than a question that would keep the U.S. Congress busy for several months. On the other hand, a group should not phrase a policy discussion question so that it demands only a "yes" or "no" answer or so that it limits the group's options for solutions. Given this criterion, "Should seat belts be required by law?" is a less satisfactory policy discussion topic than "What can be done to ensure greater highway safety?"

A third important criterion is that a policy question should be controversial. It should be an important issue worth discussing. An issue is a question about which individuals disagree. If group members disagree about how to solve a problem, they should not necessarily select another issue. If group members agreed on how to solve a problem from the beginning of the discussion, they would have nothing to discuss. Conflict, controversy, and disagreement should not always be viewed negatively. The purpose of a group discussion is to consider all alternatives and to agree on the best alternative. Therefore, don't reject a discussion question because other group members may hold contrasting points of view. Your discus-

Three Types of Group Discussion Questions

Question Type	Definition	Example
Question of fact	A question that asks whether something is true or false.	Did the university have a freshman admission policy last year?
Question of value	A question that considers the worth or desirability of something.	Is an electoral college a better system than a direct popular vote?
Question of policy	A question that considers whether a change in procedure should be made.	What should be done to stop violent crimes from being committed in our high schools?

sion will be more interesting and you will probably reach a better solution if the group examines all sides of an issue.

The three types of discussion questions (fact, value, and policy) may not appear to overlap, but as one researcher has observed, group members must concern themselves with questions of fact and value when considering questions of policy.[6] They must judge research and evidence as true or false (question of fact). Their attitudes, beliefs, and values (questions of value) will influence the decisions that they make on policy changes (questions of policy). Thus, a discussion question serves a valuable function in providing direction to group deliberations. Once groups devise discussion questions, however, they can modify those questions.

Decide whether your group is considering a question of fact, value, or policy. Identifying the type of question involved helps you understand the dynamics of the issue under discussion. If you realize that the question "Should we legalize casino gambling?" involves value judgments, you will be less likely to condemn group members who disagree with you. Even in the face of disagreement, frustration and defensiveness can yield to understanding and compromise. Remember, too, that even though a discussion question may be clearly identified as one of fact, value, or policy, your discussion will probably include other types of questions. Once your group has a well-defined problem to discuss, members should begin researching and analyzing it.

TYPES AND TESTS OF EVIDENCE

After you formulate your discussion question, you need to define key terms and gather information on the issues involved in it. As noted earlier in the chapter, a group needs to assess the present situation. Members should also know something about the four kinds of evidence available: facts, examples, opinions, and statistics.

Facts

A *fact* is any statement proven to be true. A fact cannot be a prediction about the future, because such a statement cannot be verified; it must be a report of something that has already happened or that is happening. "It will rain tomorrow" cannot be a fact because the statement cannot be verified. "The weather forecaster predicts rain" may be a fact if the weather forecaster has indeed made such a prediction; the accuracy of the forecast has nothing to do with whether the statement is a fact. Ask yourself these questions to determine whether a statement is a fact:

1. Is it true?
2. Is the source reliable?
3. Are there contrary facts?

Examples

An *example* is an illustration of a particular case or incident and is of greatest value when used to emphasize a fact. An example may be real or hypothetical. A real example can also be called a fact; it actually exists or has happened. A hypothetical example is of little use in proving a point but can add color and interest to or help explicate an otherwise dry or difficult factual presentation. Apply the following tests to examples:

1. Is it typical?
2. Is it significant?
3. Are there contrary examples?

Opinions

An *opinion* is a quoted comment. Opinions of unbiased authorities who base opinions on fact are most valuable as evidence. Like examples, opinions can dramatize a point and make it more interesting. Like examples, opinions are most effective when used in conjunction with facts or statistics. The following questions will help you determine the usefulness of opinions:

1. Is the source reliable?
2. Is the source an expert in the field?
3. Is the source free from bias?
4. Is the opinion consistent with other statements made by the same source?
5. Is the opinion characteristic of opinions held by other experts in the field?

Statistics

Because they cannot present dozens of facts or examples in a given time limit, people often rely on statistics. A *statistic* is simply a number: 10,000 people, 132 reported cases of child abuse, 57 Western nations. Statistics provide firm support for important points. Pay special attention, though, to the tests of statistics listed below, since statistics are probably the most frequently misgathered and misinterpreted type of evidence.

1. Is the source reliable?
2. Is the source unbiased?
3. Are the figures recent? Do they apply to the time period in question?
4. How were the statistics drawn? If from a sample, is the sample representative of the total population? Is the sample big enough?
5. Does the statistic actually measure what it is supposed to measure?
6. Are there contrary statistics?

Using Evidence Effectively

Once you have located and collected your evidence, keep in mind a couple of guidelines for applying it effectively. First, never take evidence out of context. Even if you find a statement that seems to be exactly the evidence you need, don't use it if the next sentence following it says something like, "However, this idea has recently been proved false." Second, try to gather and utilize evidence from as many sources as possible. Finally, use many different types of evidence to support a point.

TWO APPROACHES TO GROUP PROBLEM SOLVING

Problem-solving and decision-making groups must identify clear points of departure. Groups need to know why they exist and what their problems are. Phrasing problems as policy-oriented discussion questions helps groups solve them.

Fisher has identified two approaches to problem solving—*descriptive* and *prescriptive* approaches.

> [A descriptive problem-solving approach] attempts to document not how groups should make decisions but how they do make decisions. As its name implies, a descriptive approach involves observing actual groups interacting for the purpose of social decision making. The descriptive method seeks to describe the interactive process that is common to those groups.[7]

A **descriptive problem-solving approach,** then, does not give you guidelines and techniques for solving problems in groups; rather, it outlines how most groups go about solving problems. Fisher makes two assumptions about the descriptive approach to group problem solving: (1) There is a "natural" or normal process of group problem solving, and (2) groups will follow a normal problem-solving approach unless some external authority interferes with its freedom to solve its problem (e.g., an agenda is handed to the group or a strong-willed group leader dictates how the group should approach its task).[8]

A **prescriptive problem-solving approach** is based on a different set of assumptions. Groups use specific, predetermined agendas to solve problems efficiently and effectively. As summarized by Fisher:

> [A prescriptive approach] provides guidelines, a road map, to assist the group in achieving consensus. In one way, such a prescriptive approach is based on an assumed "ideal" process.[9]

Fisher has also noted two assumptions that underlie the prescriptive approach to problem solving: (1) Group members are consistently rational, and (2) the prescribed agenda will result in a better decision. The key difference between the two approaches is that the descriptive approach helps the group understand how groups usually solve problems, while the prescriptive approach offers specific suggestions for developing a group agenda.

Some scholars advocate the descriptive approach, pointing out that it does not constrain a group from its normal or natural process. Others contend that the prescriptive approach gives a group needed structure for solving problems. Each approach has unique advantages. It is useful for you both to understand how groups solve problems and to be acquainted with some techniques of organizing an agenda for problem-solving discussions. The remainder of this chapter gives an overview of the descriptive approach to problem solving in small groups. Chapter Eight will present several prescriptive approaches to group problem solving.

THE DESCRIPTIVE APPROACH

"Don't worry, Mom, I'm just going through a phase." Think back. Does this sound like something you may have said at one time? Apparently you were trying to alleviate your mother's concern by assuring her that your behavior was not at all uncommon and that it surely must pass in time. Implicit here is an assumption that individuals pass through several identifiable developmental stages, each of which leads to the next. Problem-solving groups, like individuals, go through several stages. With an understanding of these stages, you can learn to communicate in ways that expedite a group's passage from one stage to the next.

Several researchers have attempted to identify the phases of a problem-solving group. They have observed and recorded who speaks to whom and have categorized the comments group members exchange. Even though researchers have used various labels to describe these phases, they have reached similar conclusions. Table 7-1 illustrates the general pattern.

Of the research on developmental phases of groups, the most significant for small group communication is that of Fisher, who focused primarily on what was said throughout the development of his test groups. His terminology is used in the following sections. See Table 7-1 to compare these terms to the terms used by other researchers'.[10]

Table 7-1 Summary of Literature on Group Phases

	Phase 1	Phase 2	Phase 3	Phase 4
Thelen and Dickerman (1949)	Forming	Conflict	Harmony	Productivity
Bennis and Shepard (1956, 1961)	Dependence	Inter-dependence	Focused Work	Productivity
Tuckman (1965)	Forming	Storming	Norming	Performing
Fisher (1970, 1974)	Orientation	Conflict	Emergence	Reinforcement
Bales and Strodbeck (1951)	Orientation		Evaluation	Control
Schutz (1958)	Inclusion		Control	Affection

Phase One: Orientation

In the first phase of small group interaction "group members break the ice and begin to establish a common basis for functioning."[11] Speech communication during this phase tends to be oriented toward members getting to know one another, sharing backgrounds, and tentatively approaching the group's task. You are not likely to say anything that might prompt the rest of the group to reject you. Fisher noted that "more ambiguous comments . . . are contained in phase one than in any other phase except the third, which is also characterized by ambiguity."[12]

The research on the **orientation phase** suggests that your communication is directed at orienting yourself toward others as well as to the group's task (which can also be said about the other phases). What sets this phase apart from the others is the degree to which the social dimension is emphasized and the tentative, careful way in which the task dimension is approached.

Even the most efficient, task-motivated group will spend some time socializing and getting acquainted. Do not underestimate the importance of this type of interaction. Interpersonal trust—an essential ingredient for an effective working environment—does not happen all at once. You begin slowly, with "small talk," to determine whether it is "safe" to move on to deeper levels of interaction. The orientation phase, then, develops trust and group cohesiveness, which are so important for the group's survival in the second phase—conflict.

Phase Two: Conflict

During the first phase of orientation, group members begin to form opinions about their own positions in the group and about the group's task. By the second phase they start asserting these opinions. They have tested the water in the first phase and now are ready to jump in. On the process, or social level, this is a period in which individuals compete for status in the group. Two or more potential leaders may emerge with the support for each dividing the group into camps. In a decision-making or problem-solving group this division is reflected along the task dimension as well. During the first phase, members are hesitant to speak about the group's task, but in the second phase they begin to assert their individuality and respond favorably or unfavorably to the direction the group is taking. With such polarization of attitudes, disagreement or conflict naturally results.[13]

Communication during the **conflict phase** is characterized by persuasive attempts at changing others' opinions and reinforcing your own position. Some participants relish the idea of a good argument, while others see conflict as something to avoid at all cost. Avoiding conflict, however, means avoiding issues relevant and even crucial to the group's success. Just as individuals need to assert their own points of view, so do groups need to investigate all relevant alternatives in order to select the best solutions.

The conflict phase is necessary at both the task and the process dimensions of small group communication. Through conflict, you begin to identify the task issues that confront the group. Through conflict, you begin to clarify your own and others' roles. This clarification leads toward greater predictability, less uncertainty, and the establishment of group norms.

Phase Three: Emergence

In phase three new patterns of communication indicate a group's emergence from the conflict phase. If a group is going to function as a cohesive unit, it must resolve the conflict of phase two. Though conflict is still a part of phase three, what sets the **emergence phase** apart from the preceding conflict phase is the way in which members deal with conflict. This shift is most apparent in the reappearance of ambiguity in task-related statements.

Think of a time when a group adopted a course of action that you had at first opposed. Did you support the group decision in the end? If so, you had to change your attitude along the way. How did that take place? Can you identify a time when you suddenly turned against your former position? Probably not. The change was most likely gradual, was characterized by creeping ambivalence, and took place during the third phase of group interaction. If you argued strongly for a position in phase two, you have a hard time letting go of that position all at once. Your ego simply won't stand for it. At the same time, you may feel a need to pull the group back together. Task and process dimensions are interwoven at this stage. While the group is divided, there is also clarity. Leadership patterns and roles have been established, the issues and problems confronting the group have been identified, and the need to settle differences and reach consensus has become apparent. Here *metadiscussion*—talking about the status of the group, acknowledging differences and the need for consensus—may be a turning point. At other times, the change may occur more subtly as proponents of various positions become less tenacious in their arguments. However the change takes place, ambiguity appears to be the means by which you can comfortably shift your position toward group consensus.

Fisher noted that ambiguity in the third phase functions very differently from the way it does in the first phase. During the orientation phase, ambiguity serves as a tentative (and, therefore, safe) expression of attitudes.

> This explanation of ambiguity is not appropriate to the third phase . . . ; groups are no longer searching for attitude direction. This direction was plotted in the orientation phase and debated in the conflict phase. In the third phase, task direction is no longer an issue. . . . Ambiguity . . . functions in the third phase as a form of modified dissent. That is, the group members proceed to change their attitudes from disfavor to favor of the decision proposals through the mediation of ambiguity."[14]

In the emergence phase, then, a group settles on norms and moves toward consensus via ambiguous statements that gradually modify dissenting positions. Such ambiguous statements might take the form of qualifiers or reservations to the previous position: "I still would like to see our company merge with the Elector Electronics Corporation, but maybe we could consider a merger later in the year. Such a merger may be more appropriate next fall." Such a statement allows you to save face and still allows the group to reach consensus.

Phase Four: Reinforcement

A spirit of unity characterizes the final phase of group interaction. In the preceding three phases group members struggle through getting acquainted, building cohesiveness, expressing individuality, competing for status, and arguing over issues. The group eventually emerges from those struggles with a sense of direction, consensus of opinion, and a feeling of group identity. Not surprisingly, then, the fourth phase is characterized by positive feelings toward the group and its decisions. Finally, members feel a genuine sense of accomplishment!

Reinforcement predominates in communication:

Jim: I may have been against it at first, but I've finally seen the light. We're going in the right direction now.

Marilyn: Yes, but don't shortchange your contribution, Jim. If you hadn't opposed it so vehemently, we never would have developed the idea so fully.

Fisher noted that ambiguous and unfavorable comments all but disappear in the fourth phase, being replaced by uniformly favorable comments and reinforcement. At this time all of the hassle of group decision making and problem solving seems worthwhile. The group is at its most cohesive, individual satisfaction and sense of achievement are high, and uncertainty is at a low. Furthermore, it is a time when you find yourself in a new group with new problems.

A group in its initial stages of development is very different from that same group in its final phase. This metamorphosis can be followed and charted by carefully observing the communicative behavior of group members. Groups, like individuals, struggle through childhood and adolescence on their way to maturity.

The Process Nature of Group Phases

Even though it may appear from the discussion that a group neatly goes through four phases of development in a predictable way, group deliberations are seldom that orderly. In reality, a group may go through the phases for each issue that comes before it. For example, the first issue may be "What is the purpose of this group?" A group will probably spend some time getting oriented to this task, conflict may follow as members learn about the objectives each person has, and, after discussion, a general consensus may emerge about the group's purpose. Finally, members may assure one another that their purpose has been clearly developed.

Perhaps the next issue to come before the group is "How will we organize our work—should we have subcommittees?" Again, the members may go through orientation, conflict, emergence, and reinforcement. Since group discussions tend to hop from topic to topic, a group may get bogged down in conflict, abandon the issue, and move to another issue. Groups can either move through phases for each issue, or they can get sidetracked and abandon discussions about an issue.

Poole suggests that the phases of group problem solving, like any complex process, do not have clear-cut divisions.[15] Rather than describing group decision making as a sequence of four distinct stages, Poole builds on Fisher's research by suggesting that groups engage in three types of **activity tracks** that do not necessarily follow logical step-by-step patterns. The three types of activities that Poole believes best describe group interaction are: (1) **task process activities**, (2) **relational activities**, and (3) **topical focus**.[16] Task process activities are "those activities the group enacts to manage its task,"[17] such as analyzing a problem, becoming oriented to the issues of a problem, establishing criteria, and evaluating solutions proposed. Answering such questions as, "What's the problem here?" "How can we better understand the problem?" and "How effective will our solution be?" are examples of task process activities.

Verbal or nonverbal communication that indicates who is liked and disliked can be categorized as relational activity. These are "activities that reflect or manage relationships among group members as these relate to the group's work."[18] As noted in Chapter Four, communication has both a task and a relationship dimension. Relational activities are communication behaviors that sustain or damage interpersonal relationships among group members. Criticism, conflict, praise, and encouragement help group members understand their relationships with one another. Relational activities also affect a group's working climate.

The third type of activity, topic focus, deals with the "general themes, major issues or arguments of concern to the group at a given point in the discussion."[19]

Bormann and other researchers have noted that groups often focus their conversations on given themes or topics that serve as the actual agendas for the groups.[20] This third type of activity, then, deals with major topics that do not relate to a group's specific task or to member relationships. These three activity "tracks," as Poole calls them, do not all develop at the same rate or according to the same pattern. Some groups may spend a considerable portion of their time developing relationships before discussing their tasks in great detail. On the other hand, task-oriented groups often devote considerable energy to completing their tasks, letting relationships play minor roles in group deliberations. Groups switch activity tracks at various **breakpoints**, which occur as groups switch topics, adjourn, or schedule planning periods. Another type of breakpoint, called a delay, occurs because of group conflict or its inability to reach consensus. Whereas groups may expect and schedule some breakpoints, they usually do not schedule delays. Poole notes, "depending on the nature of the delay and the mood of the group, [a] breakpoint can signal the start of a difficulty or a highly creative period."[21] A disruption, the third type of breakpoint, results from a major conflict or a realization that a group may not be able to complete its task. A group must be flexible to manage disruption.

Poole's analysis of group phases and group activity emphasizes the process nature of group communication. While several researchers have documented chronological phases in a group's decision-making efforts, a group's communication can also be described by the three activities of task process, relational activity, and topical focus. A descriptive approach to group communication can help you better understand and explain why certain types of statements are made in groups. With an understanding of the process, you should be in a better position to evaluate and improve your participation in group meetings.

The next chapter will present prescriptive formats designed to help you organize group problem solving and decision making.

UNDERSTANDING PROBLEM SOLVING IN SMALL GROUPS: PUTTING PRINCIPLE INTO PRACTICE

If you can understand how groups go about the task of solving problems, you will be better able to manage the problem-solving process in small groups. The following suggestions should help you apply the concepts presented in this chapter.

Group Decision Making

- Groups make decisions by assessing the present situation, identifying alternative solutions for the group goal, identifying positive and negative consequences of alternatives, and selecting the best alternative.
- Group members should accurately assess the choice-making situation.
- Group members should establish clear and appropriate group goals.
- Group members should identify the positive and negative consequences of alternatives.

- Group members should have accurate information.
- Group members should draw reasonable conclusions from the information that is available.

Group Problem Solving

- Almost any problem can be phrased in terms of something you want more of or less of.
- The three elements of a problem include (1) the undesirable present, (2) obstacles, and (3) the goal.
- Effective problem solvers sees the problem from a variety of viewpoints.
- Effective problem solvers gather data and research the issues.
- Effective problem solvers evaluate the opinions and assumptions of others.
- Effective problem solvers know how to use evidence.
- Effective problem solvers are concerned for both the group task and the feelings of others.
- Effective problem solvers ask appropriate questions in order to keep a discussion on track.
- Effective problem solvers search for many alternatives or solutions to a problem.
- Effective problem solvers listen to minority arguments.
- Effective problem solvers test solutions in order to see if they meet preestablished criteria.
- Effective problem solvers take a vacation from a problem if the group can't reach a solution.

Formulating Discussion Questions

- Formulate a discussion question that focuses and directs the deliberations of your group.
- Formulate a question of fact if your group is trying to decide whether something is true or false, or whether something did or did not occur.
- Formulate a question of value if your group is trying to decide whether one idea or approach to an issue is better than another approach.
- Formulate a question of policy if your group is trying to develop a solution to a problem.

Two Approaches to Group Problem Solving

- Adopt a descriptive approach to group problem solving if you understand the phases that a group goes through to reach a solution.
- Adopt a prescriptive approach to problem solving if your group needs the structure that a problem-solving agenda provides.

- Do not be too concerned when your group takes time to orient itself to the problem-solving process. It is a normal part of group problem solving.
- Expect some conflict and differences of opinions after a group clarifies its task and passes through the orientation phase of problem solving.
- Even though conflict may appear to impede a group's efforts to solve a problem, expect a decision to emerge after a thorough discussion and analysis of the issues.
- Do not overlook the importance of the reinforcement phase of group problem solving. Group members need a sense of accomplishment after the group makes a decision.

PRACTICE

Identifying Questions of Fact, Value, and Policy

Read the following narrative, then identify and phrase the following questions: (1) the main discussion question (and label it as fact, value, or policy), (2) at least one question of fact, and (3) at least one question of value.

> A new liberal divorce law has come up for discussion in the state senate. Senator Smith, who introduced the bill, has lobbied hard for it because she has found evidence to suggest that complications in the current law do not deter divorce but only result in lengthy delays and higher fees for divorce lawyers. Senator Williams also supports the new law; he was recently divorced and experienced much frustration and aggravation in the process. Senator Schwartz, on the other hand, is happily married and quite conservative; he leads opposition to the new law.

Hurricane Preparedness Case

Although you have idly watched local meteorologists track Hurricane Bruce's destructive course through the Caribbean for several days, you have not given any serious thought to the possibility that the number 3-rated storm might directly affect your coastal city. However, at about 7 o'clock this morning the storm suddenly veered northward, putting it on course for a direct hit. Now the National Hurricane Center in Miami has posted a Hurricane Warning for your community. Forecasters are predicting landfall in approximately 9 to 12 hours. Having taken no advance precautions, you are stunned by the amount of work you now have to do to secure your three-bedroom suburban home, which is about ½ mile from the beach. You have enough food in the house for two days. You also have one candle and a transistor radio with one weak battery. You have no other hurricane supplies, nor have you taken any hurricane precautions. Your task is to rank the following items in terms of their importance for ensuring your survival and the safety of your property. Place number *1* by the first thing you should do, *2* by the second, and so on through number *13*. Please work individually on this task.

Fill your car with gas   _____

Trim your bushes and trees   _____

Fill your bathtub with water   _____

Construct hurricane shutters for your windows   _____

Buy enough food for a week   _____

Buy batteries and candles   _____

Bring in patio furniture from outside   _____

Buy dry ice   _____

Invite friends over for a Hurricane Party   _____

Drain your swimming pool   _____

Listen to TV and radio for further bulletins before doing anything   _____

Make sure you have an evacuation plan   _____

Stock up on charcoal and charcoal lighter for your barbecue grill   _____

Description of Group Process

Attend a school board, city council, or other public meeting in which problems are discussed and solutions are recommended. Prepare a written analysis of the meeting by attempting to identify phases in the group's discussions. Also, try to identify examples of the three activity tracks discussed in this chapter (task process, relational, topical). In addition, provide examples of breakpoints in the discussion of the group.

Evaluation of Group Decision Making

Use the following scales to record your response to your participation in a problem-solving or decision-making group discussion.

1. How well did the group assess the problem or decision?

1	2	3	4	5	6	7	8	9	10
not at all								a great deal	

2. How well did the group identify its goal?

1	2	3	4	5	6	7	8	9	10
not at all								a great deal	

3. How well did the group identify the positive consequences of the solutions under consideration?

1	2	3	4	5	6	7	8	9	10
not at all								a great deal	

4. How well did the group identify the negative consequences of the solutions under consideration?

1	2	3	4	5	6	7	8	9	10
not at all									a great deal

5. Did the group draw reasonable conclusions from available information?

1	2	3	4	5	6	7	8	9	10
yes									no

Evaluation of Group Problem Solving

Based upon your participation in a problem-solving group, use the following scales to evaluate your group problem-solving skills.

1. I was able to see the problem from a variety of viewpoints.
   strongly agree   agree   unsure   disagree   strongly disagree
2. I researched the issues under discussion appropriately.
   strongly agree   agree   unsure   disagree   strongly disagree
3. I evaluated the opinions and assumptions of others.
   strongly agree   agree   unsure   disagree   strongly disagree
4. I used evidence effectively to reach a valid conclusion.
   strongly agree   agree   unsure   disagree   strongly disagree
5. I was concerned for both the group task and the feelings of others.
   strongly agree   agree   unsure   disagree   strongly disagree
6. I helped to keep the discussion on track.
   strongly agree   agree   unsure   disagree   strongly disagree
7. I generated several possible alternatives or solutions to the problem.
   strongly agree   agree   unsure   disagree   strongly disagree
8. I courteously listened to minority arguments and opinions.
   strongly agree   agree   unsure   disagree   strongly disagree
9. I checked to determine if the proposed solutions met the group's preestablished criteria.
   strongly agree   agree   unsure   disagree   strongly disagree
10. If the group was not easily able to solve the problem I encouraged members to take a break so that they could have a fresh perspective.
    strongly agree   agree   unsure   disagree   strongly disagree

Fallout Shelter Exercise: Ranking Task

The possibility of a nuclear war has been announced and the alert signal has been sounded. You and your group have access to a small basement fallout shelter. When the warning signal sounds, you must immediately go to the shelter. In the meantime, you must decide what to take with you to help you survive the attack.

You are outside the immediate blast areas. The greatest danger facing you is from radioactive fallout. In order to help in your decision making, rank the following items in order of their importance to your survival in the shelter (use *1* for the most important items and *13* for the least important).[22]

_____ one large and one small garbage can with lids

_____ broom

_____ containers of water

_____ blankets

_____ canned heat stove

_____ matches and candles

_____ canned and dried foods

_____ liquid chlorine bleach

_____ vaporizing liquid fire extinguisher

_____ flashlight and batteries

_____ battery powered radio

_____ soap and towels

_____ first-aid kit with iodine and medicines

_____ cooking and eating utensils

_____ geiger counter

Stranded in the Desert Situation

You are a member of a geology club that is on a field trip to study unusual formations in the New Mexico desert. It is the last week in July. You have been driving over old trails, far from any road, in order to see out-of-the-way formations. At about 10:30 A.M. your club's specially equipped minibus overturns, rolls into a twenty-foot ravine, and burns. The driver and professional adviser to the club are killed. The rest of you are relatively uninjured.

You know that the nearest ranch is approximately forty-five miles east of where you are. There is no closer habitation. When your club does not report to its motel that evening you will be missed. Several people know generally where you are but will not be able to pinpoint your whereabouts.

The area around you is rather rugged and dry. There is a shallow waterhole nearby, but the water is contaminated by worms, animal feces and urine, and several dead mice. Before you left you heard from a weather report that the temperature would reach 108 degrees, making the surface temperature 128 degrees. All of you are dressed in lightweight summer clothing and all have hats and sunglasses.

While escaping from the minibus, each group member salvaged a couple of items; there are twelve items in all. Your group's task is to rank these items according to their importance to your survival, starting with *1* for the most important and proceeding to *12* for the least important.

You may assume that the number of club members is the same as the number of persons in your group and that the group has agreed to stick together.[23]

_____ magnetic compass

_____ a piece of heavy-duty, light-blue canvas, 20 square feet in size

_____ book, *Plants of the Desert*

_____ rearview mirror

_____ large knife

_____ flashlight

_____ one jacket per person

_____ one transparent, plastic ground cloth (6 feet by 4 feet) per person

_____ a .38-caliber loaded pistol

_____ one two-quart plastic canteen of water per person

_____ an accurate map of the area

_____ a large box of kitchen matches

Notes

1. Randy Y. Hirokawa and Dirk R. Scheerhorn, "Communication in Faulty Group Decision-Making," in Randy Y. Hirokawa and Marshall Scott Poole, *Communication and Group Decision-Making*, (Beverly Hills, California: Sage Publications, 1986), p. 67.

2. *Ibid.*, p. 69.

3. See John K. Brilhart, *Effective Group Discussion* (Dubuque, Iowa: Wm. C. Brown, 1986), p. 267; David W. Johnson and Frank P. Johnson, *Joining Together: Group Theory and Group Skills* (Englewood Cliffs, New Jersey: Prentice-Hall, 1987), pp. 99–104.

4. Charles H. Kepner and Benjamin B. Treogoe, *The Rational Manager* (New York: McGraw-Hill, 1965); also see Brilhart, *Effective Group Discussion*, p. 284.

5. See Randy Y. Hirokawa and Roger Pace, "A Descriptive Investigation of the Possible Communication-Based Reasons for Effective and Ineffective Group Decision Making," *Communication Monographs* 50 (December 1983): 363–379. The authors also wish to acknowledge Dennis A. Romig, Performance Resources, Inc., Austin, Texas, for his contribution to the discussion.

6. Dennis S. Gouran, *Discussion: The Process of Group Decision-Making* (New York: Harper & Row, Publishers, 1974), p. 72.

7. B. Aubrey Fisher, *Small Group Decision Making: Communication and the Group Process*, 2nd ed. (New York: McGraw-Hill Book Company, 1980), p. 132.

8. *Ibid.*

9. *Ibid.*, p. 130.

10. *Ibid.*, pp. 130–131.

11. Stewart L. Tubbs and Sylvia Moss, *Interpersonal Communication*, 5th ed. (New York: Random House, 1987), p. 270.

12. B. Aubrey Fisher, "Decision Emergence: Phases in Group Decision-Making," *Speech Monographs* 37 (1970): 60.

13. *Ibid.*, p. 61.

14. *Ibid.,* p. 63.

15. Marshall Scott Poole, "Decision Development in Small Groups, III: A Multiple Sequence Model of Group Decision Development," *Communication Monographs* 50 (December 1983): 321–341.

16. *Ibid.,* p. 326.

17. *Ibid.*

18. *Ibid.*

19. *Ibid.*

20. See Ernest G. Bormann, *Discussion and Group Methods* (New York: Harper & Row, 1975).

21. Poole, "Decision Development," p. 330.

22. Johnson and Johnson, *Joining Together,* p. 239.

23. *Ibid.,* p. 231

Chapter Eight

Small Group Problem-Solving Techniques

After studying this chapter, you should be able to:

☐ Use reflective thinking to solve a problem in a small group discussion.

☐ Apply brainstorming to a problem-solving group discussion.

☐ Apply the ideal solution problem-solving method to a group discussion.

☐ Apply the single question problem-solving approach to a group discussion.

☐ Determine when participative decision-making methods such as buzz groups, nominal group technique, risk technique, quality control circles, or focus groups will be useful.

☐ Determine which problem-solving approach is most suitable for a given group discussion.

Imagine that you are chairperson of a committee appointed to improve the quality of education in your community. Students' scores on standard achievement tests have declined in the past two years. School administrators complain that they do not have the funds to develop new programs or to hire more teachers. Your committee must develop a plan to deal with the problem. The last chapter introduced the concepts of descriptive and prescriptive approaches to problem solving. As committee chairperson you could adopt a descriptive problem-solving approach by cluing in group members on some of the processes that groups experience when trying to solve problems. Although giving your committee an understanding of the process may be beneficial, you feel you need to provide more structure to help the group efficiently organize its approach to solving the problem.

This chapter identifies some prescriptive approaches to problem solving that may help you organize a group's problem-solving attempts. There is no one best way to solve problems in groups. Each group is unique, and each group member is unique. No single prescriptive problem-solving formula always works. This chapter will, however, give you several suggestions for solving problems in groups, one of which should meet your group's need at any given time.

Research suggests that some method of group problem solving is better than no method at all.[1] Groups need some structure because of their members' relatively short attention spans. In separate studies researchers found that groups shift topics about once a minute.[2] As noted in the last chapter, Poole argues that group members consider task process, relational concerns, and topical shifts with varying degrees of attention.[3] Thus, they benefit from an agenda that helps reduce uncertainty by keeping the discussion focused on the group's task.

In trying to make small group communication theory practical and useful, this chapter will not only describe four problem-solving approaches but will also give you some specific suggestions for applying the approaches to your discussions. Your group will not necessarily use any one of the approaches described here exclusively. You may find several of these methods useful at various phases of the problem-solving process.

A TRADITIONAL APPROACH TO PROBLEM SOLVING: REFLECTIVE THINKING

In 1910 philosopher and educator John Dewey, in his book *How We Think,* identified the steps most people follow to solve problems. Dewey did not focus specifically on small groups,[4] but the steps he outlined, part of the process called **reflective thinking,** has been used by many groups as a way to structure the problem-solving process. Some researchers and numerous group communication textbooks recommend reflective thinking as a useful and productive way to organize group problem solving. However, many group communication theorists today believe that it is more useful as a description of the way *some* people solve problems rather than as an ideal way for *all* groups to solve problems. Dewey's reflective-thinking process consists of five steps.

Step One: Identify and Define the Problem

A group first has to recognize that a problem exists. This step may be a group's biggest obstacle. Before a PTA fund-raising committee can effectively consider suggestions for raising money, members must recognize that a need exists. Many groups don't bother to verbalize the problem facing them; each person would rather begin by offering solutions to remedy the problem. A group must clearly and succinctly agree on the problem facing it. The problem should be limited so that members know its scope and size. After members identify and limit it, they should define key terms so that they have a common understanding of the problem. The terms should be defined in light of the problem under consideration. For example, one student group recently decided to solve the problem of student apathy on campus. The students phrased their problem as a question: "What can be done to alleviate student apathy on campus?" They had identified a problem, but they soon discovered that they needed to decide what they meant by the word *apathy.* Does it mean poor attendance at football games? Does it mean a sparse showing at the recent fund-raising activity, "Hit Your Professor with a Pie"? After additional efforts to define the key word, they decided to limit their problem to low attendance at events sponsored by the student activities committee. With a clearer focus on their problem, they were ready to continue with the problem-solving process.

Consider the following questions when attempting to identify and define a problem for group deliberations:

1. What is the specific problem the group is concerned about?
2. Is the question the group is trying to answer clear?
3. What terms, concepts, or ideas need to be defined?
4. Who is harmed by the problem?
5. When do the harmful effects of the problem occur?

Step Two: Analyze the Problem

During the analysis phase of group problem solving, members need to research and investigate the problem. In analyzing the problem, a group may wish to consider the following questions:

1. What is the history of the problem? How long has it existed?
2. How serious is the problem?
3. What are the causes of the problem?
4. What are the effects of the problem?
5. What are the symptoms of the problem?
6. What methods does the group already have for dealing with the problem?
7. What are the limitations of those methods?
8. How much freedom does the group have in gathering information and attempting to solve the problem?
9. What are the obstacles that keep the group from achieving the goal?
10. Can the problem be divided into subproblems for definition and analysis?

For the group to analyze the problem effectively, members need to acquaint themselves with the basic techniques for conducting research presented in Appendix A.

Another phase in the analysis step of the reflective-thinking process is to formulate criteria for an acceptable solution. **Criteria** are standards or goals for acceptable solutions. Formulating such criteria may prevent future uncertainties and misunderstandings and may help your group sort through proposed solutions to arrive at the best possible one. Many groups begin listing solutions before they have properly analyzed problems or before they have identified adequate criteria. If you adhere to the reflective-thinking format, you will identify criteria before offering possible solutions. In listing criteria for a solution, you may wish to consider the following questions:

1. What philosophy should the group adopt with respect to solving the problem?
2. What are the minimum requirements of an acceptable solution?
3. Which criteria are the most important?
4. How should the group use the criteria to evaluate the suggested solutions?

Sample criteria for a solution may include the following:

1. The solution should be inexpensive.
2. The solution should be implemented as soon as possible.
3. The solution should be agreed on by all of the group members.

Step Three: Suggest Possible Solutions

After a group has analyzed a problem and selected criteria for a solution, it should begin to list possible solutions in tentative, hypothetical terms. Many groups suggest a variety of possible solutions without evaluating them.

Step Four: Suggest the Best Solution(s)

After a group has compiled a list of possible solutions to a problem, it should be ready to select the best solution. Members should refer to the criteria they proposed during the analysis stage of their discussion and should consider each tentative solution in light of these criteria. The group should decide which proposed solution or combination of solutions best meets the group's criteria. The following questions may be helpful in analyzing the proposed solutions:

1. What would be the long-term effects and short-term effects of this solution if it were adopted?
2. Would the solution really solve the problem?
3. Are there any disadvantages to the solution? Do the disadvantages outweigh the advantages?
4. Does the solution conform to the criteria formulated by the group?
5. Should the group modify the criteria?

If group members agree, the criteria for a best solution may need to be changed or modified.[5]

Step Five: Test and Implement the Solution

Group members should be confident that the proposed solution is valid—that is, that it will solve the problem. After a group selects the best solution, it must determine how the solution can be put into effect. You may wish to consider the following questions:

1. How can the group get public approval and support for its proposed solution?
2. What specific steps are necessary to implement the solution?
3. How can the group evaluate the success of its problem-solving efforts?

In many groups, those who choose a solution are not the same people who will implement it. If this is the case, members who select the solution should clearly explain why they selected it to members who will put the solution into practice. If they can demonstrate that the group went through an orderly process to solve the problem, they can usually convince others that their solution is valid.

Reflective Thinking

1. Identify and Define the Problem
2. Analyze the Problem
3. Suggest Possible Solutions
4. Suggest the Best Solution(s)
5. Test and Implement the Solution(s)

Applying Reflective Thinking

Dewey's reflective thinking suggests that groups work best when their discussions are organized rather than unorganized or random. Remember that you should use reflective thinking as a guide, not as an exact formula for solving every problem. As noted earlier, several group communication researchers have discovered that groups do not necessarily solve problems in a linear, step-by-step process.[6] They go through several phases of growth and development as members interact.[7] Reflective thinking is most useful in helping groups understand the phases of problem solving. As Bormann has noted, "Difficulties arise when [group] participants demand rationality from a group throughout its deliberations."[8] One researcher suggests that reflective thinking may work best if groups face a limited range of possible solutions or courses of action.[9] To add flexibility to the reflective-thinking steps, a group may return to an earlier problem-solving step to help clarify the discussion. For example, after researching and analyzing a problem, a group may decide to define it a little differently than it had previously. Perhaps after carefully trying to apply criteria to select the best solution, a group may decide that it needs to revise the criteria. Reflective thinking can serve as a general guide to the problem solving process. Hirokawa's research suggests that a systematic approach to group problem solving and decision making is better than no organized approach at all.[10]

In trying to apply reflective thinking to group problem solving, consider the suggestions listed below.

1. *Clearly identify the problem you're trying to solve.* Make sure that you are not just discussing a topic. For example, one group decided to discuss the quality of the U.S. justice system. The group selected a topic area, but it did not identify a problem. It should have focused clearly on a specific problem, such as "How can we improve the quality of the judicial system in the United States?" or "What should be done to improve the education and training of lawyers in the United States?"

2. *Phrase the problem as a question to help guide group discussion.* Identifying your group's problem as a question adds focus and direction to your delibera-

Brainstorming is a means of generating many possible solutions to a problem; group members express any ideas that come to them without judging or evaluating those ideas.

tions. When formulating a problem-solving discussion question, keep in mind the guidelines discussed in Chapter Seven.

3. *Don't start suggesting solutions until you have analyzed the problem.* Many group communication researchers agree that until your group has researched the problem, you may not have enough information and specific facts to reach the best solution.[11] You will be tempted to think of solutions to your problem almost as soon as you have identified it. By deferring the search for a solution, you will gain a greater understanding of the causes, effects, and symptoms of the problem.

4. *In the definition and analysis steps of reflective thinking, don't confuse the causes of the problem with its symptoms.* A fever and headache are symptoms and not necessarily causes of a patient's ill health. The cause may be a cold or flu virus or a number of other things. A doctor tries to identify the cause of symptoms by running tests and analyzing a patient's medical history. In other words, a doctor needs to define, analyze, and solve a problem. You should try to clarify the differences between the causes and the symptoms (effects) of a problem. Perhaps your only goal is to alleviate the symptoms.

However, you can better understand what your group is trying to accomplish if you can distinguish causes and symptoms.

5. *Constantly evaluate your group's problem-solving method.* For many years the only problem-solving method suggested to group discussion classes was reflective thinking. Some communication theorists suggest, however, that for certain types of problems alternative problem-solving methods work just as well, if not better, than reflective thinking. The remaining portions of this chapter will discuss some of these other problem-solving strategies.

A CREATIVE APPROACH TO PROBLEM SOLVING: BRAINSTORMING

Imagine that your employer assigns you to a task force whose goal is to try to increase the productivity of your small manufacturing company. Phrased as a question, the problem is, "What can be done to increase efficiency and productivity for our company?" Your group is supposed to come up with ideas to help solve the problem. Assume that your boss has clearly identified the problem for the group and has provided you with several documents analyzing the problem in some detail. Your group may decide that reflective thinking, which focuses on identifying and analyzing problems, may not be the best process to follow. Your group needs innovative ideas and creative, original solutions. Perhaps your group could benefit from brainstorming.

Brainstorming is a problem-solving approach designed to help a group generate several creative solutions to a problem. It was first developed by Alex Osborn, an advertising executive who felt the need for a problem-solving technique that instead of evaluating and criticizing ideas would focus instead on developing imaginative and innovative solutions.[12] Brainstorming has been used by businesses, committees, and government agencies to improve the quality of group decision making. Although it can be used in several phases of many group discussions, it may be most useful if a group needs original ideas or has trouble coming up with any ideas at all.

Here is a step-by-step description of how brainstorming works:

1. *Select a specific problem that needs solving.* Be sure that all group members can identify and clearly define the problem.

2. *Group members should temporarily put aside all judgments and evaluations.* The key to brainstorming is ruling out all criticism and evaluation. Osborn makes these suggestions:

   - Acquire a "try anything" attitude.
   - Avoid criticism, which can stifle creativity.
   - Remember that all ideas are thought-starters.
   - Today's criticism may kill future ideas.

Brainstorming

1. Select a problem that needs creative solutions.
2. Tell group members to withhold judgments and evaluations.
3. Tell the group to generate as many solutions as possible.
4. Tell the group it's OK to piggyback off someone else's idea.
5. Have someone record the ideas generated.
6. Evaluate the ideas when the time allotted for brainstorming has elapsed.

---

3. *After group members have a clear understanding of the problem and know the brainstorming ground rules, tell them to think of as many possible solutions to the problem as they can.* Consider the following suggestions:
   - The wilder the ideas, the better.
   - It is easier to tame ideas down than to think ideas up.
   - Think out loud and mention unusual ideas.
   - Someone's wild idea may trigger a good solution from another person in the group.
4. *Make sure that the group understands that "piggybacking" off someone's idea is useful.* Combine ideas; add to previous ideas. Adopt this philosophy: Once an idea is contributed to the group, no one owns it. It belongs to the group and anyone can modify it.
5. *Have someone record all of the ideas mentioned.* Ideas could be recorded on a chalkboard or an overhead projector so that each group member can see them. You could also tape-record your discussions.
6. *Some groups evaluate ideas at later sessions.* Consider these suggestions:
   - Approach each idea positively, and give it a fair trial.
   - Try to make ideas workable.
   - If only a few of the ideas generated by a group are useful, the session has been successful.

Applying Brainstorming

While you should now understand how brainstorming works, you may still have some questions about how you can apply this method of creative problem solving to your group discussions. Consider the following suggestions:

1. *Be certain each group member understands the specific problem that the group is trying to solve.* A problem must be clearly defined and understood and must also be limited in size and scope. A broad, vaguely worded problem must be clarified before a group attempts to identify possible solutions.

2. *Brainstorming works best as part of an overall problem-solving strategy.* As with reflective thinking, group members need to define and analyze the problem under consideration, provided it has not already been identified for them. One difference between a creative problem-solving method like brainstorming and traditional reflective thinking is that those using the former method apply criteria for solutions after they generate possible solutions. Otherwise criteria may put a damper on group creativity. Instead of developing solutions according to established criteria, members evaluate solutions after they are developed.

3. *Make sure that each group member follows the brainstorming rules.* Brainstorming will be most effective if group members stop criticizing and evaluating ideas. Don't forget that group members can criticize nonverbally through tone of voice, facial expression, or posture. Everyone in the group must feel completely free to communicate ideas that may solve the problem. What should you do if a few members just can't stop evaluating the ideas that are suggested? You may have to: (1) remind them courteously to follow the rules, (2) ask them to be quiet, (3) ask them to record the ideas of others, or (4) ask them to leave the group.

4. *If brainstorming doesn't work for your group, consider this alternative: Have each group member work individually.* One team of researchers has discovered that group members' creative talents may be restricted when they are around others.[13] Groups may collect more solutions if members first work alone and then regroup. After they meet as units again, groups can modify, elaborate on, and evaluate ideas.

5. *If you are serving as the group's leader, try to draw less talkative group members into the discussion and compliment them when they come up with good ideas.* Call people by name: "Curt, you look like you've got some good ideas. What do you suggest?" You can also compliment the entire group when members are doing a good job of generating ideas: "Good job, group! We've got thirty ideas so far. Let's see if we can come up with thirty more."

6. *Set aside a definite amount of time for brainstorming.* Decide, as a group, how much time you want to devote to brainstorming. Be sure to give yourself plenty—it's better to have too much than too little. You may want to set a goal for a certain number of ideas that should be recorded: "We'll stop brainstorming when we get sixty ideas."

7. *Make sure your group needs a creative problem-solving format.* Brainstorming can help generate ideas, but if your group does not have a lot of time to devote to it, a simpler, more conventional problem-solving method (such as reflective thinking) may be best. Don't avoid brainstorming when it may be useful as part of an overall problem-solving plan (e.g., it can be used to generate possible solutions in the third step of the reflective-thinking format).

Some researchers believe that five people is an ideal size for a brainstorming group. If the group is too large, members may feel inhibited and may not contribute creative ideas. Therefore, make sure that brainstorming is the problem-solving format your group needs.

QUESTION-ORIENTED APPROACHES TO PROBLEM SOLVING

As discussed earlier, a group adopts a problem-solving format mainly to organize its deliberations and reach its goal more efficiently. Thus far, the chapter has discussed a traditional problem-solving format (reflective thinking) and a method of generating creative ideas (brainstorming). A third approach to problem solving requires groups to consider a series of questions to keep them oriented toward their goal. Two such approaches, discussed in the following sections, can help groups develop strategies for solving problems. Both formats have groups consider series of questions to help identify the critical issues that they need to resolve. The questions also provide an orderly sequence of thought to help groups formulate the best possible solutions. After you study both of these formats, the chapter will offer some specific suggestions for applying these approaches to your group discussions.

Ideal-Solution Format

Obviously, problem-solving groups want to identify the best solutions to problems. In the ideal-solution format, groups answer questions designed to help them identify ideal solutions. Goldberg and Larson have devised the following agenda of questions:

1. Do all members agree on the nature of the problem?
2. What would be the ideal solution from the point of view of all the parties involved in the problem?
3. What conditions within the problem could be changed so that the ideal solution might be achieved?
4. Of the solutions available, which one best approximates the ideal solution?[14]

These questions help groups recognize the barriers that the problems under consideration have created. The questions also encourage groups to analyze their problem's cause and to evaluate proposed solutions. The advantage of the ideal-solution format over other problem-solving approaches is its simplicity. Group members simply consider each of the questions listed previously, one at a time. Brilhart recommends the ideal-solution format for discussions that involve people with varied interests. He also believes that the format can work best when acceptance of a solution is important.[15] The format enables group members to see the problem from several viewpoints in their search for the best solution.

Here is a situation in which the ideal-solution format might prove valuable. Sean is personnel director for the Barnett Chemical Company. Mr. Barnette, the company president, has asked Sean to organize a committee to investigate the problem of low morale among workers. Employee turnover has been high, and most employees are not satisfied with working conditions at the chemical plant. Sean asked three supervisors from the production line to serve on the committee. He also organized the committee's problem-solving agenda, using the ideal-solution format. Since each supervisor probably has different ideas about how the problem can best be solved, Sean thinks the ideal-solution format will keep the committee's discussion focused. After explaining the purpose for the meeting, Sean asked, "Do we all agree on the nature of the problem?" This question encouraged each supervisor to talk about the problem and gave the others an opportunity to hear each viewpoint. After considerable discussion, committee members agree that the main cause of worker dissatisfaction is that employees do not participate in the decisions affecting their work. Employees think their opinions aren't respected. Following the ideal-solution format for problem solving, the group next considers, "What would be the ideal solution to this problem?" Since the group has already agreed on the probable cause of the problem, they soon agree that they need a job enrichment program that permits employees greater opportunity to convey their ideas and suggestions to their managers. Specifically, the group recommends that each supervisor should have more time to talk with employees on a one-to-one basis in order to listen to employee suggestions for solving problems and increasing productivity. The committee members agree that employees need greater opportunity to be heard. After the ideal solution has been described, Sean asks the committee, "What do we need to change about our present way of managing our employees so that the ideal solution we have identified can be put into practice?"

Note that the group has considered each question in the ideal-solution format separately. The group has first agreed on the problem, then considered why the problem exists, and finally, noted how the problem can be solved. Now it is ready to consider a question that will help it formulate specific steps for implementing the ideal solution that it has identified. After considering all of the suggestions and recommendations made by the supervisors, Sean asks them, "Which of the specific recommendations that we've made will best help us achieve the ideal solution that we've identified?" This question directs the group discussion toward specific practical suggestions that will enable the group to formulate a detailed set of recommendations for the company president.

While the ideal-solution format is similar to reflective thinking, its chief value is that it uses questions to help a group systematically identify and analyze a problem, pinpoint the best possible solution, and formulate specific methods for achieving a solution. Like the other problem-solving formats presented in this chapter, it helps a group, particularly one with varying viewpoints and experiences, focus on a problem and devise ways to solve it.

Single-Question Format

Like the ideal-solution format, the **single-question format** requires considering answers to a series of questions designed to guide the group toward a best solution. Goldberg and Larson suggest that the answers to the following five questions can help a group achieve its goal:

1. What is the question whose answer the group needs to know in order to accomplish its purpose?
2. What subquestions must be answered before the group can answer the single question it has formulated?

3. Does the group have sufficient information to answer the subquestions confidently? (If yes, answer them. If no, continue below.)

4. What are the most reasonable answers to the subquestions?

5. Assuming that the answers to the subquestions are correct, what is the best solution to the problem?[16]

A key difference between the single-question format and the ideal-solution format is that the former requires a group to formulate a question to help gain information needed to solve a problem. The single-question format also helps a group identify and resolve issues that must be confronted before it can reach a solution. As noted by Goldberg and Larson, "An assumption of the single question form seems to be that issues must be resolved, however tentatively."[17] Thus, the single-question format would probably work best if a group is capable of reaching reasonable agreement on the issues and is able to agree on how the issues can be resolved. A group characterized by conflict and contention would probably not find the single-question approach productive.

A school board is meeting to decide on next year's budget. Lucy Jones, chairperson of the board, thinks that the board can use the single-question format to agree on a budget. Because the board will have to consider many subquestions, she knows that they need a problem-solving plan that will help resolve those subissues. But she also knows that she must keep the discussion focused on the main problem—agreeing on next year's budget. Another reason she thinks the single-question format would work well for the meeting is that she knows the board members generally work well together.

The budget is complex and controversial. The board must first agree on budget requests from the numerous departments and divisions in the school system before they can agree on a final dollar figure. Chairperson Jones opens the meeting by saying, "If we can agree on our ultimate objective for this meeting, I think it would help keep our discussion on track. First, we really need to identify the specific question that we are trying to answer during this meeting. Remember, agreeing on our ultimate objective will help keep our discussions focused."

Board member Smith replies, "Our main objective is to agree on the budget for next school year. Phrased as a question, we want to know: 'What is next year's school budget?' "

Jones then asks the board to consider the next question in the single-question format: "What subquestions must be answered before we can answer the single question we have formulated?"

"Well," responds member Brown, "we need to ask whether we can agree on the budget requests submitted to us from each of the departments and divisions. If we can agree on these individual budgets, then we will probably be able to agree on the total budget."

Jones asks, "But do we have enough information to approve the individual departments' budget requests?"

"Yes, I think we do," answers another member. "We've got the budget requests for the last five years. We also have a record of the amount of money spent by each department."

The board then considers the budget requests of each department. After reaching consensus on the subquestions, the board is ready to consider the final phase of its problem-solving process. "Assuming that we are satisfied with the recommendations for individual department budgets, let's see if we can agree on the total budget for the coming year," says Jones. The group can now readily agree on the final budget for next year.

The success of the single-question format depends on a group's agreeing on the subissues before trying to agree on the major issues. If you are working with a group that has difficulty reaching agreement, the single-question format may not be the best approach. The group may become bogged down arguing about trivial matters while the major issues go unanswered. Decide whether your group will be able to reach agreement on the minor issues before you decide to use the single-question format. If your group can't reach agreement, either the ideal-solution format or reflective-thinking format may be a better method of organizing your group's deliberations.

Applying Question-Oriented Approaches

You may have noticed some similarities among the single-question, the ideal-solution, and the reflective-thinking formats. All of these approaches suggest that a group should begin its deliberations by trying to define the problem or attempting to formulate a question that will focus the discussion. After a group zeroes in on key issues, members must next analyze the problem. The ideal-solution format suggests that the group formulate criteria to direct its search for a solution, while the single-question format asks a group to identify and answer subquestions to help formulate a solution.

By guiding groups toward their goals with questions, the ideal-solution and single-question formats help groups agree on minor issues before they try to agree on solutions to problems. Larson tried to find out whether an ideal-solution format, single-question format, reflective-thinking format, or no format at all would produce better solutions.[18] His study indicates that ideal-solution and single-question formats generated better solutions than did the reflective-thinking approach. All three approaches fared better than no approach at all. While just one laboratory study does not prove that the single-question and ideal-solution formats are superior to the reflective-thinking format, it does suggest that under certain conditions goal-oriented approaches may have certain advantages. In Larson's study, when groups were given alternatives and told to choose the best solution to a problem, their discussions lasted only about twenty minutes. Thus, by considering specific questions, members were able to solve problems efficiently. Maier also concluded that a problem-solving approach that has a group consider minor issues before major issues can improve group decisions.[19] Clearly, theorists need to conduct additional research before they can prescribe specific formulas to ensure efficiency in group problem solving.

If you are going to lead a group discussion, the following suggestions may help you apply the ideal-solution and single-question approaches to problem solving:

1. *If you are going to use the ideal-solution or single-question approach, provide group members with copies of the questions that will guide your discussion.* Since these approaches rely on a series of questions to guide discussion, you can reduce some of the uncertainty that occurs by making sure that each person has a copy of the questions. Tell the group to use the questions as a guide.

2. *Explain why you are using the format you have selected.* Most groups are willing to go along with a particular discussion agenda, especially if you give them reasons for having selected a specific approach. Tell the group that considering specific questions in a developmental format can keep the discussion on track. If your group has a specified time period in which to meet, you can explain that using questions to guide the discussion can help make the discussion more efficient.

3. *Keep the discussion focused on the specific question under consideration.* If you have provided copies of the questions for either the ideal-solution or single-question format, some group members may be tempted to skip a question or may want to discuss an unrelated issue. You may have to help orient the group by focusing on one question at a time. Several studies suggest that groups with members who try to keep participants aware of the pertinent issues by summarizing the discussion and requesting clarification have a good chance of agreeing on a solution and of being satisfied with their discussion.[20]

AGENDAS FOR PARTICIPATIVE GROUP PROBLEM SOLVING

One of the key responsibilities of a problem-solving discussion leader is to encourage all group members to participate in the discussion. Several specific methods have been devised to encourage all individuals, particularly in larger groups or organizations, to become involved in the problem-solving process. Whether you are a corporate executive, church leader, or committee chairperson, the following agendas can help you maximize group participation.

Buzz Sessions

Have you ever been in an audience during a speech, symposium, or panel discussion and wished that you could contribute more to the discussion? Even a public forum, which permits an audience to question a panel or speaker, often offers an audience too little time to participate. One technique that improves audience participation is called a **buzz session**. This technique, frequently used in conferences and large group meetings, is quite simple. To conduct a buzz session, the leader or chairperson of a large gathering should make sure that everyone present has a general understanding of the problem or issue facing the group. The leader should pose a specific question for the group to address. The audience is then divided into small groups of about six people to respond to the question. One member of each small group should write down the suggestions that group developed. After a specific time period, the recorder of each group reports the results of the discussion to the large group. The results can also be written either on paper to be distributed or on a chalkboard for all to see and evaluate.

When allowed to participate in the decision process, an audience is more likely to produce, implement, and support a better decision. Buzz sessions foster member involvement whenever a large group assembles to reach a decision, recommend a solution, or strive for enlightenment.

RISK Technique

The Industrial Chemical Company is considering a change from a five-day to a four-day workweek. Management believes that a four-day workweek would save energy, increase productivity, and reduce equipment maintenance costs. Managers are, however, uncertain about how employees would react to the schedule change. To help managers reach a decision, a communication consulting firm has suggested that the **RISK technique** be used to assess employee reactions. Developed by group communication researcher Norman Maier, the RISK technique is designed to determine how proposed policy changes would affect employees or any group that may experience a change in procedure.[21] By encouraging employees or group members to voice concerns over proposed changes, the RISK technique can suggest the impact of changes on those who would be affected by them. In the case of the Industrial Chemical Company, employees could be placed in small groups and asked to list their concerns about switching to a four-day workweek. Brilhart and Galanes suggest the following steps for implementing the RISK technique:

1. Present in detail the proposed change of procedure or policy to the group.
2. Explain the purpose and procedures to be followed in the RISK technique, being sure to describe the leader's nonevaluative role.
3. Invite and post all risks, fears, problems, doubts, and concerns. The leader should allow no evaluation, verbal or nonverbal. The leader or other members of the group may clarify or simplify a member's statement but should never modify its meaning. The wording of a risk as posted should be acceptable to its presenter. Allow plenty of time. Often members do not name the most significant items, the most threatening and disturbing ones, until late in the session, often after periods of silence. The leader should keep encouraging members to think of more risks. Members will be feeling out the leader and each other to determine if it is safe to express these, or if they might be in some way ridiculed or punished for speaking.
4. After the initial meeting, reproduce and circulate the list to all participants, inviting any additions they may have thought of in the interim.
5. At the next meeting of the group, add any further risks mentioned.

6. Have the group decide if each risk is serious and substantive. The group should consider a risk to be the property of the group, not of its presenter. Often participants can resolve many of each other's concerns by sharing experiences, ideas, and points of view. Such concerns should now be removed from the list.

7. Remaining risks are now processed into an agenda. The group can resolve some by obtaining information; the group can deal with the problems remaining one at a time in problem-solving discussions.[22]

Nominal Group Technique

Researchers suggest that individuals can solve some problems better than groups can. They note that when one person talks during a group discussion, other members stop thinking and listen to the idea presented.[23] They also found that people work more diligently if they have an individual assignment than if they have a group assignment. As noted in Chapter One, a disadvantage of group work is that it spreads responsibility, thereby increasing the probability that some group members will shirk their responsibilities. **Nominal group technique** is one procedure for overcoming this disadvantage. A group is nominal in the sense that members work on problems individually, rather than during sustained group interaction.

After group members have worked individually on a specific idea or question, they report their ideas to the group for discussion and evaluation. Members then work individually to rank proposed solutions, and their group discusses the rankings. The following steps summarize the procedure:

1. Make sure all group members know the problem under consideration. Each member should be able to define and analyze the problem.

2. Working individually, group members should write down possible solutions to the problem.

3. Have individuals report solutions. Each idea should be noted on a chart, chalkboard, or overhead projector.

4. Discuss each idea as a group to make sure it is clear to all.

5. After discussing all proposed solutions, have individuals rank the solutions; tabulate the results.

6. Discuss the results of the ranking. If the first ranking is inconclusive, have individuals rank the options again after additional discussion.

This technique has the advantage of involving all group members in deliberations. It can be a useful method if some group members are unwilling to make or are uncomfortable in making contributions because of status differences in the group. Also, alternating group discussion with individual deliberation can be useful in groups plagued by conflict and tension. Some may believe that because the method relies heavily on individual work rather than on group interactive work, it is not really a group communication problem-solving approach.

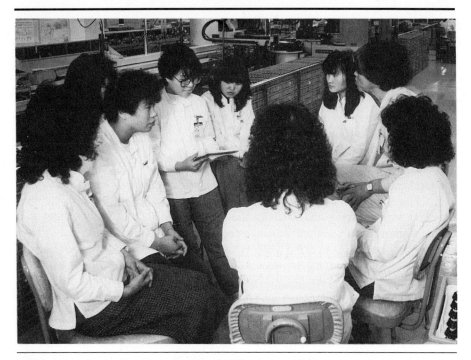

Quality circles are small groups of employees who meet regularly to suggest ways of improving productivity, morale, and work quality.

Quality Circles: A Participative Decision-Making Agenda

Several organizations use **quality circles** to involve employees in group problem solving and decision making. A quality circle consists of a group of five to fifteen employees who meet on a regular basis for the purpose of improving productivity, morale, and overall work quality.[24] Tasks of quality circles include:

Improving the quality of services or products
Reducing the number of work-related errors
Promoting cost reduction
Developing improved teamwork
Developing better work methods
Improving efficiency in the organization
Improving relations between management and employees
Promoting participants' leadership skills
Enhancing employees' career and personal development
Improving communication throughout the organization
Increasing everyone's awareness of safety

The concept of quality circles was developed in Japan in the late 1940s by W. Edward Deming, a professor from the United States who was invited to Japan to help improve industry. Based on the success of the program in Japan, it eventually was implemented in the United States.

Employees trained in quality circles receive basic information about group communication theory and skills. Many of the concepts presented in this text, such as group relationships, cohesiveness, roles, consensus, decision making, and problem solving, are part of the training of quality circle members. Members are also given training in statistics to help them analyze production and quality.

Leaders of quality circles are given additional training in leading groups and in conflict management. Quality circle leaders are primarily procedural leaders responsible for developing agendas, scheduling meetings, and ensuring equal participation by all group members.

Participative decision making is one of the most valuable approaches to analyzing, managing, and solving problems in business and industry. Evidence suggests that quality circles are effective if employees are comfortable being involved in the decision-making process.

Focus Groups

Focus groups are small groups of individuals selected to discuss topics so that group leaders can better understand how individuals view topics. Advertisers often use focus groups for market research. The objective of most focus groups is to gather information and help analyze products or issues. The information gleaned from focus groups helps later on when decisions need to be made about problems related to topics of discussion.

If a soap company wants to understand how consumers like the soap it sells, it could form a focus group to tap individual attitudes and reactions to the product. Seven to ten people could be invited to discuss what they like and dislike about the soap. The focus group leader, who is trained in group communication skills, engages the group in discussion and listens carefully to members talk about the product. Written questionnaires can collect consumer attitudes about the soap, but a live focus group lets the focus group leader probe for more detail. The group session can help the company better understand how to sell its product.

In some ways, a focus group discussion is like a group interview, in which a leader asks members for information. Many universities and large corporations use focus groups to understand how the public views them. Political candidates also use focus groups to understand how their constituents stand on issues.

SMALL GROUP PROBLEM-SOLVING TECHNIQUES: PUTTING PRINCIPLE INTO PRACTICE

In this chapter we discussed several prescriptive approaches that a group can use to solve a problem. Groups often need some plan or structure to help its members define, analyze, and solve a problem. We described nine different kinds of problem-solving formats: (1) reflective thinking, (2) brainstorming, (3) ideal solution,

Participative Group Problem Solving

Buzz Session	A small group, formed from a larger group, that responds to a question or problem. After deliberation, the small group appoints a representative to report back to the large group.
RISK Technique	A group discussion format that assesses how individuals may respond to and manage a change in policy or procedure.
Nominal Group Technique	Group members work individually on a specific task and then report their ideas to the group for discussion; suggested ideas or solutions are ranked individually by group members and then presented for summary ranking.
Quality Circle	A small group that participates in corporate decision making by meeting on a regular basis for the purpose of improving productivity, morale, and work quality, using brainstorming and other group problem-solving methods.
Focus Group	A small group of individuals selected to discuss a particular topic, issue, person, organization, or consumer product; the members of the group help a group leader understand how individuals perceive the topic of discussion.

(4) single question, (5) buzz sessions, (6) RISK technique, (7) nominal group technique, (8) quality control circles, and (9) focus groups. Review the following suggestions for applying these problem-solving approaches to the groups in which you participate.

Reflective Thinking

- To help your group define and limit a problem, phrase it as a question.
- Don't start suggesting solutions until your group has thoroughly analyzed a problem.
- Formulate criteria for a good solution before you begin suggesting solutions.
- Use brainstorming to help your group generate possible solutions.
- If the other group members agree, you may need to change the criteria you have selected during the analysis phase of reflective thinking.
- Make sure that reflective thinking is the best method for your group; another problem-solving approach may work better.

Brainstorming

- Make sure all group members understand the ground rules for brainstorming. Don't evaluate solutions until you have finished brainstorming.
- If group members do not follow the brainstorming rules, you may have to (1) restate the rules, (2) ask them to keep quiet, (3) ask them to record the ideas of others, or (4) ask them to leave the group.

"Then it's settled. We'll make 7 million with blue handles, 5 million with red handles, 4 million with purple handles and 2 million with green handles."

- If brainstorming doesn't work, consider having each member of the group work individually.
- Try to draw less talkative group members into the discussion; compliment members when they come up with good ideas.
- Set aside a definite amount of time for brainstorming.
- Make certain that brainstorming is the best problem-solving approach for your group.

Ideal Solution and Single Question

- If you are the leader of the group, tell the group why you have selected either the ideal-solution format or the single-question approach to problem solving.
- Use the ideal-solution format to help the group come to an agreement on the nature of the problem.
- Use the single-question format if you are sure that your group is capable of agreeing on the issues and on how the issues can be resolved.
- Provide members with copies of the questions used in the ideal-solution format or the single-question format; this will help to keep your discussion on track.
- Remind group members to address only those questions and issues that are relevant to the discussion.

Participative Decision Making

- Use buzz groups to involve a large group of people in the process of problem solving.
- Use the RISK technique to help manage uncertainty that occurs when new policy and procedures are suggested.
- Use the nominal group technique as a decision-making agenda when status differences, conflict, or stress prohibit full group interaction.
- Consider using quality control circles in business and industry to improve productivity, morale, and overall work quality.
- Focus groups are useful in gathering information about products, organizations, people, and ideas.

PRACTICE

The Bomb Shelter Case

Divide into groups of three to six people. Individually read the case study and follow the directions. Do not confer with anyone in your group until everyone has analyzed the case study and made individual choices. Then discuss the case study as a group. Try to reach agreement. After a given amount of time your instructor will ask you to discuss your decision-making process. Which problem-solving techniques did you use? Did you formulate a discussion question? How could you and your group improve the problem-solving process?

One evening two years from now you invite eight acquaintances to your home to talk with a psychologist you know personally. In the midst of your discussion you hear an air raid siren. You turn on the radio and the Civil Defense station says that enemy planes are approaching your city. Fortunately you have a well-equipped bomb shelter in your basement. You, the psychologist, your eight companions, and a mechanic who has been repairing the air-conditioner go downstairs. Shortly after you are all in the shelter, a terrific blast shakes the earth, and you realize that a bomb has fallen. For four frantic hours you get static on the radio. Finally you hear the following announcement: "A bomb of great magnitude has hit ten miles from your city. Damage is extensive. Radiation is intense. Those not in shelters may have suffered fatal doses of radiation. All persons in shelters are warned that they should not leave for at least a month. Further bombing is anticipated. This may be the last broadcast you will hear for some time."

You realize that you have eleven people in a shelter that is equipped with enough food, water, and, most important, oxygen to last eleven people two weeks or six people a month. When you tell them this, the others unanimously decide that in order for anyone to survive, five must be sacrificed. Because it is your shelter, all agree that you must stay and choose the other five who are to be saved.

- *Mary,* a psychologist, is a few years older than the others. They all respect her and recognize her ability to take control. Although she is rather cold and impersonal, she has helped quiet the group and has settled an argument between Don and Hazel. Even though no one seems close to her, you think she would be valuable as an organizer and a pacifier.
- *Hazel* is studying home economics—nutrition and dietetics. She is a very attractive woman. One of the first things she did was to appraise the food supply. You realize that her training has given her practical knowledge of how to ration food to avoid waste; also, she is an imaginative cook who can fix even canned foods appealingly. She is efficient to the point of being domineering and bossy.
- *Alberta* is a brilliant woman who has been given a graduate assistantship to do research on radiation. She has been pampered all her life and is horrified at wearing the same clothes for a month, being unable to take a bath or wash her hair, and sleeping in a room with five other people.
- *Laura* is a literature major, has read extensively, and writes well herself. Already she has entertained and diverted the group by retelling one of the books she has recently read.
- *Nancy,* Chet's wife, has a pleasant personality generally. However, she has been the most nervous of the group. She is expecting a baby in two months.

- *Chet,* Nancy's husband, has had two years of medical school, three summers in a camp as a medical assistant, and a close association with his father, who is a doctor. You realize he would be a great aid; however, he refuses to stay unless Nancy also stays.

- *Jack,* the mechanic, also has a great deal of practical know-how. Although his education ended with high school, he has had experience with air-filtration systems, air purifiers, and oxygen supplies. He does not, however, see the need to control the food and water supply.

- *Paul,* a young minister, is easygoing. His calmness, optimism, and faith are an inspiration to the group. His presence is reassuring. He helped quiet Nancy's tearful outburst. He revealed that he has learned to remain calm, of necessity, because he has diabetes.

- *Joe* is a clean-cut, husky football player, the star center of the college team. He is highly respected by everyone on campus. Joe was the only one able to lift the heavy metal plate over the shelter door. At one point, when Chet tried to set the oxygen tank valve, Jack flew at him, shoved him out of the way, and reset the valve properly. A fight might have ensued had Joe not parted the two.

- *Don* is an incurable romantic. His smile, lively guitar music, and sense of humor have helped improve everyone's mood. He gets along well with everyone but antagonized Hazel by flirting. The others have also noticed his flirting eyes as he sings.

Evaluating Your Ability to Solve Problems in Groups

How effectively do you solve problems in small groups? Take this brief test to rate yourself on the various skills needed to work in problem-solving groups. The results should give you a clearer understanding of how well or how poorly you perceive your problem-solving abilities. Keep in mind that in this test there are no right or wrong answers.

1. I like to work with a small group of people to solve problems.
   often _____ usually _____ seldom _____ never _____
2. I do a good job of helping to define and limit the problem that a group is discussing.
   often _____ usually _____ seldom _____ never _____
3. I enjoy conducting research to help solve problems.
   often _____ usually _____ seldom _____ never _____
4. I usually start thinking of possible solutions to a problem before a group has finished analyzing its causes and effects.
   often _____ usually _____ seldom _____ never _____
5. I analyze problems better than I suggest solutions.
   often _____ usually _____ seldom _____ never _____

6. I like to assume some leadership responsibilities when I participate in a problem-solving discussion.
   often _____ usually _____ seldom _____ never _____
7. I am usually satisfied with the contributions that I make to a problem-solving
   group discussion.
   often _____ usually _____ seldom _____ never _____
8. I try to encourage less talkative members to participate in the group problem-
   solving process.
   often _____ usually _____ seldom _____ never _____
9. I like to work in a problem-solving group when a specific agenda has been
   formulated and I am aware of the steps that the group is taking in order to
   solve the problem.
   often _____ usually _____ seldom _____ never _____

Do you note any consistent pattern in your responses to this questionnaire? What
group problem-solving skills do you need to improve? How might you improve
your problem-solving ability?

The Kidney Machine

Each patient below needs a kidney machine. Only five machines are available
because of the cost of manufacturing them. No more machines will be available
in time to save all of these patients. Your panel, which consists of doctors, must
decide, based on the information given, which patients will receive treatment and
which will not. Those who do not receive treatment will die.

Mrs. Maria
Vasquez:
29 years old; married, with six children ranging in age from 2
to 10 years; her husband is a printer who, along with his
brother-in-law, owns a print shop.

Mrs. Mary
Fortran:
31 years old; director of foods research for NASA; former
Rhodes scholar with a Ph.D. in physics; working on a formula for a food capsule to be used in space travel; divorced,
with no children.

Mike
Carbona:
39 years old; an ex-convict, convicted for tax evasion; served
seven years; active in local politics in New Jersey, known as
the spearhead behind the minority rights program in his area;
suspected of having criminal connections; the nine Korean
orphans he supports do not know of his former involvement
in crime.

Peter
Maximo:
9 years old; has an IQ of 160, but is severely mentally dis-
turbed at having witnessed the car accident that killed two of
his parents' friends; has not spoken a word for over two years.

Mrs. Terry McBride: 27 years old; an instructor at a local university working on her M.S. in communication; her husband is partially blind and receives disability payments from the Army; no children; debts include car loans and a 30-year mortgage on a house.

Dick Constable: 35 years old; a bachelor and federal narcotics agent in Chicago, primarily arresting heroin dealers; active in community youth organizations; engaged to be married.

Father Mussello: 53 years old; a Dominican friar and headmaster of a parochial school; organizes missions to help with Indian education in New Mexico; counsels juvenile delinquents.

Thomas Washington: 19 years old; a freshman at New York University; lives with his family in Harlem; his father died when he was very little; insurance money is paying for his education; a member of a radical group whose avowed purpose is to foster anarchy in America.

Using Problem-Solving Agendas

As a class, identify a problem that needs to be solved. It could be a university, local, state, or national problem. Then divide into groups of five or six members. Each group should attempt to solve the problem using a different problem-solving format (reflective thinking, brainstorming, etc.). After the groups have deliberated, have one member from each summarize how the problem-solving format worked for the group. Which format was the easiest to use? Did some groups take more time than others to solve the problem? Did the problem-solving format help or hinder the group's effort to solve the problem? Note other differences and similarities in the groups' problem-solving process.

Exercise: Creativity

Solving this problem requires creativity. The class should divide into groups of three. Each group's assignment is to connect all nine dots with only four straight and connected lines.[25]

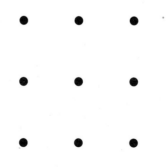

Different problem-solving agendas work better than others in different groups. Which ones work better for you?

Evaluation of Group Problem Solving

Use the following scales to assess your skills in applying problem-solving agendas to group deliberations.

1. I helped the group identify the specific problem it was trying to solve.
   strongly agree   agree   unsure   disagree   strongly disagree

2. I helped phrase the problem as a question to guide the group's discussion.
   strongly agree   agree   unsure   disagree   strongly disagree

3. I analyzed the problem throughly before suggesting possible solutions.
   strongly agree   agree   unsure   disagree   strongly disagree

4. I was able to distinguish clearly between causes of the problem and symptoms of the problem.
   strongly agree   agree   unsure   disagree   strongly disagree

5. I evaluated the problem-solving approach the group used to determine if it was the best way to organize the discussion.
   strongly agree   agree   unsure   disagree   strongly disagree

Postdecision Reaction

Use the following scales to record your reactions to participating in a small group problem-solving or decision-making activity.

1. I was satisfied with my individual contribution to the group task.

1	2	3	4	5	6	7	8	9	10
very satisfied								not at all satisfied	

2. I was satisfied with my individual skill in helping group members feel comfortable in participating in the group.

1	2	3	4	5	6	7	8	9	10
very satisfied								not at all satisfied	

3. I was satisfied with the way other group members helped to complete the group's task.

1	2	3	4	5	6	7	8	9	10
very satisfied								not at all satisfied	

4. I was satisfied with the way other group members helped to make group members feel comfortable in participating in the discussion.

1	2	3	4	5	6	7	8	9	10
very satisfied								not at all satisfied	

Postmeeting Group Evaluation Form

Use the following form to evaluate your group discussion. Compare your evaluation with those of other group members.

1. Identify effective uses of group communication skills in today's discussion.

2. Identify the weaknesses in today's discussion.

3. Identify ways in which the group meeting could be improved.

Notes

1. Dennis S. Gouran, Candace Brown, and David R. Henry, "Behavioral Correlates of Perceptions of Quality in Decision-Making Discussion," *Communication Monographs* 45 (1978): 60–65; Linda L. Putnam, "Preference for Procedural Order in Task-Oriented Small Groups," *Communication Monographs* 46 (1979): 193–218.

2. David M. Berg, "A Descriptive Analysis of the Distribution and Duration of Themes Discussed by Task-Oriented Small Groups," *Speech Monographs* 34 (1967): 172–175; also see Ernest G. Bormann and Nancy C. Bormann, *Effective Small Group Communication,* 2nd ed. (Minneapolis: Burgess Publishing Company, 1976), p. 132.

3. Marshall Scott Poole, "Decision Development in Small Groups III: A Multiple Sequence Model of Group Decision Development," *Communication Monographs* 50 (1983): 321–341.

4. See R. Victor Harnack, "John Dewey and Discussion," *Western Speech* 32 (Spring 1969): 137–149.

5. For evidence to support this modification of the reflective-thinking pattern, see John K. Brilhart, "An Experimental Comparison of Three Techniques for Communicating a Problem-Solving Pattern to Members of a Discussion Group," *Speech Monographs* 33 (1966): 168–177.

6. For example, see Robert F. Bales and Fred L. Strodtbeck, "Phases in Group Problem-Solving," *Journal of Abnormal and Social Psychology* 46 (1951): 485–495; Thomas M. Schiedel and Laura Crowell, "Idea Development in Small Groups," *Quarterly Journal of Speech* 50 (1964): 140–145; and B. Aubrey Fisher, "Decision Emergence: Phases in Group Decision-Making," *Speech Monographs* 37 (1970): 53–66.

7. Chapter Seven discusses the phases of a group's growth and development in detail.

8. Ernest G. Bormann, *Discussion and Group Methods: Theory and Practice,* 2nd ed. (New York: Harper & Row, Publishers, 1975), p. 282.

9. John K. Brilhart and Gloria J. Galanis, *Effective Group Discussion,* 6th ed. (Dubuque, Iowa: Wm. C. Brown, 1989), p. 280.

10. Randy Y. Hirokawa, "Consensus Group Decision-Making, Quality of Decision and Group Satisfaction: An Attempt to Sort Fact from Fiction." *Central States Speech Journal* 33 (1982): 407–415; Randy Y. Hirokawa, "Why Informed Groups Make Faulty Decisions: An Investigation of Possible Interaction-Based Explanations," *Small Group Behavior* 18 (1987): 3–29.

11. Norman R. F. Maier, *Problem-Solving and Discussions and Conferences* (New York: McGraw-Hill Book Company, 1963), p. 123.

12. Alex F. Osborn, *Applied Imagination* (New York: Charles Scribner's Sons, 1962).

13. Gerry Philipsen, Anthony Mulac, and David Dietrich, "The Effects of Social Interaction on Group Generation of Ideas," *Communication Monographs* 46 (June 1979): 119–125.

14. Alvin A. Goldberg and Carl E. Larson, *Group Communication: Discussion Processes and Applications* (Englewood Cliffs, New Jersey: Prentice-Hall, 1975), p. 149.

15. John K. Brilhart, *Effective Group Discussion,* (Dubuque, Iowa: Wm. C. Brown, 1986), p. 306.

16. Goldberg and Larson, p. 150.

17. *Ibid.*

18. Carl E. Larson, "Forms of Analysis and Small Group Problem-Solving," *Speech Monographs* 36 (1969): 452–455.

19. Norman R. F. Maier, "An Experimental Test of the Effect of Training on Discussion Leadership," *Human Relations* 6 (1953): 166–173.

20. Dennis G. Gouran, "Variables Related to Consensus in Group Discussions of Questions of Policy," *Speech Monographs* 36 (1969): 385–391; Thomas J. Knutson, "An Experimental Study of the Effects of Orientation Behavior on Small Group Consensus," *Speech Monographs* 39 (1972): 159–165; John A. Kline, "Orientation and Group Consensus," *Central States Speech Journal* 23 (1972): 44–47; Steven A. Beebe, "Orientation as a Determinant of Group Consensus and Satisfaction," *Resources in Education* 13 (October 1978): 19–25.

21. Norman R. F. Maier, *Problem-Solving Discussions and Conferences: Leadership Methods and Skills* (New York: McGraw-Hill Book Company, 1963), pp. 171–177.

22. Brilhart and Galanes, *Effective Group Discussion,* p. 323.

23. Andre L. Delbecq, Andrew H. Van de Ven, and David H. Gustafson, *Group Techniques for Program Planning: A Guide to Nominal Group and Delphi Processes* (Glenview, Illinois: Scott, Foresman and Company, 1975), pp. 7–16.

24. *Positive Personnel Practices: Quality Circles' Participant's Manual* (Prospect Heights, Illinois: Waveland Press, 1982).

25. David W. Johnson and Frank P. Johnson, *Joining Together: Group Theory and Group Skills* (Englewood Cliffs, New Jersey: Prentice-Hall, 1987), p. 258.

Chapter Nine

Conflict Management in Small Groups

After studying this chapter, you should be able to:

☐ Explain why conflict occurs in small groups.

☐ Describe the negative impact that conflict has on group communication.

☐ List three myths about conflict.

☐ Identify strategies for managing different types of conflict.

☐ Define the concept *groupthink*.

☐ Identify six symptoms of groupthink.

☐ Apply techniques for reducing groupthink.

☐ Define consensus.

☐ Apply techniques for managing conflict and reaching consensus in small groups.

Social psychologists say that people inevitably disagree and experience conflict when they interact. Neither centuries of peace propaganda nor human behavioral research has been able to eliminate disagreement and conflict. Throughout history, people have been involved in conflicts ranging from family feuds to international wars. Whether groups are negotiating international trade or deciding how to repave a parking lot, their members experience disagree.

This chapter gives you some ideas about the causes of conflict and presents some strategies for managing it. You will not learn how to eliminate group conflict, but to understand it and its importance in your group deliberations.

This chapter will examine the role of conflict in small group discussions. First, it will define conflict and note why it occurs so often. Second, it will look at three common myths about conflict in small groups. Third, it will examine three types of conflict and offers suggestions for managing each type. Fourth, it will discuss consensus and offer suggestions for helping groups to reach agreement. Finally, it will discuss groupthink, a phenomenon that occurs when small groups have too little disagreement or controversy. The prime objective of this chapter is to help you understand how conflict in groups can be both useful and detrimental to group decision making.

WHAT IS CONFLICT?

Conflict occurs when members disagree over two or more options that a group can take in trying to resolve a problem. Conflict also occurs when an individual's goal is incompatible with the goals of others. Folger and Poole define conflict as "the interaction of interdependent people who perceive incompatible goals and interference from each other in achieving these goals."[1]

If a group experienced no conflict, it would have little to discuss. One value of conflict is that it makes a group test and challenge ideas. Conflict can also, however, be detrimental to group interaction and group decision making. Conflict has a negative impact on a group when it: (1) keeps the group from completing its task, (2) interferes with the quality of the group's decision or productivity, or (3) threatens the existence of the group.[2]

What causes conflict in groups? Why does it exist? Conflict results from differences between group members—differences in personality, perception, information, and power or influence. Because people are unique, their different attitudes, beliefs, and values will inevitably surface and cause conflict. No matter how much they try to empathize with others, people still have individual perspectives on the world. People also differ in the amount of knowledge they have on various topics. In groups, they soon realize that some members are more experienced or more widely read. This difference in information contributes to different attitudes. People also have different amounts of power, status, and influence over others—differences that can increase conflict. People with power often try to use that power to influence others, and most do not like to be told what to do or think.

Myths About Conflict

Many small group communication textbooks published just a few years ago included few references to conflict. Some texts did offer suggestions for reaching agreement, but few discussed the functions or positive aspects of disagreement among group members. Conflict management is a relatively new area of communication research, and many misunderstandings about the nature and function of conflict exist.

People have several misconceptions about the role of conflict in communication because they think that conflict is bad and should be avoided. With higher rates of divorce, crime, and international political tensions, it is understandable that people view conflict negatively. The following sections will examine some of the feelings you may have about conflict and determine whether a different attitude can improve the quality of your group discussions.[3]

Myth #1: In Group Discussions, Conflict Should Be Avoided at All Costs.
Do you feel uncomfortable when conflicts occur in a group? You may believe that groups should not experience conflict, that conflict is unnatural, that if people express conflicting points of view, you should try to squelch disagreement. Conflict, however, is a natural by-product of communication; unless in your group participants share the same attitudes, beliefs, and values (an unlikely situation), there will be some conflict. Of course, members may privately disagree with other group members, but because they regard disagreement as inappropriate, they may not admit their negative feelings. Several researchers have discovered that conflict is an important, indeed useful, part of group communication.[4] In a group's efforts to solve a problem, members experience conflict and tension. Members who believe that conflict is unnatural and unhealthy become frustrated when conflict erupts in a group. They should realize that conflict probably will occur and that it is not an unnatural or unhealthy part of group communication.

Myth #2: All Conflict Occurs Because People Do Not Understand Each Other.
Have you ever been in a heated disagreement with someone and then shouted, "You just don't understand me!"? You easily assume that conflict occurs because another person does not understand your position. Not all conflict occurs

because of misunderstandings, however. You may believe that if others really understood you they would agree with you. As Robert Doolittle observed,

> . . . many conflicts result from more than mere misunderstandings. Indeed, some of the most serious conflicts occur among individuals and groups who understand each other very well but who strongly disagree.[5]

Conflict can result from not understanding another group member's message, but some conflicts intensify when that person clarifies his or her point. For example, Mayor Johnson wanted to rezone a certain area in the city. Potter, a city council member, opposed the rezoning; he thought the master zoning plan developed by the city three years ago was a good one. Johnson and Potter had several heated arguments about the rezoning. When Potter realized that Johnson wanted to rezone the land to allow for industrial development, Potter became even more entrenched in his position. He understood the mayor's position on the issue; he simply disagreed with it. Further clarification of the issue would not resolve the conflict. The two needed to discuss the reasons for their differing viewpoints. Not all conflict occurs because people misunderstand one another's viewpoints; conflict can occur because they do understand. If you experience such conflict, remember to discuss the evidence and the validity of the arguments and not just to restate your position.

Myth #3: All Conflict Can Be Resolved. Perhaps you consider yourself an optimist. You like to think that problems can be solved. You may also feel that if a conflict arises, a compromise will resolve it. However, you should realize that not all conflicts can be resolved. Realistically, many disagreements are not simple. Fundamental differences between evangelist Billy Graham and atheist Madaline Murray-O'Haire would probably not be resolved easily, if at all. Some ideologies are so far apart that resolving conflicts between them is unlikely. This does not mean that whenever a conflict arises in your group you should despair, "Oh, well, no use trying to solve this disagreement." That position also oversimplifies the conflict-management process. Because some conflicts cannot be resolved, group members may have to focus on differences over which they are most likely to reach agreement.

If you find yourself arbitrating a conflict in a small group, first decide which issues are most likely to be resolved. If you assume that all conflict can be resolved just by applying the right techniques, you may get frustrated. On the other hand, you must be wary of the self-fulfilling prophecy, too. If you hastily reach the conclusion that the conflict cannot be resolved, you may behave in a way that fulfills your prediction.

Consider, for example, the hypothetical, but very possible, case of Bob and Freda. Bob has lived in a large industrial city for several years, and Freda has lived in a small rural community. When the two recently disagreed about how to reduce crime in the United States, Bob unabashedly announced, "There is no use continuing this discussion. A girl from the country just can't understand the problems of a large urban metropolis." With an attitude like that, Bob did not make much

Groups must find some means of managing conflict among members so that energy can be channeled constructively and not be allowed to degenerate into personal attacks.

headway in his discussion with Freda. His mind was made up, and the two could not resolve the conflict. You must take time to understand all of the conflicting points of view before you decide whether or not a conflict can be resolved. Even though not all conflicts can be resolved, do not dismiss a disagreement as unsolvable too quickly.

MANAGING DIFFERENT TYPES OF CONFLICT

Miller and Steinberg have identified three common types of interpersonal conflict: **pseudo-conflict, simple conflict,** and **ego-conflict**.[6] They suggest that by identifying the type of conflict in a group, you will be better able to manage it. The following sections look at these three types of conflict in the context of a small group.

Managing Pseudo-conflict: When Misunderstandings Occur

Some conflict occurs because of misunderstandings. **Pseudo-conflict** occurs when individuals agree, but, because of poor communication, they appear to each other to disagree. *Pseudo* means fake or false. Thus, pseudo-conflict is conflict between people who really agree on issues but who don't understand that their differences are caused by misunderstandings or misinterpretations. "Oh, I see," said Mark after several minutes of heatedly defending a position he had suggested to the group. "I just misunderstood you. I guess we really agree."

To manage pseudo-conflict you need to be able to describe ideas and feelings to others, listen accurately to others, and check your understanding of a message's meaning. To describe your feelings to others accurately, you need to develop a supportive rather than defensive climate. The key to managing pseudo-conflict is to make sure all group members clearly understand the issues under consideration. Good listening skills are important assets in managing conflicts that result from misunderstandings.

Active listening, a technique for helping you check your understanding of another's point of view, enables you to check your perceptions of both the content of a message and the feelings of another person. To sharpen your active listening skills, you need to: (1) stop, (2) look, (3) listen, (4) question, (5) paraphrase content, and (6) paraphrase feelings. These steps were discussed in detail in Chapter 5.

Managing Simple Conflict: Disagreeing on Issues

Simple conflict occurs when each of two individuals knows what the other wants, but neither can achieve a goal without preventing the other from achieving a goal. "Simple conflict involves one person saying, 'I want to do X,' and another saying, 'I want to do Y,' when X and Y are incompatible forms of behavior."[7] While the conflict may seem far from simple, it is called simple conflict because the issues are clear and each party understands the problem. For example, in a corporation with only a limited amount of money to invest in new product expansion, one board member may want to invest in real estate while another may want to make capital improvements. The issue is clear; the individuals simply believe the company should take different courses of action.

When you are involved in a disagreement in a group, first make sure that you clearly understand the other individual's point of view; make certain the conflict is not a pseudo-conflict. Listen to the arguments the other person makes and try to clarify how you define the issues. Keep the discussion focused on the issues rather than on personalities. Name-calling and emotional tirades will make conflict worse and make it more difficult to manage. Also, try to reach agreement on the goal each side wants to accomplish. Treat the difference of opinion as a problem to be solved, rather than as a conflict in which someone wins and someone loses. Go through the problem-solving process reviewed in the last chapter. Define the problem, analyze it, establish criteria, identify several possible options, apply criteria in selecting the best option, and implement the solution. Another suggestion for managing simple conflict is to determine which areas of disagreement are the most important to resolve. Putnam has noted, "Some conflicts are fundamental to a group's decisions and to its survival, while others are tangential to its goal and maintenance. The ability to choose which conflicts to consider and which ones to ignore is an important step in managing disagreements."[8] Rely on facts to support your arguments, rather than opinions alone. Also, make the conflict a group concern rather than an individual one. If the conflict cannot be resolved or does not need be resolved immediately, call for a cooling-off period and tackle the problem at a later meeting.

Managing Ego-Conflict: Unraveling Personality Clashes

Of the types of conflict under discussion, the third is the most difficult to manage. **Ego-conflict** occurs when individuals become defensive about their positions because they think they are being personally attacked. Ego-conflicts are charged with emotion, and defensiveness in one individual often causes defensiveness in others. "Just because you're the chairman of the group doesn't give you the right to railroad decision making," snaps Frank. "Well, you're just jealous. You think *you* should have been elected chairperson," retorts Ed. This exchange suggests that the conflict is not over a substantive issue but is over ego. When egos are involved and personalities are attacked, well-practiced feedback techniques or clarifying issues will not resolve conflict.

If you are trying to mediate a conflict, try to find issues the disagreeing parties agree on. Identify and emphasize the common ground between them, and encourage them to describe the sequence of events that created the conflict.

The conflicting parties need to express their concerns. They should not, however, personally attack one another. As Miller and Steinberg suggest, the first thing to do in managing ego-conflict is to:

> . . . give people a chance to bring out relevant concerns and then stop. The parties should not be prevented from expressing primary concerns, even if they are highly emotional, but they should be discouraged from escalating the conflict into violent personal attacks and counter attacks. When an ego-conflict looms stormily on the horizon, take control of the communication situation and let each person have his say, but do not allow either one to carry on too far.[9]

Encourage active listening and try to keep the discussion focused on the issues. Turn the conflict into a problem to be solved rather than a win-lose situation between two factions of the group. One way to change an emotionally charged climate in a group is to speak slowly and softly. Loud, fast-paced talk adds to a climate of agitation.

If personality differences are so intense that nothing relieves the ego-conflict, the group could adopt rules or procedures that allow for the differences. If, for example, the feud between Frank and Ed simply can't be resolved, the group could assign Frank and Ed specific duties that contribute to the group's goal but that minimize the amount of time the two have to spend together. Frank could gather information on one topic, and Ed could research a different topic. If Frank's role as chairperson becomes so controversial that the group is unable to accomplish its task, other group members need to recommend a change in group leadership.

Summary of Three Conflict Types

	Pseudo-Conflict	Simple Conflict	Ego-Conflict
Source of conflict	Misunderstanding individuals' perceptions of the problem.	Individual disagreement over which course of action to pursue.	Defense of ego: Individual believes he or she is being attacked personally.
Suggestions for managing conflict	1. Ask for clarification of perceptions. 2. Establish a supportive rather than a defensive climate. 3. Employ active listening: *Stop* *Look* *Listen* *Question* *Paraphrase content* *Paraphrase feelings*	1. Listen and clarify perceptions. 2. Make sure issues are clear to all group members. 3. Use a problem-solving approach to manage differences of opinion. 4. Keep discussion focused on the issues. 5. Use facts rather than opinions for evidence. 6. Look for alternatives or compromise positions. 7. Make the conflict a group concern, rather than an individual concern. 8. Determine which conflicts are the most important to resolve. 9. If possible, postpone the decision while additional research can be conducted. This delay also helps relieve tensions.	1. Let members express their concerns but do not permit personal attacks. 2. Employ active listening. 3. Call for a cooling-off period. 4. Try to keep discussion focused on issues (simple conflict). 5. Encourage parties to be descriptive, rather than evaluative and judgmental. 6. Use a problem-solving approach to manage differences of opinion. 7. Speak slowly and calmly. 8. Develop rules or procedures that create a relationship which allows for the personality difference.

GROUPTHINK: WHEN CONFLICT DOES NOT OCCUR

Frank Baxter, chairman of the board of Eastern Oil Company, was meeting with the board of directors to decide whether Eastern Oil would merge with Southern Oil Company. Baxter called the meeting to order. After the reading and approval of the minutes from the last meeting, Baxter stated that he thought the merger would benefit both companies. As soon as Baxter finished speaking, other board members quickly chimed in, offering their support for the merger. No board members stated any objections to the deal; they fully supported Baxter's decision. One member, however, thought that the merger might violate antitrust laws by creating a monopoly in the southeastern United States. He also noted that the government would probably oppose the merger. Other board members quickly tried to gloss over the potential problem, one member confidently stating, "The government should not have any power to affect how we run our corporation. After all, it's our company."

After additional supportive comments from board members, the group voted to approve the merger. After the meeting, one member commented, "I wish all the group meetings I participated in would go as smoothly as our board meetings. We always seem to get along so well together. Baxter does a great job as chairperson." "Yes," observed another member, "he certainly has our respect. We always support what he has to say."

Upon first analysis of this meeting, you might think it effective. The chairperson appears to have the support of his group, whose members have little uncertainty. Looking at the meeting more closely, however, you see that the group is not functioning as well as it should; it is not taking advantage of the benefits of working together. This board of directors is a victim of groupthink.

Groupthink occurs when a group strives to minimize conflict and reach a consensus without critically testing, analyzing, and evaluating ideas. When a group reaches decisions too quickly, it does not properly consider the implications of its decisions. Groupthink results in an ineffective consensus; too little conflict often lowers the quality of group decisions. When a group does not take time to examine the positive and negative consequences of alternative decisions the quality of its decision is likely to suffer. Sociologist Irving Janis believes that many poor governmental decisions and policies are the result of groupthink.[10] After studying minutes of meetings and transcripts of conversations, he concluded that a lack of healthy disagreement contributed to inept decisions, such as the Bay of Pigs invasion in 1962. The Kennedy administration's decision to attack Cuba came from a group of advisers who were reluctant to voice their private doubts about invading Cuba. Janis has also noted that a group plagued by groupthink perpetrated the Watergate break-in. Members of the Committee to Reelect the President believed that they needed information at Democratic headquarters in the Watergate office complex. Again, even though some members privately thought that breaking into Democratic headquarters was wrong, they did not raise their objections. The decision to launch the flawed space shuttle *Challenger* on that unforgettable January morning in 1986 was also tinged by groupthink. Corporate executives and others did not

"We have to find another way to break these deadlocks at school board meetings."

challenge assumptions in the construction and launch procedures; disaster resulted. The pressure for consensus resulted in groupthink.

Groups most prone to groupthink have leaders who are held in high esteem. Since these leaders' ideas are often viewed as sacrosanct, few members disagree with them. A group may also suffer from groupthink if its members consider themselves highly cohesive and take pride in getting along so well with one another in providing support and encouragement to members' ideas.

Symptoms of Groupthink

Can you identify groupthink when it occurs in groups you belong to? Do you know how to guard against too strong a tendency to reach consensus in a group? Can you help reduce the likelihood that groupthink will occur in your group? Here are some of the common symptoms of groupthink.[11] See if you can think of some group communication experiences that exemplify groupthink.

Critical Thinking is not Encouraged or Rewarded. If you are working in a group that considers disagreement or controversy counterproductive, the chances are that groupthink is alive and well in that group. One advantage of working in groups is having the opportunity to evaluate ideas so that you can select the best possible solution. If group members seem proud that peace and harmony prevail at their meetings, they may suffer from groupthink.

Members Believe that their Group Can Do No Wrong. Members of the Committee to Reelect the President did not consider that they might fail to obtain information from Democratic headquarters. They thought their group was invulnerable. This sense of invulnerability is a classic symptom of groupthink. Another symptom is that members dismiss potential threats to the group as minor problems. In the example of the Eastern Oil Company merger, board members quickly dismissed the potential problem of government intervention. The group thought that their decision was a good one and that no outside threat could interfere with their plans. If your group is consistently overconfident in dealing with problems that may interfere with its goals, it may suffer from groupthink.

Group Members Are too Concerned About Justifying Their Actions. Members of highly cohesive groups like to feel that they are acting in the best interests of their group. Therefore, groups that experience groupthink like to rationalize their positions on issues. Members are particularly susceptible to feeling tension and dissonance. If a group's position is attacked, the group may respond by dealing with the resulting tension and conflict. First, a group may try to destroy the credibility of the person attacking it. For example, students working on a group project for a small group communication class received some negative feedback from their instructor about their progress. The students responded by saying that the instructor was not a good teacher and would not know a good group if he saw one. They tried to rationalize their poor performance by attacking the credentials of the person who criticized them. A group may also ignore information that contradicts its opinion. The star of a Broadway production received poor reviews from one local paper and responded by refusing to read the rest of the review and vowing never to read that paper again. Similarly, if a group is criticized by someone, it may not seek advice from that person again. Finally, a group may listen only selectively to less-than-positive information about a decision it has reached. If a group is criticized, it may rationalize the criticism to diminish the impact of the adverse comments. A group susceptible to groupthink is too concerned about convincing itself that it has made proper decisions in the past and will make good decisions in the future.

Members Apply Pressure to Those Who Do Not Support the Group. Have you ever voiced an opinion contrary to the majority opinion and quickly realized that other members were trying to pressure you into going along with the rest of

---

Symptoms of Groupthink

Critical thinking is not encouraged or rewarded.

Group members think that their group can do no wrong.

Group members are too concerned about justifying their actions.

Group members apply pressure to those who do not support the group.

Group members often believe that they have reached a true consensus.

Group members are too concerned about reinforcing the leader's beliefs.

---

the group? Groups prone to groupthink have a low tolerance for members who do not go along with the group. Controversy and conflict injected by a dissenting member threaten esprit de corps. Therefore, a person voicing an idea different from the group's position is often punished. Sometimes pressure is subtle, taking the forms of frowns or grimaces. Group members may not socialize with the dissenting member, or they may not listen attentively to the dissident. Usually their first response is to try to convince this member to reconsider his or her position. Members may try to persuade the dissident to conform; if the member still does not agree with the others, he or she may be expelled from the group. Of course, if a group member is just being stubborn the others should try to reason with the dissenter. Don't, however, be too quick to label someone as a troublemaker simply because he or she has an opinion different from that of other group members.

Group Members Often Believe that They Have Reached a True Consensus.
A significant problem in groups that suffer from groupthink is that members are not aware of groupthink. They think they have reached genuine consensus. For example, suppose you and your friends are trying to decide which movie to rent on Friday night. Someone suggests, "Why don't we see *Gone with the Wind*?" Even though you have already seen the movie on television, you don't want to be contentious, so you agree with the suggestion. Other group members also agree.

After your group has seen the movie and you are returning the tape to the video store, you overhear another one of your friends say, "I enjoyed the movie better when I saw it the first time." After a quick poll of the group, you discover that most of your friends have already seen the movie! They agreed to see it only because they did not want to hurt anyone's feelings. They thought everyone else was in agreement. While the group appeared to reach consensus, only a few people actually agreed with the decision. Therefore, even if you think that the rest of the group agrees and that you are the only person who thinks that a different solution would be best, your group could still be experiencing groupthink. Just because your group seems to have reached a consensus does not necessarily mean that all of the members truly agree.

Group Members Are Too Concerned About Reinforcing the Leader's Beliefs. Leaders of small groups often emerge because they suggest some of the best ideas, motivate group members, or devote themselves to group goals more than others do. If group members place too much emphasis on the credibility or infallibility of their leader, groupthink may occur. Leaders who like to be surrounded by people who always agree with their ideas lose the advantage of working in small groups. Most people do not like criticism and do not like to be told that their ideas are inept or inappropriate. Therefore, group leaders are understandably attracted to those who agree with them. Leaders sensitive to the problem of groupthink will solicit and tolerate all group viewpoints, since testing the quality of solutions requires different opinions.

Suggestions to Reduce Groupthink

You may think that groupthink, which is characterized by a lack of conflict or controversy, should not occur in an effective task-oriented group, but what you really want to know is, "How can I reduce the chances of groupthink occurring in my group?" You expect theory to do more than just describe what happens; it should also suggest ways of improving communication. In order to help prevent groupthink, consider the following specific suggestions based on Janis's initial observations, as well as on the theories and the research of other small group communication researchers.

The Group Leader Should Encourage Critical, Independent Thinking. One characteristic of groupthink is that members generally agree with a group leader. The leader of a small group can help alleviate groupthink by encouraging members to think independently. The leader should make clear that he or she does not want the group to reach agreement until each member has critically evaluated the issues. Most group leaders want to command the respect of their groups, but a leader's insisting that the group always agree with him or her does not constitute respect; instead, it may demonstrate a fear of disagreement. Thus, if you find yourself as a leader in a small group, you should encourage disagreement not just for the sake of argument but to eliminate groupthink. Even if you are not a leader, you can encourage a healthy discussion by voicing any objections that you have to the ideas being discussed. Don't permit instant, uncritical agreement in your group.

Group Members Should Be Sensitive to Status Differences That May Affect Decision Making. Imagine that you are a young architect assigned to help design a new dinner theater for a large futuristic shopping center. When you first meet with the other architects assigned to the project, the senior member of your firm presents the group with a rough sketch of a theater patterned after a nineteenth-century American opera house. While the design is practical and attractive, you feel that it doesn't fit in with the ultramodern design of the rest of the center.

Because of the difference in status between the younger architects and the senior architect, you and your contemporaries are tempted to laud the design and keep your reservations to yourselves. Doing so would result in groupthink. Groups should not yield to status differences when evaluating ideas, issues, and solutions to problems. Instead, they should consider the merits of suggestions, weigh evidence, and make decisions about the validity of ideas without being too concerned about the status of those making suggestions. Of course, this is easier to suggest than to implement. Numerous studies suggest that a person with more credibility is going to be more persuasive.[12] Cereal companies know this when they hire famous athletes to sell breakfast food. The message is, "Don't worry about the quality of the product. If this Olympic gold medal winner eats this stuff, you'll like it too." The athlete's fame and status do not necessarily make the cereal good, however. You still might buy the cereal, making a decision based on emotion rather than on fact. Group members sometimes make decisions this way too. Avoid agreeing with a decision just because of the status or credibility of the person making it. Evaluate the quality of the solution on its own merits.

Invite Someone From Outside the Group to Evaluate the Group's Decision-Making Process. Sometimes an objective point of view from outside the group can help avoid groupthink. Many large companies hire consultants to evaluate organizational decision making. You don't have to be part of a multinational corporation to ask someone to analyze your group's decision-making process. Ask someone from outside your group to sit in on one of your meetings. At the end of the meeting, ask the observer to summarize his or her observations and evaluations of the group. An outside observer may make some members uncomfortable, but if you explain why the visitor is there, the group will probably accept the visitor and eagerly await objective observations. Sometimes an outsider can identify unproductive group norms more readily than group members can. Chapter Eleven offers additional criteria for observing and evaluating small group communication.

Assign a Group Member the Role of Devil's Advocate. If no disagreement develops in a group, members may enjoy always getting along and may never realize that their group suffers from groupthink. If you find yourself in a group of pacifists, play devil's advocate by trying to raise objections and potential problems. You might also ask someone else to play the role. If someone periodically assumes the role of disagreer, the group will more likely consider available alternatives.

The Peterson Plastics Company has been steadily losing employees to its competitor, Wilson Plastics. Peterson executives met to discuss how to retain employees. The vice president for personnel strongly advocated offering substantial pay bonuses to employees after six months, one year, and five years, arguing that employees about to receive such bonuses will probably not change jobs. Several junior executives in the group, however, know that money is not really an issue in this case. Peterson is losing employees because its plant is neither air-conditioned nor well ventilated, while Wilson offers employees an air-conditioned working

Suggestions to Reduce Groupthink

A group leader should encourage critical, independent thinking.

Group members should be sensitive to status differences that may affect decision making.

Invite someone from outside the group to evaluate the group's decision-making process.

Assign a group member the role of devil's advocate.

Ask group members to subdivide into small groups (or to work individually) and to consider potential problems with suggested solutions.

environment. The junior executives hesitate to counter the vice president's proposal. Because of groupthink, the group reached a less than satisfactory decision to offer pay bonuses. If the management group had considered the negative consequences of its decision by having someone play devil's advocate, it might have opted for a better way to retain employees. Again, the myth that conflict and disagreement have a negative influence on a group's productivity results in a poor solution. Assign someone to consider the negative aspects of a suggestion before it is implemented. It could save the group from groupthink and enhance the quality of the group's decision.

Ask Group Members to Subdivide Into Small Groups (or to Work Individually) and to Consider Potential Problems with the Suggested Solutions. In large groups all members will most likely not be able to voice their objections and reservations. The U.S. Congress does most of its work in small committees. Members of Congress realize that in order to hear and thoroughly evaluate bills and resolutions, small groups of representatives must work together in committees. If you are working in a group too large for everyone to discuss the issues, suggest breaking into groups of two or three, each group to compose a list of objections to the proposals. The lists could be forwarded to the group secretary, who could then weed out duplicate objections and identify common points of contention. Even in a group of seven or eight, two subcommittees can evaluate the recommendations of the group. Group members should be able to participate frequently and evaluate the issues carefully. Individuals could also write down their objections to the proposed recommendations and then present them to the group.

The previous clues for identifying and correcting groupthink should help improve the quality of your group's decisions by capitalizing on opposing viewpoints. A textbook summary of suggestions for dealing with groupthink may lead you to think that groupthink can easily be corrected. It cannot. Because people think that conflict should be avoided, they need specific guidelines for identifying and avoiding groupthink. In essence, be critical of ideas, not people. Some controversy is useful. Ideally, groups should strive for an optimum amount of controversy so that they will not be lulled into groupthink. The group should not, however, create new conflict. A decision-making group seeks the best unanimous decision possible—it seeks consensus. The last section of this chapter will discuss managing conflict in the search for consensus.

CONSENSUS: A GOAL OF TASK-ORIENTED SMALL GROUPS

Some conflict is inevitable in groups, but this does not mean that all group discussions are doomed to end in disagreement and conflict. Conflict can be managed. **Consensus**—when all group members agree with and are committed to a decision—can occur. Even if a group does not reach consensus on key issues, it is not necessarily a failure. Good decisions can certainly emerge from groups whose members do not all completely agree on decisions. The U.S. Congress, for example, rarely achieves consensus; that does not mean, however, that its legislative process is ineffective.

After reading this chapter's discussion of conflict, you may be skeptical that a group can agree on anything. Many, if not most, groups do not reach total agreement, but it can be achieved. While conflict and controversy can improve the quality of group decision making, it is worthwhile to aim for consensus. Ideally, a certain level of tension can improve a group's decisions. A few words about consensus may help you form more realistic expectations about working in small groups. The following sections will also suggest some specific ways to help your group reach agreement.

Nature of Consensus

Consensus should not come too quickly. If it does, your group is probably a victim of groupthink. Nor should consensus come easily. Sometimes group agreement is built on agreements on minor points raised during the discussion. To achieve consensus, group members should try to emphasize these areas of agreement. This can be a time-consuming process, and some members may lose patience before they reach agreement. Regardless of how long a group takes to reach consensus, it generally results from careful and thoughtful communication between discussion members in the group.

To achieve consensus, some personal preferences must be surrendered for the overall well-being of the group. Group members must decide, both individually and collectively, whether they can achieve consensus. If two or three members refuse to change their minds on their positions, the rest of the group may decide that reaching consensus is not worth the extra time. Some group communication theorists suggest that groups might do better to postpone a decision if consensus can't be reached, particularly if the group making the decision will also implement it. If several group members oppose the solution, they will be less anxious to put it into practice. Ultimately, if consensus cannot be reached, a group should abide by the decision of the majority.

Suggestions for Reaching Consensus

Communication researchers agree that members usually go through considerable effort and patience before reaching consensus in a decision-making or problem-solving small group. However, guidelines may help members foster consensus in small group meetings.[13] Consider these specific suggestions for managing conflict and reaching consensus.

Avoid Always Arguing for Your Own Position. You often defend a solution or suggestion just because it is yours. Here is a suggestion that may help you develop a more objective point of view: If you find yourself becoming defensive over an idea you suggested, assume that your idea has become the property of the group; it no longer belongs to you. Present your position as clearly as possible, then listen to other members' reactions and consider them carefully before you push for your point. Just because people disagree with your idea does not necessarily mean that they respect you less.

Don't Assume That Someone Must Win and Someone Must Lose. When discussion becomes deadlocked, try not to view the discussion in terms of "us" versus "them" or "me" versus "the group." Try not to view communication as a game in which someone wins and others lose. Be willing to compromise and modify your original position. Of course, if compromising means finding a solution that is marginally acceptable to everyone but does not really solve a problem, then seek a better solution.

To be most effective, a group should try to cooperate and work together. The National Training Laboratories describes this type of group behavior as *integrative*—a group tries to integrate individual goals into the group goal. Group members who strive for integrative approaches to conflict management have the following attributes:

1. They attempt to pursue a common goal rather than individual goals.
2. They openly and honestly communicate with other group members.
3. They do not try to manipulate the group.
4. They do not use threats or bluffs to achieve their goals.
5. They try to understand themselves and the needs of others accurately.
6. They evaluate ideas and suggestions on their own merits.
7. They try to find solutions to problems.
8. They strive for group cohesiveness.[14]

Don't Change Your Mind Too Quickly Just to Avoid Conflict. While you may have to compromise to reach agreement, beware of changing your mind too quickly just to reach consensus. Groupthink occurs when group members do not test and challenge the ideas of others. When agreement seems to come too fast and too easily, be suspicious. Make certain that you have explored other alternatives and that everyone accepts the solution for basically the same reasons. Beware of the tendency to avoid conflict. Of course, you should not produce conflict just for the sake of conflict, but don't be upset if disagreements arise. Reaching consensus takes time and often requires compromise. Be patient.

Avoid Easy Techniques that Reduce Conflict. You may be tempted to flip a coin or to take a simple majority vote when you cannot resolve a disagreement. Resist that temptation. If possible, avoid making a decision until the entire group can agree. Of course, at times a majority vote is the only way to resolve a conflict. Just be certain that the group explores other alternatives before it makes a hasty decision to avoid conflict. Consensus through communication is best.

Seek Out Differences of Opinion. Remember that disagreements may help improve the quality of a group's decision. With a variety of opinions and information, a group has a better chance of finding a good solution. Also remember that complex problems seldom have just one solution. Perhaps more than one of the suggestions offered will work. Actively recruit opposing viewpoints if everyone seems to be agreeing without much discussion. You could appoint someone to play the role of devil's advocate if members are reluctant to offer criticism. Of course, don't belabor the point if you think that, after considerable discussion, group members genuinely agree. Test ideas that a group accepts too eagerly.

Try to Involve Everyone in the Discussion; Frequently Contribute to the Group. Again, the more varied the suggestions, solutions, and information, the greater the chance that a group will reach quality solutions and will achieve consensus. Encourage less talkative members to contribute to the group. Several studies suggest that members will be more satisfied with a solution if they have an opportunity to express their opinions and to offer suggestions.[15] Remember not to dominate the discussion. Good listening is important, too, and you may need to encourage others to speak out and assert themselves.

Use Group-Oriented Pronouns Rather than Self-Oriented Pronouns. Harry liked to talk about the problem as *he* saw it. He often began sentences with phrases like, "*I* think this is a good idea," or, "*My* suggestion is to. . . ." Studies suggest that groups that reach consensus generally use more pronouns like *we, us,* and *our,* while groups that do not reach consensus use more pronouns like *I, me, my,* and *mine.*[16] Using group-oriented words can foster cohesiveness.

Use Metadiscussional Phrases. Metadiscussion literally means "discussion about discussion." In other words, a metadiscussional statement focuses on the discussion process rather than on the topic under consideration.[17] Metadiscussional statements include, "Aren't we getting a little off the subject?" or "John, we haven't heard from you yet. What do you think?" or "Let's summarize our areas of agreement." These statements contain information and advice about the problem-solving process rather than about the issue at hand. Several studies show that groups whose members help orient the group toward its goal by (1) relying on facts

REVIEW BOX

Suggestions for Reaching Group Consensus

Effective Group Members	Ineffective Group Members
Avoid always arguing for their own position.	Argue for an idea because it is their own.
Approach conflict as a problem to be solved rather than a win-lose situation.	Assume that someone will win and someone will lose the argument.
Do not change their minds quickly just to avoid conflict.	Give in to the opinion of group just to avoid conflict.
Avoid easy conflict-reducing techniques.	Find easy ways to reduce the conflict, such as taking a quick vote without holding a discussion.
Seek out differences of opinion.	Do not ferret out a variety of viewpoints.
Try to involve everyone in the discussion and make frequent, meaningful contributions to the group.	Permit one person to monopolize the discussion or fail to draw out quiet group members.
Use third-person pronouns to talk about the group.	Talk about individual accomplishments rather than group accomplishments.
Use metadiscussional phrases; they talk about the discussion process.	Do little to help summarize or clarify the group discussion.
Orient the group toward its goal.	Do little to keep the group members focused on their task.
Avoid opinionated statements that are not based on facts or evidence.	Are closed-minded and inflexible.
Clarify misunderstandings.	Do not clarify misunderstandings or check to see whether their message is understood.

rather than on opinions, (2) making useful, constructive suggestions, and (3) trying to resolve conflict are more likely to reach agreement than groups whose members do not try to keep the group focused on its goal.[18]

Orient the Group Toward its Goal. Many groups fail to reach consensus because they lose sight of their objectives. If, however, members continually make constructive suggestions supported by factual evidence, they will more likely agree.

Avoid Opinionated Statements that Indicate a Closed Mind. Communication scholars consistently find that opinionated statements and low tolerance for dissenting points of view often inhibit agreement. This is especially apparent when the opinionated person is the discussion leader. A group with a less opinionated leader is more likely to reach agreement. Of course, it is easier to realize that opinionated statements hamper consensus than it is to solve a problem. Remember that using facts and relying on information obtained by direct observation are probably the best ways to avoid being too opinionated.

Make an Effort to Clarify Misunderstandings. All conflicts and disagreements do not arise because conflicting parties do not understand one another. Misunderstanding another's meaning does sometimes create conflict and adversely affect group consensus. Dealing with misunderstanding is simple. Ask a group member to explain a particular word or statement that you do not understand. Constantly solicit feedback from your listeners. For example, repeat the previous speaker's point before you state your position on an issue. This procedure can be overused, time-consuming, and stilted and artificial, but it can help when misunderstandings about meanings arise. It may also be helpful for you to remember that meanings are in people, not in words. Stated another way, the meaning for a word comes from a person's unique perspective, perception, and experience.

CONFLICT MANAGEMENT IN SMALL GROUPS: PUTTING PRINCIPLE INTO PRACTICE

Conflict can have both positive and negative effects on a group. Conflict occurs because people are different, because they have their own ways of doing things. These differences affect the way people perceive and approach problem solving.

Groupthink

The absence of conflict or a false sense of agreement is called groupthink. It occurs when group members are reluctant to voice their feelings and objections to issues.

To help reduce the likelihood of groupthink, review the following suggestions:

- The group leader should encourage critical, independent thinking.
- Group members should be sensitive to status differences that may affect decision making.
- Invite someone from outside the group to evaluate the group's decision-making process.
- Assign a group member the role of devil's advocate.
- Ask members to subdivide into small groups to consider potential problems with suggested solutions.

Consensus

Consider applying the following suggestions to help reach consensus and to help manage the conflicts and disagreements that arise in groups.

- Avoid always arguing for your own position.
- Don't assume someone must win and someone must lose.

- Don't change your mind too quickly just to avoid conflict.
- Avoid easy conflict-reducing techniques.
- Seek out differences of opinion.
- Try to involve everyone in the group discussion; be a frequent contributor to the group.
- Use group pronouns (e.g., *we, us, our*), rather than self-oriented pronouns (e.g., *I, me, mine*).
- Use metadiscussional phrases.
- Orient the group toward its goal.
- Avoid opinionated statements that indicate a closed mind.
- Make an effort to clarify misunderstandings.

PRACTICE

Agree-Disagree Statements About Conflict

Read each statement once, and mark whether you agree (A) or disagree (D) with it. Take five or six minutes to do this.

_____   1. Most people find an argument interesting and exciting.

_____   2. In most conflicts someone must win and someone must lose. That's the way conflict is.

_____   3. The best way to handle a conflict is simply to let everyone cool off.

_____   4. Most people get upset at a person who disagrees with them.

_____   5. Most hidden agendas are probably best kept hidden to ensure a positive social climate.

_____   6. If people spend enough time together, they will find something to disagree about and will eventually become upset with one another.

_____   7. Conflicts can be solved if people just take the time to listen to one another.

_____   8. Conflict hinders a group's work.

_____   9. If you disagree with someone in a group, it is usually better to keep quiet than to get the group offtrack with your personal difference of opinion.

_____ 10. When a group can't reach a decision, members should abide by the decision of the group leader if the leader is qualified and competent.

_____ 11. To compromise is to take the easy way out of conflict.

_____ 12. Some people produce more conflict and tension than others. These people should be restricted from decision-making groups.

After you have marked the above statements, break up into small groups and try to agree or disagree unanimously with each statement. Especially try to find reasons for differences of opinion. If your group cannot reach agreement or disagreement, you may change the wording in any statement to promote consensus. Assign one group member to observe your group interactions. After your group has attempted to reach consensus, the observer should report how effectively the group used the guidelines suggested in this chapter.

Consensus Evaluation Form

1. Group members always argued for their own positions.
   strongly agree   agree   undecided   disagree   strongly disagree
2. Group members assumed that someone must win and someone must lose an argument.
   strongly agree   agree   undecided   disagree   strongly disagree
3. Group members did not change their minds to avoid conflict.
   strongly agree   agree   undecided   disagree   strongly disagree
4. As a group, we avoided easy conflict-reducing techniques like flipping a coin or taking a quick vote.
   strongly agree   agree   undecided   disagree   strongly disagree
5. Group members sought out differences of opinion.
   strongly agree   agree   undecided   disagree   strongly disagree
6. All group members were involved in the discussion.
   strongly agree   agree   undecided   disagree   strongly disagree
7. Group members used group-oriented words *(we, us, our)* more than they used self-oriented words *(I, me, mine).*
   strongly agree   agree   undecided   disagree   strongly disagree
8. Group members used metadiscussional phrases.
   strongly agree   agree   undecided   disagree   strongly disagree
9. Group members tried to orient the group toward its goal.
   strongly agree   agree   undecided   disagree   strongly disagree
10. Group members avoided making opinionated statements and were generally open-minded.
    strongly agree   agree   undecided   disagree   strongly disagree
11. Group members made an effort to clarify misunderstandings.
    strongly agree   agree   undecided   disagree   strongly disagree

Win As Much As You Can

This activity is designed to explore the effects of trust and conflict on communication.[19] Your instructor will explain how this exercise is to be conducted.*

---

*The *Instructor's Manual* explains how this activity should be conducted.

4 X's: Lose $1.00 each
3 X's: Win $1.00 each 1 Y: Lose $3.00
2 X's: Win $2.00 each 2 Y's: Lose $2.00 each
1 X: Win $3.00 3 Y's: Lose $1.00 each
4 Y's: Win $1.00 each

Directions: For ten successive rounds you and your partner will choose either an "X" or a "Y." Each round's "pay-off" depends on the pattern made in your cluster. *Strategy:* You are to confer with your partner on each round to make a joint decision. Before rounds 5, 8, and 10 you confer with the other pairs in your cluster. There are three key rules:

1. Do not confer with the other members of your cluster unless you are given specific permission to do so. This applies to nonverbal and verbal communication.
2. Each pair must agree on a single choice for each round.
3. Make sure that the other members of your cluster do not know your pair's choice until you are instructed to reveal it.

Round	Time Allowed	Confer with	Choice	$Won	$ Lost	$ Balance	
1	2 min.	partner					
2	1 min.	partner					
3	1 min.	partner					
4	1 min.	partner					
5	3 min. 1 min.	cluster partner					Bonus Round pay is multiplied by 3
6	1 min.	partner					
7	1 min.	partner					
8	3 min.	cluster					Pay is multiplied by 5
9	1 min.	partner					
10	3 min.	cluster					Pay is multiplied by 10

The Case of Johnny

Read the following case study about Johnny, a youth with several problems. Following the case study are a range of possible solutions to Johnny's problem. Your task is to decide, as a group, on the best solution. Strive for total group agreement. After a given amount of time, your instructor* will lead you in a discussion of your group's ability to reach consensus.

Johnny was born in a large midwestern industrial city. There were already nine other children in Johnny's family when Johnny was born; one more child, David, came after Johnny. His family lived in one of the worst slums in the city, known for its high crime rate and juvenile delinquency. It was a neighborhood of factories, junkyards, poolrooms, cheap liquor joints, and broken homes.

By the time Johnny's father died, four of the older children had married and moved away. The rest of the family continued in its dismal course; the children were getting into one difficulty after another, and Johnny's mother, sick and confused, was tired of trudging from school to police station to court, listening to complaints about them. Of the remaining children only Georgie, the oldest, assumed any responsibility toward the others. However, when the rest of the children got out of hand, he beat them brutally.

Johnny's mother tried to pacify landlords by keeping her screaming children on the streets as much as possible. Five of Johnny's brothers, starting in childhood, ran up police records covering charges of disturbing the peace, breaking and entering, larceny, perjury, assault and battery, and malicious injury.

"I was in the police station, too, plenty," Johnny says. "Saturdays they had kids' day. We'd be in this long corridor, there'd be all little kids sitting down. They'd bring us in and those jerks, the cops, they'd be sitting there and this cop here, he was always insulting us. 'You little creep,' he'd tell me, and he'd belt me."

Johnny was a trial to his teachers. They complained that he was "nervous, sullen, obstinate, cruel, disobedient, disruptive." "Teachers can stand him for only one day at a time," one said. "He talks to himself. He fights. He attempted to kick Ms. Clark. He isn't going to be promoted. He knows this and refuses to study."

With every new failure Johnny committed some new misbehavior. Once, at the beginning of a new semester, he told his teacher, "I wasn't promoted. OK! This year I'm going to make plenty of trouble." With every new punishment Johnny's conviction that his teachers, like everybody else, were "against him" grew. Johnny had been seeing his parole officer, Mr. O'Brien, for some time now.

During the months of Mr. O'Brien's friendship with Johnny, his teachers found that he was making a tremendous effort to behave himself but that he was "like a kettle of boiling water with the lid about to blow off." Johnny managed to get through that term of school without too much trouble and was promoted, but school had not been out long before he fell into trouble with the police again, this time for breaking into a house and stealing fifty dollars' worth of jewelry. Before

---

*Note to instructor: The *Instructor's Manual* explains how this activity should be conducted.

Johnny appeared in court, Mr. O'Brien visited him. Johnny, O'Brien reported, seemed "unhappy, but stolid and apathetic, though once or twice as we talked, he verged on tears."

Johnny didn't deny the theft and, as his confession poured out, Mr. O'Brien asked, "Even when I thought you were being a good boy, Johnny, were you stealing all the while?" Johnny, verging on tears, replied. "Yes, sometimes. But lots of times I didn't steal because I thought of you."

Suggested Solutions: Love-Punishment Scale

1. Love, kindness, and friendship are all that are necessary to make Johnny a better youth. If he can be placed in a more agreeable environment, such as a warm, friendly foster home, his trouble will clear up.
2. Johnny should be put into warm and affectionate surroundings where he will be punished if he really gets out of hand.
3. Johnny should be sent into a warm and affectionate environment where discipline and punishment will be frequent if his behavior warrants it.
4. Johnny needs an equal measure of both love and discipline. Thus, he should be placed in an atmosphere where he will be disciplined and punished if he does wrong but rewarded and given affection if he behaves himself, and where equal emphasis will be placed on both love and discipline.
5. Though they should not be too strong and frequent, punishment and discipline should be emphasized more than kindness and affection. Johnny should be placed in an atmosphere where he will be seriously disciplined but where he will also be allowed warmth and kindness.
6. Johnny should be sent into surroundings where he will be disciplined and punished, but where he will receive praise and kindness if he behaves himself.
7. There is very little you can do with a youth like this; put him in an extremely severe disciplinary environment. Only by punishing him strongly can we change his behavior.

Exercise: Identifying Your Conflict Strategies

Different people learn different ways of managing conflict.[20] The strategies you use to manage conflict may be different from those used by your friends and acquaintances. This exercise gives you an opportunity to increase your awareness of what strategies you use and how they compare with those strategies of others. The procedure is as follows:

1. With your classmates, form groups of six. Make sure you know the other members of the group; do not join a group of strangers.
2. Working by yourself, complete the following questionnaire.

3. Working by yourself, read the accompanying discussion of conflict strategies. Then make five slips of paper. Write the names of the other five members of your group on the slips of paper, one name to a slip.

4. On each slip of paper write the conflict strategy that best fits the actions of the person named.

5. After all group members are finished, pass out your slips of paper to the people whose names are on them. In turn you should end up with five slips of paper, each containing a description of your conflict style as seen by another group member. Likewise, each member of your group should end up with five slips of paper describing his or her conflict strategy.

6. Score your questionnaire, using the table that follows the discussion of conflict strategies. Rank the five conflict strategies from the one you use the most to the one you use the least. This will give you an indication of how you see your own conflict strategy. The second most frequently used strategy is your backup strategy, the one you use if your first one fails.

7. After drawing names to see who goes first, one member describes the results of his or her questionnaire. This is his view of his or her own conflict strategies. The member then reads each of the five slips of paper on which are written the views of the group members. Next the member asks the group to give specific examples of how they have seen him or her act in conflicts. The group members should use the rules for constructive feedback. The person to the left of the first member repeats this procedure, and so on around the group.

8. Each group discusses the strengths and the weaknesses of each of the conflict strategies.

How You Act in Conflicts

The proverbs listed below can be thought of as descriptions of some of the different strategies for resolving conflicts. Proverbs state traditional wisdom, and these proverbs reflect traditional wisdom for resolving conflicts. Read each carefully. Using the following scale, indicate how typical each proverb is of your actions in a conflict.

5 = very typical of the way I act in a conflict
4 = frequently typical of the way I act in a conflict
3 = sometimes typical of the way I act in a conflict
2 = seldom typical of the way I act in a conflict
1 = never typical of the way I act in a conflict

_____ 1. It is easier to refrain than to retreat from a quarrel.
_____ 2. If you cannot make a person think as you do, make him or her do as you think.

_____ 3. Soft words win hard hearts.

_____ 4. You scratch my back, I'll scratch yours.

_____ 5. Come now and let us reason together.

_____ 6. When two quarrel, the person who keeps silent first is the most praiseworthy.

_____ 7. Might overcomes right.

_____ 8. Smooth words make smooth ways.

_____ 9. Better half a loaf than no bread at all.

_____ 10. Truth lies in knowledge, not in majority opinion.

_____ 11. He who fights and runs away lives to fight another day.

_____ 12. He hath conquered well that hath made his enemies flee.

_____ 13. Kill your enemies with kindness.

_____ 14. A fair exchange brings no quarrel.

_____ 15. No person has the final answer, but every person has a piece to contribute.

_____ 16. Stay away from people who disagree with you.

_____ 17. Fields are won by those who believe in winning.

_____ 18. Kind words are worth much and cost little.

_____ 19. Tit for tat is fair play.

_____ 20. Only the person who is willing to give up his or her monopoly on truth can ever profit from the truths that others hold.

_____ 21. Avoid quarrelsome people; they will only make your life miserable.

_____ 22. A person who will not flee will make others flee.

_____ 23. Soft words ensure harmony.

_____ 24. One gift for another makes good friends.

_____ 25. Bring your conflicts into the open and face them directly; only then will the best solution be discovered.

_____ 26. The best way of handling conflicts is to avoid them.

_____ 27. Put your foot down where you mean to stand.

_____ 28. Gentleness will triumph over anger.

_____ 29. Getting part of what you want is better than not getting anything at all.

_____ 30. Frankness, honesty, and trust will move mountains.

_____ 31. There is nothing so important you have to fight for it.

_____ 32. There are two kinds of people in the world, winners and losers.

_____ 33. When someone hits you with a stone, hit him or her with a piece of cotton.

_____ 34. When both give in halfway, a fair settlement is achieved.

_____ 35. By digging and digging, the truth is discovered.

Scoring

Withdrawing	Forcing	Smoothing	Compromising	Confronting
1. _____	8. _____	15. _____	22. _____	29. _____
2. _____	9. _____	16. _____	23. _____	30. _____
3. _____	10. _____	17. _____	24. _____	31. _____
4. _____	11. _____	18. _____	25. _____	32. _____
5. _____	12. _____	19. _____	26. _____	33. _____
6. _____	13. _____	20. _____	27. _____	34. _____
7. _____	14. _____	21. _____	28. _____	35. _____
Total	Total	Total	Total	Total
_____	_____	_____	_____	_____

The higher the total score for each conflict strategy, the more frequently you tend to use that strategy. The lower the total score for each conflict strategy, the less frequently you tend to use that strategy.

Notes

1. Joseph P. Folger and Marshall Scott Poole, *Working Through Conflict: A Communication Perspective* (Glenview, Illinois: Scott, Foresman and Company, 1984), p. 4.

2. Michael Burgoon, Judee K. Heston, and James McCroskey, *Small Group Communication: A Functional Approach* (New York: Holt, Rinehart & Winston, 1974), p. 76.

3. Portions of the following discussion of myths about conflict were adapted from Robert J. Doolittle, *Orientations to Communication and Conflict* (Chicago: Science Research Associates, 1976), pp. 7–9.

4. See Fred E. Jandt (ed.), *Conflict Resolution Through Communication* (New York: Harper & Row Publishers, 1973).

5. Doolittle, p. 8.

6. Gerald R. Miller and Mark Steinberg, *Between People: New Analysis of Interpersonal Communication* (Chicago: Science Research Associates, Inc., 1975), p. 264.

7. *Ibid.*

8. Linda L. Putnam, "Conflict in Group Decision-Making," in Randy Y. Hirokawa and Marshall Scott Poole (eds.), *Communication and Group Decision-Making* (Beverly Hills, California: Sage Publications, 1986), p. 195.

9. Miller and Steinberg, p. 269.

10. Irving L. Janis, *Victims of Groupthink* (Boston: Houghton Mifflin Company, 1973).

11. Adapted from Irving L. Janis, "Groupthink," *Psychology Today* 5 (November 1971): 43–46, 74–76.

12. See Kenneth Andersen and Theodore Clevenger, Jr., "A Summary of Experimental Research in Ethos," *Speech Monographs* 30 (1963): 59–78.

13. Portions of the following section on consensus were adapted from John A. Kline, "Ten Techniques for Reaching Consensus in Small Groups," *Air Force Reserve Officer Training Corps Education Journal* 19 (Spring 1977): 19–21.

14. *1968 Reading Book* of the National Training Laboratories Institute of Applied Behavioral Sciences.

15. See Henry W. Riecken, "The Effect of Talkativeness on Ability to Influence Group Solutions of Problems," *Sociometry* 21 (1958): 309–321.

16. See John A. Kline and James L. Hullinger, "Redundancy, Self Orientation, and Group Consensus," *Speech Monographs* 40 (March 1973): 72–74.

17. See Dennis S. Gouran, "Variables Related to Consensus in Group Discussions of Questions of Policy," *Speech Monographs* 36 (August 1969): 385–391; Thomas J. Knutson, "An Experimental Study of the Effects of Orientation Behavior on Small Group Consensus," *Speech Monographs* 39 (August 1972): 159–165; John A. Kline, "Orientation and Group Consensus," *Central States Speech Journal* 23 (Spring 1972): 44–47.

18. Gouran, pp. 385–391; Knutson, pp. 159–165; Kline, pp. 44–47.

19. J. William Pfeiffer and John E. Jones (eds.), *A Handbook of Structured Experiences for Human Relations Training,* vol. 2 (La Jolla, California: University Associates, 1974), pp. 62–67.

20. David W. Johnson and Frank P. Johnson, *Joining Together: Group Theory and Group Skills* (Englewood Cliffs, New Jersey: Prentice-Hall, 1987), p. 270.

Chapter Ten

Leadership

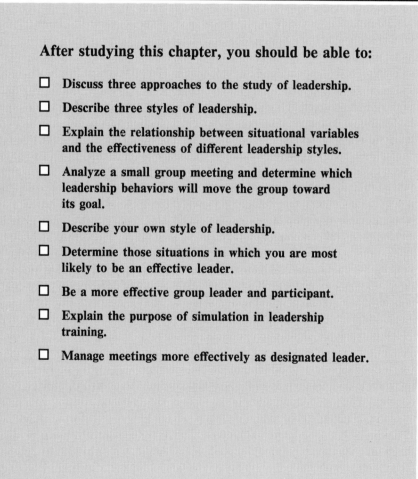

After studying this chapter, you should be able to:

☐ Discuss three approaches to the study of leadership.

☐ Describe three styles of leadership.

☐ Explain the relationship between situational variables and the effectiveness of different leadership styles.

☐ Analyze a small group meeting and determine which leadership behaviors will move the group toward its goal.

☐ Describe your own style of leadership.

☐ Determine those situations in which you are most likely to be an effective leader.

☐ Be a more effective group leader and participant.

☐ Explain the purpose of simulation in leadership training.

☐ Manage meetings more effectively as designated leader.

$\mathbf{B}$efore beginning this chapter, consider the following statements about leadership:

> Leaders are born and not made.
>
> An effective leader is always in control of the group process.
>
> A leader is a person who gets others to do the work.
>
> Leadership is a set of functions distributed throughout the group.
>
> The leader should know more than other group members about the topic of discussion.
>
> An authoritarian leader is better than one who allows the group to function without control.
>
> It's best for a group to have only one leader.
>
> A person who has been appointed leader *is* the leader.

What do you think about these statements? With which ones do you agree? Disagree? If it hasn't happened already, be assured that one day you will find yourself in a leadership position—on a committee, in an organization, or perhaps in the military. In fact, whenever you participate in a decision-making group your attitudes about leadership will affect your behavior, the behavior of others, and the effectiveness of the group.

This chapter will provide you with information about the nature of leadership in groups to help you become a more effective group participant and will make some specific suggestions to help you become an effective leader.

WHAT IS LEADERSHIP?

When you think about "leadership," what comes to mind? A fearless commanding officer leading troops into battle? The president of the United States addressing the country on national television? The student body president coordinating and representing student efforts? Perhaps you think of the chairperson of a committee you're on. Traditionally, the study of leadership has centered on people who are successful in leadership positions. Researchers argued that by looking at successful leaders they could identify attributes or individual traits that best predict good leadership ability. Identifying such traits would be tremendously valuable to those in business, government, or the military who are responsible for promoting others to positions of leadership.

TRAIT PERSPECTIVE

Over the last several decades, researchers have conducted scores of trait studies. These studies indicated that leaders often have attributes such as intelligence, enthusiasm, dominance, self-confidence, social participation, and equalitarianism.[1] Other researchers found that physical traits were related to leadership ability. Leaders seemed to be larger, more active, energetic, and better looking than others.[2] Still other researchers found that leaders possess tact, cheerfulness, a sense of justice, discipline, versatility, and self-control. One alleged study conducted by a branch of the military determined that leaders love good, red meat and aggressively pursue desserts.

The **trait perspective** of leadership seemed like a good idea at the time but actually yielded very little useful information. While correlations between traits and leadership have generally been positive, they have occasionally been weak.[3] Traits useful in one situation, such as leading troops into battle, are not necessarily the traits required for other leadership positions, such as conducting a business meeting.

A further problem with the trait approach is that it does not identify which traits are important to become a leader and which are important to maintain the position. These studies also do not adequately distinguish between leaders and followers who possess the same traits and do not prove useful to group participants wishing to improve their leadership skills. After all, people cannot make themselves larger, more energetic, or more aggressive pursuers of desserts. Therefore, this book will consider the trait approach to be a "historical perspective" and proceed from there.

FUNCTIONAL PERSPECTIVE

The **functional perspective** to studying leadership has proven to be informative to students of small group communication. Rather than focusing on the characteristics of individual leaders, the functional approach examines leadership as behaviors that may be performed by any group member to maximize group effectiveness. Barnlund and Haiman identify leadership behaviors as those that guide, influence, direct, or control others in a group.[4] This is a much more fruitful approach for those interested in improving their leadership abilities. Whereas the trait approach might help identify the sort of person who should be appointed to a leadership position, the functional approach describes the specific communicative behaviors a leader needs in order for a group to function effectively. By understanding these behaviors people can more effectively participate in group discussions.

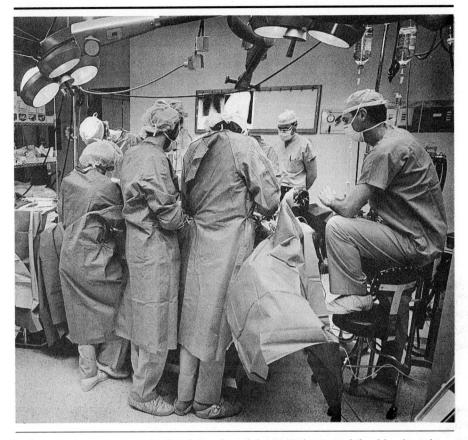

In the operating room, the role of each member of the surgical team is defined by the tasks required of him or her.

According to advocates of the functional approach, leadership behaviors fall into two categories. The major distinctions are between **task leadership** and **process leadership** (also called group building or maintenance). Task-oriented behaviors aim specifically at accomplishing a group goal. Process-oriented behaviors help maintain a satisfactory interpersonal climate within a group. Both types of leadership are essential.

Task Leadership

When groups convene to solve problems, make decisions, plan activities, or determine policy, they are frequently hampered by group members' random behavior. Even when they get down to business, group process strays. Discussion becomes tangential, and groups lose track of where they are going. Sometimes one person monopolizes the conversation while others remain silent. Sometimes groups just can't seem to get started. At times like these, members may blame their designated leaders for their failure.

A group leader has a responsibility to keep a group moving, but research in group process has shown that behaviors which keep the group on track are behaviors which anyone can perform. Just because a person has the title "leader" does not necessarily mean that that person is best equipped to do the job. If leadership is a set of functions that are often distributed, a group is still quite capable of getting its job done regardless of who is designated leader. If you are a member of a disorganized group, you can provide the leadership the group needs even though you are not the leader.

Chapter Four listed functional leadership roles. The following sections will look at a few task-leadership behaviors and consider ways that these behaviors help a group toward its goal.

Initiating. Task-oriented group discussions need to generate ideas. Sometimes ideas are related to procedural matters; at other times a group needs to generate ideas to solve problems. If, for example, you just finished Chapter Eight on problem solving and can see that your group has not adequately defined its problem before suggesting solutions, you might say: "Listen. I'm afraid that we're all proposing solutions before we've really agreed on the nature of the problem itself. Let's take a few minutes and talk some more about the problem so that we know we're all discussing the same thing."

By proposing a change in the group's deliberations you are initiating a procedural change, in this case one that will probably benefit the group. To "initiate" means to "begin." If you say: "Let's get this meeting under way," you have begun a change (assuming the group follows your suggestion). If, later in the meeting, you offer: "Let's consider an alternate plan" or "Let's generate some more ideas before evaluating what we have here," again you will probably alter the course of the group's action. You are initiating. Without someone who initiates discussion, a group has no direction. The ability to initiate is an important group behavior and one that anyone can contribute.

Coordinating. Different people bring different expectations, beliefs, attitudes, values, and experiences to a group. The contributions of each member are unique, yet all are directed toward a common group goal. Given the diversity in small groups, coordinating is often an important leadership function. Communicative behavior that helps a group explore the contributions of all members is valuable. If, for example, you see a tie between the ideas brought to the group by two of its members, you should point it out to help focus the group. Coordinating members' efforts can help group members see the "groupness" of their efforts and reduce their uncertainty about the group, its problem, and its solutions.

Summarizing. Groups can get long-winded. Often in the middle of a discussion members cannot tell just where the discussion began and where it is going. It doesn't take many tangential remarks to get the group off track. Even when the

Process-leadership behaviors maintain good interpersonal relations so that the group climate is satisfying to members and allows them to achieve their goals.

group is on track it is sometimes useful to stop and assess its progress. Summarizing reduces group uncertainty by showing how far the discussion has progressed and what it still needs to accomplish. By understanding when a group needs a summary—and then providing it—you can help move the group toward its goal. Even if your summary is not accepted by the group, you will still reveal discrepancies among group members' perceptions, thus opening the door to more clarification and less uncertainty.

Elaborating. Sometimes good ideas fall on deaf ears until they are elaborated enough to be visualized. Suppose you are at a meeting of your fraternity or sorority, which is trying to determine ways of increasing next year's pledge class. Someone in the group suggests that redecorating the recreation room might help. Several things might happen in the discussion: (1) Members might begin to evaluate the idea, some being in favor and some not, (2) another idea might be suggested and recorded, or (3) you (or someone else) might elaborate on the idea by describing how the room might look with new carpeting, a pool table, soft lighting, and a new sofa. Whereas redecoration might have fallen flat by itself, your elaboration gives it a fighting chance. Good ideas are often left unexplored because people fail to elaborate on them.

Initiating, coordinating, summarizing, and elaborating are types of communicative behaviors. While these are some of the more important types of contributions you can make, the list is by no means complete. Task leadership is any behavior or behaviors that influence group process and help accomplish the group's task. Making suggestions, offering new ideas, giving information or opinions, asking for more information, and making procedural observations or recommendations are all task-oriented leadership behaviors that can contribute to a group's effort. Viewing leadership from the functional approach, leadership skill is associated with your ability to analyze a group's process and to choose appropriate behaviors.

Process Leadership

For a group to accomplish its task, members must address themselves to it. For a group to function effectively, it needs to concern itself *with itself!* Groups are composed of people, and people have needs. (In fact, the family is a small group specifically adapted to meeting individual needs.) People don't leave their needs at home when they come to a meeting; they bring those needs along. Effective group communication must be addressed to the external task of the group and to the needs of its members. Effective groups not only solve problems and make decisions but also satisfy their members. Failing to maintain a satisfying group climate can lead to a breakdown in a group's performance. In this respect, small groups resemble automobiles. Cars are great for getting you where you want to go, but they require regular tuning and maintenance in order to run reliably and efficiently. In fact, if an owner doesn't maintain a car it will eventually break down. So it is with groups: They, too, need tuning and maintaining.

Leadership research consistently indicates that groups have both task and process needs. The process dimension is often called "group building and maintenance." Process-leadership behaviors maintain interpersonal relations in a group and facilitate a climate satisfying to members and conducive to accomplishing the group's task. Process leaders are really communication facilitators.

Chapter Five discussed group climate from the perspective of individual and interpersonal needs. The following sections look at some specific process-leadership behaviors from the perspective of leadership and group needs.

Tension Release. Think of times you've studied for exams. You cram more and more information into your head until you reach a point where it all seems futile. Everything runs together; ideas blur. You know it's time for a break, and after a cup of coffee and some relaxing conversation you return to your books with renewed energy.

Sometimes the most effective leadership you can provide for a group is suggesting a coffee break. When a group is tired, when its task is difficult, when the hour is late, when tension and stress are high, a group needs relief. A joke, a bit of humor, a break, or even a move for adjournment can often provide just what a group needs—tension release. An occasional break or a good laugh can renew a group's energy and improve member satisfaction.

Some people seem to be naturally sensitive to a group's need for tension release. Knowing that tension release is a necessary leadership function can alert anyone—even the most task-oriented individual—to that need.

Gate Keeping. As noted in Chapter One, an advantage of working in small groups is that several heads are better than one. The very diversity that makes group communication so complex also gives it strength. A group possesses more experience and intelligence than does any individual, but experience and individual insight are only useful to a group if they are shared.

Some people like to talk more than others, and in some groups two or three people monopolize the conversation while others remain relatively silent. This fairly common occurrence poses a problem for a group in two ways: First, quiet members are just as likely to possess useful information and ideas as are more vocal group members, and their ideas may never surface unless they say something. Second, people who talk more tend to be more satisfied with a group. Members that don't talk much can have a negative effect on a group at both the task and process dimensions.

Gate keeping is aimed at coordinating discussion so that members can air their views. It may take the form of eliciting input ("Harvey, you must have given this a lot of thought. What are your views of the problem?") or even of limiting the contributions of more verbal group members ("Can we perhaps limit our comments to two or three minutes so that we can get everyone's ideas before we have to adjourn?"). Gate keeping is an important leadership function because it insures more input along the task dimension and higher member satisfaction along the process dimension.

Encouraging. People like praise. They feel good when someone recognizes them for their contributions. Encouraging is a leadership behavior aimed at increasing the esteem of group members and raising their hopes, confidence, and aspirations. Improving the morale of a group can increase cohesiveness, member satisfaction, and productivity.

Mediating. Conflict is a normal, healthy part of group interaction. However, mismanaged conflict can lead to hurt feelings, physical or mental withdrawal from a group, reduced cohesiveness, and general disruption. Mediating is aimed at resolving conflict between group members and releasing any tension associated with the conflict. Whenever conflict becomes person-oriented rather than issue-oriented, it is a particularly appropriate time for mediation.

> Wanda: I think that the plan I'm proposing has considerable merit and meets our needs.
> Harold: That's ridiculous. It'll never work.
> Wanda: Get off my case, Bozo! I don't see you proposing any better solutions.

This potentially volatile situation could easily disrupt the group. You often have to work in groups with people you don't especially like. Obviously, Harold and Wanda don't get along well, but groups can function effectively in spite of personality clashes. They need to focus discussion on issues rather than on personalities. At times interpersonal difficulties become so severe that they cannot be resolved by simply focusing on a group's task. Such difficulties can be a serious encumbrance to a group and need to be dealt with either within or outside the group; ignoring problems won't make them go away.

The above list of behaviors that contribute to a group's process or maintenance needs is not complete. More complete lists appear in Chapters Four and Eleven. The behaviors described above are some of the more essential task and process leadership behaviors. They are included here to illustrate their importance and to help you examine your own leadership behavior in groups.

Both task and process leadership are essential to the success of a small group. If a group does not make progress on its task, members will probably feel frustrated and unsatisfied. In addition, if a group does not maintain a comfortable environment, members tend to focus their attention and energy on their own dissatisfaction with the group rather than on their assigned task.

SITUATIONAL PERSPECTIVE

Thus far the chapter has discussed the trait and functional approaches to leadership study and has explored some task and process leadership roles. The **situational perspective** to group leadership accommodates all of these factors—leadership behaviors, task needs, and process needs—but also takes into account leadership style and situation. When you complete the task process leadership questionnaire at the end of this chapter, you may have some new insights about your own leadership behavior in groups. In interpreting the results of that questionnaire, you will find that the degree of your concern for task and for people are related to **leadership style**.

Leadership Style

Your beliefs and attitudes about leadership will affect your behavior in small groups. Leadership style is a relatively consistent pattern of behavior reflecting a leader's beliefs and attitudes. While no two people act as leaders precisely the same way, people do lead with three basic styles: authoritarian (or autocratic), democratic, and laissez-faire.

Authoritarian leaders assume positions of intellectual and behavioral superiority in groups. They make the decisions, give the orders, and generally control all activities. *Democratic leaders* have more faith in the group than authoritarian leaders and consequently try to involve members in making decisions. *Laissez-faire leaders* see themselves as no better or no worse than other group members. They assume the group will direct itself. Laissez-faire leaders avoid dominating groups. In one of the earliest studies of the effects of leadership style, researchers compared groups of schoolchildren led by graduate students who had been specifically trained

Table 10-1   Leader Behavior in Three "Social Climates"[5]

Authoritarian	Democratic	Laissez-faire
1. All determination of policy made by leader.	1. All policies a matter of group discussion and decision, encouraged and assigned by leader.	1. Complete freedom for group or individual decision; minimum of leader participation.
2. Techniques and activity steps dictated by the authority, one at a time, so that future steps are always largely uncertain.	2. Activity perspective gained during discussion period; general steps to group goal sketched, and when technical advice needed, leader suggests alternative procedures.	2. Various materials supplied by leader, making it clear he would supply information when asked, but taking no other part in discussion.
3. Particular work task and work companion of each member usually dictated by leader.	3. Members free to work with anyone; division of tasks left up to the group.	3. Complete nonparticipation of leader.
4. Dominator tending to be "personal" in praise and criticism of work of each member; remaining aloof from active group participation except when demonstrating.	4. Leader "objective" or "fact-minded" in praise and criticism, trying to be regular group member in spirit without doing too much of the work.	4. Infrequent, spontaneous comments on member activities unless questioned; no attempt to appraise or regulate course of events.

in one of the three leadership styles. The researchers defined the styles as shown in Table 10-1.

Briefly, here are the results of the study:

1. Groups with democratic leaders generally were more satisfied and functioned in a more orderly and positive way.
2. Groups with authoritarian leaders were more aggressive and more apathetic (depending on the group).
3. Members of democratic groups were more satisfied than members of laissez-faire groups; a majority of group members preferred democratic to authoritarian, although some members were more satisfied in authoritarian groups.
4. Authoritarian groups spent more time engaged in productive work, but only when the leader was present.

It is tempting to conclude that humanistic, participatory, democratic leadership will invariably lead to greater satisfaction and higher productivity. Unfortunately, the evidence does not warrant such a generalization. Several studies have shown that no leadership style is effective in all situations. What works at General Motors may not work at a local church. An effective student body president may be a poor camp counselor. The expectations of one group differ from those of others groups.

Recent research on the effectiveness of different leadership styles has suggested that effective leadership is contingent on a variety of interrelated factors, such as culture, time constraints, group compatibility, and the nature of a group's task. While the functional approach reveals the importance of fulfilling various leadership roles in a group, it does not explain which roles are most appropriate in which situation. It is clear that you need to consider the setting in which leadership behavior occurs.

Situational Factors in Leadership Behavior: A Case Study

The situational approach views leadership as an interaction between style and various situational factors. Consider the following case study.

> Having been offered some very attractive extra retirement benefits by top management, Arthur agreed to take early retirement at age sixty-two. Once an ambitious and young junior executive for the company, Arthur had, in recent years, taken a rather relaxed, anything goes attitude as director of his division. As a result, his group had been showing the lowest productivity record in the company, and his subordinates were not receiving attractive salary increments and other rewards from top management. Morale was very low, and employees were discontented.
>
> Hoping to rejuvenate the group, management replaced Arthur with an extremely bright, dynamic, and aggressive young manager named Marilyn. Marilyn's instructions were these: Get your group's productivity up by 20 percent over the next twelve months or we'll fire the whole group and start from scratch with a new manager and new employees.
>
> Marilyn began by studying the records of employees in her group to determine the strengths and weaknesses of each. She then drew up a set of goals and objectives for each employee and made assignments accordingly. She set a rigid timetable for each employee and made all employees directly accountable to her.
>
> Employee response was overwhelmingly positive. Out of chaos came order. Each person knew what was expected and had tangible goals to achieve. Employees felt united behind their new leader as they all strove to achieve their objective of a one-year, 20 percent increase in productivity.
>
> At the end of the year, productivity was up not 20 percent but 35 percent! Management was thrilled and awarded Marilyn a large raise and the company's certificate of achievement.
>
> Feeling that she had a viable formula for success, Marilyn moved into the second year as she had into the first—setting goals for each employee, holding them accountable, and so forth. However, things went less smoothly the second year. Employees who had been quick to respond the first year were less responsive. While the work she assigned was usually completed on time, the quality of the work was declining. Employees had a morale problem: Those who had once looked up to Marilyn as "Boss" were now sarcastically calling her "Queen Bee" and reminiscing about "the good old days" when Arthur was their manager.

Figure 10-1   Relation of Stress, Goal Structuring, and Leadership Patterns

Marilyn's behavior as manager had not changed, yet her leadership was no longer effective. Something needed to be done, but what?

David Korten has proposed that under certain conditions groups are pressured to have centralized, authoritarian leadership but that as these conditions change, groups often develop a more democratic, participative form of leadership. Korten's work may give us an answer to Marilyn's problem.

Korten says that groups with highly structured goals and high stress move toward authoritarian leadership. The above case study is an example of this. When Marilyn took over as manager, the group was given a very specific goal—to raise productivity by 20 percent. At the same time, employees had a good deal of stress; if they failed, they would lose their jobs. In such situations, groups appreciate an authoritarian style, and it is effective. Think of times when you were in a group with clear goals but with members uncertain of how to achieve them. Remember when a group felt a good deal of stress because of an impending deadline or a group grade. At such times a group will gladly follow any leader who can give direction and show them the means to that goal. When the situation changes—that is, when the group feels less uncertain, has less stress, and has less highly structured goals— the group has less of a need for authoritarian leadership and instead needs more participative democratic leadership. To clarify this point, return to the case study.

While Marilyn's style of leadership the first year was appropriate, the situation changed at the end of that year. Employees had reached their goal and replaced it with a much more loosely structured goal—that of continuing what they had been doing. Simultaneously, employees felt less external stress. They no longer operated under the "20 percent ultimatum." Having learned what they had to do as a group to succeed, employees were now ready to attend to their individual needs. They needed a more democratic, people-oriented style of leadership.

Figure 10-1 represents Korten's situational leadership model. The model is applicable even on an international scale. Consider the differences between leadership and goal structure in the Soviet Union and in the United States. The Soviets have been seeking a new way of life that they as yet have not attained, therefore their goals are structured, concrete, and operational. By contrast, Americans focus on maintaining processes rather than on changing them. The relationship of these goals to leadership styles in the two countries is obvious.

A coach who is respected, well liked, and trusted by his team usually has little trouble motivating players.

In the case study above, if Marilyn is to lead effectively, she has two basic options. She can either change her leadership style and encourage more participation from her employees (more process, less task); or she can continue her authoritarian style by creating new stress or the illusion of stress. The latter solution may seem unethical, but it is not uncommonly used.

A Contingency Model of Leadership Effectiveness

After fifteen years of examining over sixteen hundred small groups, Fred Fiedler developed a theory of leadership effectiveness that relates a group's effectiveness to the situational variables that enable a leader to exert influence. His major finding was this: Most people are effective leaders in some situations and ineffective in others. Fiedler related two leadership styles ("task-oriented" and "relationship-oriented") to three situational variables (leader-member relations, task structure, and position power). Defining leadership, then, involves looking at a leader's situational control. A good deal of control gives people the feeling that they can get what they want. If they want to accomplish a task, then they need to concern themselves with successfully completing a job. They feel insecure when the task outcome is uncertain. What makes a leader certain that a job will be done? The leader must answer three important questions: (1) "Will group members do what I tell them; are they reliable, and do they support me?" (2) "Do I know what I am supposed to do and how the job is to be done?" (3) "Do I have the support and backing of the 'big boss' and the organization in dealing with subordinates?[6]

Figure 10-2   Determinants of Situational Control

	1	2	3	4	5	6	7	8
Leader-Member Relations		GOOD				BAD		
Task Structure	HIGH		LOW		HIGH		LOW	
Leader Position Power	Strong	Weak	Strong	Weak	Strong	Weak	Strong	Weak

Figure 10-2 describes the ways in which situational control may be related to the three situational variables.[7]

Leader-member relations is the most influential dimension of situational control. A leader liked, respected, and trusted by group members has little trouble exerting influence in that group.

Task structure ranks second in importance. Fiedler observed that organizations form most groups to perform tasks. Since organizations have large stakes in the successes or failures of groups, they can get groups to comply with their objectives by giving group leaders standard sets of operating instructions to follow, or step-by-step ways of tackling problems. According to Fiedler:

> One important feature of the highly programmed or structured task is that the organization through the leader can maintain quality control over the process and over group behavior at every step. This also enables the organization to back up the leader whenever someone gets out of line. In effect, by structuring the task the organization is able to provide the leader with power, irrespective of the power of the position which he may occupy.[8]

Position power is the least influential of Fiedler's three determinants of situational control. Fiedler cautions students that they must not view this hierarchy as being "eternally fixed." Large differences in rank or status may outweigh task structure in some situations; however, these situations are considered exceptions to the rule.

The model in Figure 10-2 describes all possible combinations of conditions along these three dimensions. Cell 1, indicating all dimensions high, represents the most situational control. Cell 8, with all dimensions low, represents the least situational control. The intervening cells, particularly 4 and 5, describe situations of intermediate situational control.

Fiedler researched and described the relationship between leadership style and situational control in terms of a leader's motivations. As pointed out earlier in the chapter, most people are primarily motivated by either task concerns or maintenance concerns. Different group members usually perform these two functions. Fiedler identified individuals who were primarily motivated by task concerns and those who were primarily motivated by human relations. Then he studied the different individuals' effectiveness as leaders in situations of varying favorableness. Here is what he found:

> Leaders who are task motivated and task-controlling perform best under conditions that are very favorable or are relatively unfavorable for them. Considerate, relationship-motivated leaders perform best under conditions that are intermediate in favorableness.[9]

In other words, if you are highly task-oriented and authoritarian, you are likely to be most effective as a leader in groups with very favorable or very unfavorable situations. Consider an unfavorable situation such as a fire in a theater. A leader considerate of the feelings and attitudes of the audience, who will not act before discussing decisions with the group, is not going to gain a great deal of esteem from the panicking crowd. Rather, the people need decisive, authoritarian direction: "Let's get out of here! Follow me!" In a highly favorable situation where leader-member relations are strong, the task is clear-cut, and the leader has a position of authority, the task-motivated leader is operating under optimum conditions because the group is ready to work.

In the intermediate range of situational favorableness a process-oriented democratic leader is most effective. With weak position power, leaders' influence must be based on the respect group members hold for them. Democratic leaders are more likely to gain respect. Groups with poor leader-member relations or confusion over tasks need the confidence and cohesiveness that democratic leadership can foster. Again, when a situation is so bad that it appears hopeless, strong, authoritarian leadership saves a group.

In his contingency model, Fiedler suggests that while people are primarily motivated by task or process concerns, they are secondarily motivated by whichever concern is not their primary concern. If Harold is a real taskmaster as a leader and finds himself with a task that is easily accomplished, he can then be more congenial toward his workers and satisfy both his primary and secondary needs. Harold will be satisfied *and* effective. If Wanda finds herself in a group with relationship problems, she can satisfy her process motivational needs by helping resolve conflicts and then, secondarily, helping accomplish the group's task.

People are motivated by both task and process concerns, but one of the two is a primary motivation. Highly task-oriented individuals seem to function best in highly favorable or unfavorable situations, while more process-oriented individuals are more effective in situations of intermediate favorableness. Matching style to situation allows people to fulfill their motivation needs in order of their primacy.

You can use Fiedler's theory and research to assess the situation in which you are working, to determine the leadership style that will be most effective. Of course, changing your personality is no easy task, but often you can bring about changes in the situation that will help you become a more effective leader. In situations where you know you are not effective, you can lend your support to those in the group who are best equipped to deal with the situation. Furthermore, at times in your life you may have to appoint a group leader. Fiedler's theory can help you select the most appropriate person for the job.

Hersey and Blanchard's Situational Model

Like other situational leadership theories, Hersey and Blanchard's model uses various combinations of task and relationship-oriented leadership behavior to describe leadership style as it relates to different situations.[10] In this case, the maturity of the group is the situational variable.

Take a few minutes to examine their model in Figure 10-3. Note that the two axes of the model represent the now-familiar task and relationship (process) dimensions of leadership behavior, reflecting different leaders' orientations. Both dimensions can be high in concern for task and relationship, both can be low, or one can be high and one low. To these various combinations Hersey and Blanchard gave the terms *telling, selling, participating,* and *delegating.* A telling style is extremely directive. A selling style is also directive, but a leader is concerned that the group accept and internalize orders given. A participating style is driven primarily by concern for relationships and a need for all group members to share in decision making. In a delegating style a leader takes a hands-off attitude and allows the group to direct itself.

According to Hersey and Blanchard, these four leadership styles are more or less appropriate depending on a group's maturity. As groups mature, effective leadership allows for more autonomy. "Just as parents should relinquish control as a function of the increasing maturity of their children, so too should leaders share more decision-making power as their subordinates acquire greater experience with and commitment to their tasks."[11]

Communication scholar Sarah Trenholm offers the following example of how the theory might apply to a classroom:

> Consider teaching style as a form of leadership. Hersey and Blanchard would suggest that at the beginning of a course of study, with inexperienced students, a highly directive telling style is best. The teacher who tells a freshman class, "You decide what and how you want to learn. It's entirely up to you," is using a delegating style, which will fail, because at this point, students are not yet ready to take full responsibility for their own learning. As the course progresses, however, and as the students feel more comfortable with the course and each other, the teacher might use selling and participating styles, and perhaps end up with a delegating approach. More mature students may be ready for autonomy and may even resent being told what to do.[12]

The Hersey and Blanchard model is widely used in training managers and executives, probably because it shows how managers can change styles according to their subordinates' maturity level. A delegating style can be used with one employee or group and a telling style with another.[13]

Some Observations on the Situational Approach to Leadership

At first glance, the situational approach seems to cover all bases. It looks at the style, task needs, process needs, and situational variables that influence groups. Unfortunately, most research utilizing this approach has focused on the behavior of leaders rather than on leadership as a process of realizing group goals.[14] Thus,

Figure 10-3   Hersey and Blanchard's Situational Leadership Model

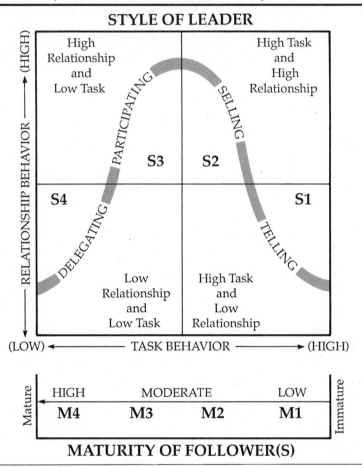

STYLE OF LEADER

	High Relationship and Low Task	High Task and High Relationship
	PARTICIPATING S3	SELLING S2
S4		S1
DELEGATING	Low Relationship and Low Task	High Task and Low Relationship TELLING

RELATIONSHIP BEHAVIOR ⟶ (HIGH)

(LOW) ◀———— TASK BEHAVIOR ————▶ (HIGH)

Mature	HIGH	MODERATE		LOW	Immature
	M4	M3	M2	M1	

MATURITY OF FOLLOWER(S)

From Paul Hersey and Kenneth Blanchard. *Management of Organizational Behavior: Utilizing Human Resources,* 4th ed. Englewood Cliffs, New Jersey: Prentice-Hall, 1982. Reprinted by permission.

while the situational approach is useful, it is, perhaps, not as helpful to the student of small group communication as is the functional approach. Achieving a group goal involves everyone in the group, not just the leader. Students and scholars continue to be concerned over the influence group members' verbal and nonverbal statements have on group goals.

EMERGENT LEADERSHIP IN SMALL GROUPS

A fascinating series of leadership studies begun at the University of Minnesota (called the Minnesota Studies) sought the answer to the question: "Who is most likely to emerge as the perceived leader of a leaderless discussion group?" Led by

Professor Ernest Bormann, the Minnesota Studies formed and observed "test-tube groups" that engaged in leaderless group discussions.

Most people think of a leader as someone who takes charge and organizes a discussion. Predictably, group members often perceive as leaders those who actively participate in the group and who direct comunication toward procedural matters. While studies show a clear correlation between perceived leadership and talkativeness, especially task-oriented talkativeness,[15] those who talk most are not the only ones who become leaders in leaderless groups. In fact, most groups do not select leaders at all. The Minnesota Studies show that leaders emerge through a method of residues in which group members are rejected until only one remains. The first members to go are the quiet ones who do not actively participate in the early stages of a group's discussion. The next to go are the talkative but overaggressive or dogmatic group members who are perceived to be too inflexible for leadership positions.

After this initial phase of elimination, a group enters a second phase in which roughly half the group members remain in contention for the leadership role. This phase moves much more slowly than the first phase, and it is a good deal more painful and frustrating. One by one, the group rejects contenders until only one or two remain. Often, members reject would-be leaders because their style is perceived as disturbing. In the Minnesota Studies' classroom discussion groups, members often rejected an authoritarian style on the grounds that the person was "too bossy" or "dictatorial." Of course, some people may consider the authoritarian style inappropriate in a classroom discussion group, but they may consider it highly appropriate in other situations, especially those that involve extreme stress. In this second phase of role emergence the Minnesota Studies also found that, to some extent, groups with two or more men rejected female contenders. Groups containing only one man often selected a female leader and isolated the man—a pattern that may be changing.

Task-motivated group members often rejected a contender who was perceived as too process-oriented—that is, too concerned about everyone's feelings and moods to be decisive. Likewise, process-oriented members tended to reject those they saw as too concerned with the task.

According to Bormann:

> In the final analysis groups accepted the contender who provided the optimum blend of task efficiency and personal consideration. The leader who emerged was the one that others thought would be of most value to the entire group and whose orders and directions they trusted and could follow.[16]

The Minnesota Studies give fascinating insight into the process through which group leaders emerge. While this information doesn't tell you how to behave in order to rise to leadership positions, it does alert you to the process through which such things take place. These studies also highlight the complexity of small groups and explain, to an extent, why a person who assumes a leadership role in one group may not do so in another and why a person who is perceived to be a leader in two groups may not assume the same role in each.

LEADERSHIP TRAINING

Research consistently indicates that the productivity of a group improves if its members are trained.[17] **Training** involves instruction to develop skills. Whereas most of the instruction you receive in university classrooms involves what and how you think, training emphasizes what you can do.

The simplest form of leadership training provides members with feedback on their performance.[18] Evidence suggests that when members receive such feedback, they tend to work harder, particularly when they are being evaluated by an expert.[19] This technique of observation and feedback is the mainstay of most leadership training programs. Whether other group members provide feedback, or an observer or a video monitor does, people need a more objective eye than their own to see what they are doing and how they can do it better. Beyond the basics, leadership training ranges from the simple and inexpensive to the elaborate and expensive. Given the various definitions of leadership outlined in this chapter, training may justifiably encompass any or all of the principles and skills outlined in this book. Often, training will include a **simulation** exercise.

A simulation is a structured exercise that creates conditions that participants might confront outside of the training environment. A simulation provides a context in which participants can experiment with new behaviors without any risks. The war games that are a part of military training are one example of simulation; the conditions of war are re-created so that trainees can try out new behaviors in a situation that is not life threatening. Likewise, many leadership and management training programs re-create conditions of the work environment— through written reports, financial documents, and background information—in which trainees can experiment. Thus simulations are important to leadership training because they add a context that approximates the actual circumstances for which participants are trained.

While most training focuses more on behavior than it does on cognition, good training is multidimensional; that is, it incorporates more than one level of learning. Good training should provide you with an expanded set or repertoire of behaviors and the understanding and awareness to make judgments about why, how, and when to use those behaviors. To learn effectively, you need be aware of principles and practice.

LEADERSHIP: PUTTING PRINCIPLE INTO PRACTICE

Leadership, whether viewed as functions distributed throughout a group or as the behavior of a leader, is an interplay among the needs of the group, the needs of individuals within the group, and the ability of a person or persons to meet the needs and expectations of all.

This chapter has presented a variety of theories about leadership. Your attitudes toward leadership affect your behavior in small groups. For example, if you believe that a group leader should be the ultimate boss, you will probably be a bossy leader. This chapter provides you with more realistic and flexible attitudes (and, therefore, behaviors) about group leadership. To review the chapter:

- There are three perspectives to the study of group leadership. The trait approach attempts to identify specific characteristics common to successful leaders. The functional approach views leadership as a set of behaviors that may be shared by all group members. The situational approach relates effective leadership to an interaction between leadership style and a group's situation.
- Three styles of leadership are authoritarian, democratic, and laissez-faire. Each has its benefits and drawbacks. The authoritarian style, for example, may be most efficient in many situations but often results in reduced member satisfaction over a longer period of time.
- Studies made at the University of Minnesota give insight into the way leaders emerge in a leaderless group discussion. These studies suggest that those perceived by other group members to be leaders are not chosen by the group *per se,* but are selected as leaders after a process of elimination.
- Considerable evidence suggests that leadership training improves the productivity of small groups. Most leadership training involves the processes of observation, evaluation, and feedback.

All of the theory and research points to the conclusion that the most effective leadership behavior is that which best meets the needs of the group. Groups have both task and process needs; these and other situational variables determine the most appropriate type of leadership behavior for groups. Here are some suggestions on how to apply what you've learned.

If you are the designated leader or chairperson of a group:

- The rest of the group will have certain expectations of you as leader. For example, they will probably expect you to be particularly influential on matters of procedure. You should meet such expectations.
- Prepare a realistic agenda well in advance and distribute it to all group members. At the meeting, help the group stick to its agenda.
- Analyze the group's situation—its time constraints, goal structure, task structure, stress, leader-member relations, position power, and so on.
- Consider your own orientation toward group work. Are you motivated primarily by task concerns or by people concerns? Some situations call for decisive, authoritarian action. Is this what you're good at? If not, you may want to delegate authority to someone who is more task-oriented, at least until the crisis has passed. Does your concern for task outweigh your concern for group-member relations? You may at times want to follow a laissez-faire leadership style and let members of the group who are person-oriented take

over for a while. Adapt your style to the situation and use the resources of the group to everyone's advantage.

- In an ad hoc group that meets only once or twice, the style of leadership you choose is not nearly as important as it is in a committee that meets regularly over a long period of time. In most long-term situations, a democratic style of leadership is preferable. Provide procedural structure for the group, but encourage as much participation as possible. Increased member participation can breed a better solution.

- Remember that groups have task and process needs. Members need to get the job done, but they also need encouragement, praise, and thanks.

If you are not the designated leader or chairperson of the group:

- While you have less control in this situation because of the different expectations the group has of you, you are still influential. You can still demonstrate leadership behavior.

- Use your knowledge about small group communication—leadership, problem solving, growth, and development—to analyze what is going on in the group. Consider your own strengths as a group member. What roles do you fulfill best in the group? Use your strengths to provide what the group needs and to support those who have other needed skills.

- Occasionally a group suffers a leadership void. This often occurs when leaders are appointed by an outside source or when leaders are elected at the first meeting before group members have a chance to evaluate one another as potential leaders. In these cases, rely on the functional approach, since any member of the group (including yourself) can provide leadership. Watch out for delicate egos. When people don't live up to your expectations, you disapprove of them. In a small group this can result in an attempt to overthrow a leader or in a resentful and ineffectual group climate. Members set aside the group's task while they hassle over who's in charge. Almost invariably, such groups produce unsatisfactory results and bruised egos. For a more effective strategy, work around an ineffectual leader (every rule, of course, has exceptions). Any group member can provide leadership while leaving a leader's self-esteem intact.

- Sometimes a small group contains a wealth of leadership talent. Leadership is not (or should not be) a contest for status and power. Individual goals must be placed behind group goals. Good leaders need good followers and supporters.

In every group the effectiveness of your leadership depends on the situation, your sensitivity to the group's needs, and your ability to adapt your communicative behavior to meet those needs.

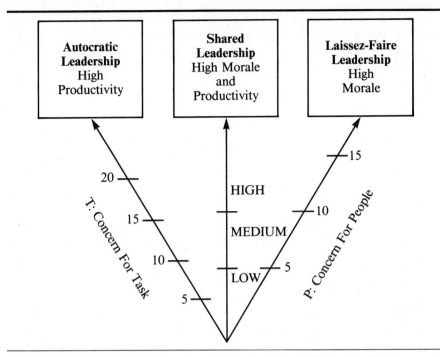

Shared Leadership Results from Balancing Concern for Task and Concern for People

PRACTICE

Task Process Leadership Questionnaire

The following items describe aspects of leadership behavior. Respond to each according to the way you would most likely act if you were the leader of a group. Circle whether you would most likely behave in the described way: always (A), frequently (F), occasionally (O), seldom (S), or never (N).[20]

A F O S N   1. I would most likely act as the spokesperson of the group.

A F O S N   2. I would encourage overtime work.

A F O S N   3. I would allow members complete freedom in their work.

A F O S N   4. I would encourage the use of uniform procedures.

A F O S N   5. I would permit members to use their own judgment in solving problems.

A F O S N   6. I would stress being ahead of competing groups.

A	F	O	S	N	7.	I would speak as a representative of the group.
A	F	O	S	N	8.	I would needle members for greater effort.
A	F	O	S	N	9.	I would try out my ideas in the group.
A	F	O	S	N	10.	I would let the members do their work the way they think best.
A	F	O	S	N	11.	I would be working hard for a promotion.
A	F	O	S	N	12.	I would tolerate postponement and uncertainty.
A	F	O	S	N	13.	I would speak for the group if visitors were present.
A	F	O	S	N	14.	I would keep the work moving at a rapid pace.

Leadership Exercises

1. Observe a working group and analyze the situation from the perspective of Fiedler's contingency model. What type of leadership is most appropriate for this situation? What type of leadership is actually taking place?

2. Consider the stages in problem solving that are described in Chapter Seven. Identify which leadership functions might be the most appropriate at each stage of development.

3. At some time you have probably been in a position of leadership. How does the style of leadership you choose relate to the way you feel about yourself as a person, a leader, or a discussant? How does it relate to the way you feel about groups? Other people? Do you want to assume leadership?

4. Consider the dialogue between Harold and Wanda presented early in this chapter. List five responses that would help the group, and especially Harold and Wanda, resolve the conflict.

Notes

1. A. Paul Hare, *Handbook of Small Group Research,* 2nd ed. (New York: The Free Press, 1976).

2. Dane Archer, "The Face of Power: Physical Attractiveness as a Non-Verbal Predictor of Small-Group Stratification," *Proceedings of the 81st Annual Convention of the American Psychological Association* 8, Part 1: 177–178.

3. Hare, p. 278.

4. Dean Barnlund and Franklyn Haiman, *The Dynamics of Discussion* (Boston: Houghton Mifflin Company, 1960), pp. 275–279.

5. Ralph White and Ronald Lippitt, "Leader Behavior and Member Reaction in Three 'Social Climates' " in Darwin Cartwright and Alvin Zander (eds.), *Group Dynamics,* 3rd ed. (New York: Harper and Row, Publishers, 1968), p. 319.

6. Fred E. Fiedler and Joseph E. Garcia, *New Approaches to Effective Leadership: Cognitive Resources and Organizational Performance* (New York: John Wiley and Sons, 1987), p. 52.

7. Adapted from Fred Fiedler, "Personality and Situational Determinants of Leadership Effectiveness" in *Group Dynamics,* Cartwright and Zander (eds.)

8. Fred Fiedler, *A Theory of Leadership Effectiveness* (New York: McGraw-Hill Book Company, 1967), p. 144.

9. Fiedler, "Personality and Situational Determinants of Leadership Effectiveness," p. 372.

10. Paul Hersey and Kenneth Blanchard, *Management of Organizational Behavior: Utilizing Human Resources,* 4th ed. (Englewood Cliffs, New Jersey: Prentice-Hall, 1982).

11. Victor H. Vroom and Arthur G. Jago, *The New Leadership: Managing Participation in Organizations* (Englewood Cliffs, New Jersey: Prentice-Hall, 1988), p. 52.

12. Sarah Trenholm, *Human Communication Theory* (Englewood Cliffs, New Jersey: Prentice-Hall, 1986).

13. Vroom and Jago, p. 52.

14. Dennis Gorman, "Conceptual and Methodological Approaches to the Study of Leadership," *Central States Speech Journal* 21 (Winter 1970): 217–223.

15. J. Kevin Barge, et al. "Relational Competence and Leadership Emergence: An Exploratory Study." Paper presented at the annual conference of the Central States Speech Association, Schaumberg, Illinois, April 14–16, 1988.

16. Ernest Bormann, *Discussion and Group Methods,* 2nd ed. (New York: Harper and Row, Publishers, 1975), p. 256.

17. For a list of studies that support this assertion, see A. Paul Hare, *Handbook of Small Group Research,* 2nd ed. (New York: The Free Press, 1976), p. 354.

18. Rita Spoelde-Claes, "The Effect of Varying Feedback on the Effectiveness of a Small Group on a Physical Task," *Psychologica Belgica* 13 (1): 61–68.

19. Murray Webster, Jr., "Source of Evaluations and Expectations for Performance," *Sociometry* 32 (3): 243–258.

20. The T-P Leadership Questionnaire was adapted from Sergiovanni, Metzcus, and Burden's revision of the Leadership Behavior Description Questionnaire, *American Educational Research Journal* 6 (1969): 62–79.

21. *Ibid.,* p. 12.

—— Chapter Eleven ——

Observing and Evaluating Group Communication

After studying this chapter, you should be able to:

☐ Explain the relationship between group communication theory and systematic observation of small group phenomena.

☐ Describe three classes of observational systems and the circumstances under which each is appropriate.

☐ Record group interaction with an interaction diagram, apply one or more category systems, and interpret the results.

☐ Use at least two self-report instruments to measure role perceptions and group cohesiveness.

☐ Explain why self-report measures can be helpful to a group.

☐ Observe, record, and interpret group interaction using Bales' Interaction Process Analysis.

☐ Observe and evaluate group leadership using one of the systems presented in this chapter.

☐ Design and implement a post-meeting reaction sheet.

$\mathbf{B}$y reading the first ten chapters of this book and by participating in classroom activities you have learned about a variety of factors that contribute to effective communication in small groups. You have learned what you need to observe in studying small group communication; now you will learn how to observe these variables in a systematic way. Having such knowledge can benefit both you and the small groups in which you participate. While few of you will become serious theorists and researchers of small group communication, all of you will find ample opportunity to apply your knowledge and skills. What you have learned so far should make you more sensitive to the dynamics that affect small group communication. The material presented in this chapter will provide you with a way to validate your observations, thereby giving you an additional tool with which to help your groups. For example, if you see a particular communication network or distribution of roles emerging in a group, making an interaction diagram and applying a category system can confirm your observations and offer you a means of recording changes in those patterns over time. If terms like *interaction diagram* and *category system* are new to you, read on.

THEORY AND OBSERVATION: A NATURAL RELATIONSHIP

As pointed out in Chapter Two, building theories is a basic human process that takes place whenever people try to make sense of the events and phenomena surrounding them. Theories are explanations that can lead people to more successful predictions. Theories reduce uncertainty. This book has presented a lot of theoretical material: theories about group formation, growth and development; theories about leadership effectiveness; theories about conflict and "groupthink," and so forth. These theories give you a way of breaking down group process into constituent elements and some guidance in analyzing the relationships among them. Before you took this course you were, no doubt, aware of the frustrations of working in small groups, but you did not have the tools to explain what was happening. Now you do. Theories serve as tools to explain—they are observation systems unto themselves. Once you have a theoretical description of small groups you no longer look at group phenomena, you look *for* them. Your theoretical understanding guides your practical observations. In essence, then, this entire book has been devoted to enhancing your skills in observing and evaluating communication in small groups. Each chapter has taken one or more components of group process and has theoretically described how these components combine to enhance or detract from group effectiveness.

This chapter will provide you with some tools with which you can validate the observations you make. Some of these tools you can readily use during any small group meeting; others require more preparation and structure. All of these tools will enable you to describe systematically many of the variables discussed in this book as they apply to working groups.

OBSERVING COMMUNICATION NETWORKS: INTERACTION DIAGRAMS

Chapter Five suggested that communication networks—who talks to whom—have an effect on group cohesiveness, leadership patterns, and group productivity. A few minutes spent observing small group interaction can show you clearly that members infrequently address the group as a whole; instead, they tend to address specific group members. An **interaction diagram** can reveal a lot about the interaction patterns in your group. It tells you who is talking to whom and how often. You can identify the most active and the more reticent members. You can pattern the relationships that form between group members. By combining an interaction diagram with a **category system**, you can recognize the contributions each member makes to the group. Interaction diagrams are extremely useful tools. Here's how to make one:

1. Draw a circle for each member of the group, arranging your circles in the same relative positions as that in which group members are seated (Figure 11-1).
2. Refer to Figure 11-1. If Nancy were to open the meeting by asking Phil for the minutes from the last meeting, you would draw an arrow from Nancy's circle to Phil's, indicating the direction and destination of Nancy's communication. Each subsequent remark made by Nancy to Phil would then be indicated by a short crossmark at the base of the arrow.
3. Repeat this process each time someone in the group addresses someone else. If Phil were to address the minutes to Nancy, you would put an arrowhead at the other end of the line that connects the two.
4. Indicate communication addressed to the group as a whole with a line pointing away from the center of the group. Again, note subsequent remarks with crossmarks.
5. Figure 11-2 is an example of what a completed interaction diagram might look like.

If you take a few moments to examine Figure 11-2, you will see some patterns beginning to emerge. For example, Phil seems to be the most vocal member of the group. Furthermore, most members address their remarks to Phil, which suggests

Figure 11-1   Interaction Diagram

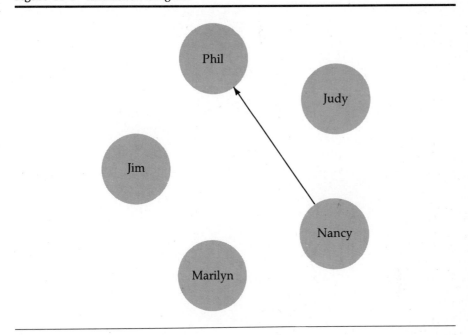

that they perceive Phil to be the group's leader. The frequency with which Phil addresses the group as a whole supports this observation. The amount of communication between Phil and Jim indicates a strong relationship there, perhaps that of a leader and his "lieutenant."

The interaction diagram is an easy way to describe graphically the interaction patterns in a group. Also, this method of observation can be used without seriously disrupting the regular workings of the group. By updating the interaction diagram during several meetings, you can observe changes in group interaction and, as we shall soon see, the addition of a category system to the interaction diagram renders this a most powerful descriptive tool.

OBSERVING GROUP CLIMATE

Groups tend to be more cohesive when all members participate actively. The interaction diagram is a way to measure this dynamic and a good deal more. If you apply a **category system** to the interaction diagram you can make some observations about the content of the communication in addition to measuring its amount and direction.

As noted earlier, interaction categories are classifications of behavior in which your various communicative attempts may fall. Chapter Five introduced you to two such systems: Gibb's categories of defensive and supportive communication

Figure 11-2 Completed Interaction Diagram

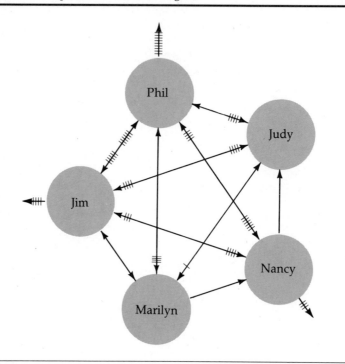

and Sieburg's categories of confirming and disconfirming responses. Consider Sieburg's categories and see how they might be used in conjunction with an interaction diagram.

Confirming and Disconfirming Responses

As you may recall, Sieburg described the types of responses that cause people either to value themselves more or to value themselves less. Clearly understanding these "confirming" and "disconfirming" typologies can assist you in improving a group's climate. After all, when people treat you in ways that devalue you, they don't exactly create warmth and friendship between you. If a group has little cohesiveness, if members feel little interpersonal trust, and if the group is going nowhere, the ways in which members respond to one another may be to blame. You can use Sieburg's system for charting interpersonal responses in the group to find out.

If you wanted to analyze this phenomenon in detail, you could videotape a group in action and carefully analyze each interpersonal response according to Sieburg's system. More informally, you can note types of responses on an interaction diagram as they occur.

The first step in this endeavor is to become thoroughly familiar with the different kinds of responses so that you can recognize them. Secondly, as you draw

Figure 11-3   Interaction Diagram

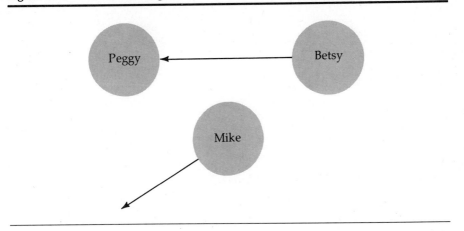

the interaction diagram, take note of types of responses and keep a list of them next to the circle representing the person who elicited each response. For example:

Mike: Well gang, I stayed up all night working on the problem and I think I've finally figured out a way to rig the boat to get that extra wind power we need to win the race this weekend.

Betsy: Peggy, did you get around to pricing those new winches we need for the foredeck?

In Figure 11-4, note that Betsy's "impervious response" is recorded next to Mike's name. This may seem a bit illogical at first, but there's good reason for it. Sieburg's theory describes the effects of Betsy's "impervious response" on Mike. If you are going to examine the group's cohesiveness or morale, you need to look at particular communicative behaviors in terms of their effects on the receivers of those acts.

There's another good reason for recording confirming and disconfirming responses in this way. Imagine that at a group meeting a member is busily taking notes and drawing interaction diagrams. Toward the end of the meeting, he reports that he would like to provide the group with a little feedback. He presents his interaction diagram, then turns to you and says, "I don't suppose that you were aware that you gave three tangential responses, one impervious response, two irrelevant responses, and interrupted others eleven times?" How would you feel? A bit defensive, eh?

By focusing attention on the receivers of disconfirming responses, you can identify behaviors that may be detrimental to the group climate without attacking the *senders.* If you openly criticize others, you are likely to increase defensiveness in the group. Many people inadvertently disconfirm other group members' responses. They interrupt and often fail to acknowledge what others have said before

Figure 11-4 Interaction Diagram with Categories

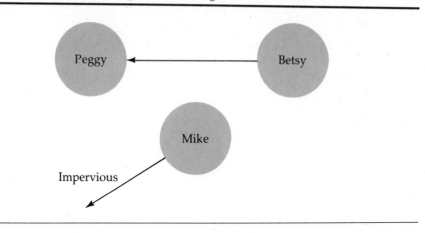

throwing in their two cents. Someone in the group should bring these behaviors to the attention of those who commit them, but those people should not be openly criticized. Note, however, that at times, with the group's consent, you might benefit from identifying confirming or disconfirming behaviors with those who show them.

Many category systems may be used effectively with interaction diagrams. If you suspect a problem in your group, such a system provides tangible evidence for the group and detaches you from your observations—important considerations if you don't want your group to respond defensively to you. Be careful, though, not to cast yourself as an outsider. If you are a part of the group you are observing, use observational systems only with the group's consent. Then, with the information you provide, the group can achieve greater insight into its process and, ideally, can communicate more effectively.

OBSERVING ROLES AND ROLE PERCEPTIONS

Chapter Four and Chapter Ten discussed the importance of role formation, role perceptions, role expectations, role enactment, and role behaviors as leadership functions. This section will describe some methodologies for clarifying role behavior in small groups: Group Role Inventory and Benne and Sheats's categories of Functional Roles.

Group Role Inventory

When you see yourself differently from the way others see you, when there is a difference between role perception and role enactment, and when your expectations of people cloud your perceptions of them, there is a potential source of uncertainty, confusion, frustration, and conflict. The Group Role Inventory was designed to help members become more aware of the roles they play and of how others perceive those roles. It is time-consuming—it takes at least forty-five minutes—but often worth the time and effort it takes, particularly when a group is having trouble establishing norms. The Group Role Inventory can also be an effective means for dealing with one or two problem members by bringing everyone's role expectations into the discussion rather than by ganging up on the troublemakers.

Objectives:	To become aware of the roles you play in your group and of how others perceive your roles
Materials:	Group Role Inventory Sheet (attached)
Time:	Forty-five minutes
Participants:	Ongoing groups
Procedures:	1) Fill out Group Role Inventory Sheet.
	2) Go over the list and check the role you would like to have performed but did not perform.
	3) Go over the list again and star (*) the role you performed but would rather not have performed.
	4) Discuss results with your group.
Application:	The exercise should make members aware of how roles are used in their groups.

Group Role Inventory Sheet

Who in your group, including yourself, is most likely to:

1. Take initiative, propose ideas, get things started?
2. Set back and wait passively for others to lead?
3. Express feelings most freely, frankly, openly?
4. Keep feelings hidden, reserved, unexpressed?
5. Show understanding of other members' feelings?
6. Be wrapped up in personal concerns and not very responsive to others?
7. Interrupt others when they are speaking?
8. Daydream, be lost in private thoughts during group sessions, be "far away"?
9. Give you a feeling of encouragement, warmth, friendly interest, support?
10. Converse privately with someone else while another member is speaking to the group?
11. Talk of trivial things, superficial chitchat?
12. Criticize you, put you on your guard?
13. Feel superior to other members?
14. Be listened to by everyone while speaking?
15. Feel inferior to other members?

16. Contribute good ideas?
17. Contradict, disagree, argue, raise objections?
18. Sulk or withdraw when the group is displeasing?
19. Be the one you would like to have on your side if a conflict arose in the group?
20. Agree or conform with whatever is said?
21. Be missed, if absent, more than any other member?

Functional Roles

If you consider leadership as behaviors distributed throughout a group, you should be able to observe group interaction and identify leadership roles. Such observations can help you pinpoint which leadership roles are being filled and which are not, thus showing how leadership roles function in relation to a group's purpose or task.

Kenneth D. Benne and Paul Sheats designed a category system that was discussed in Chapters Four and Ten. Their system includes *group task roles, group building and maintenance roles,* and *individual roles.*[1] Used alone or in conjunction with an interaction diagram, these categories of functional roles are powerful observational tools.

OBSERVING GROUP COHESIVENESS

Self-Report Measure: A Cohesiveness Index

As stated in Chapter Five, cohesiveness is often described as the attraction a group holds for its members. You can measure this variable by asking individual group members to describe their feelings toward a group. Self-report measures are easy to design and can provide a great deal of useful information. Table 11-1, Seashore's Index of Group Cohesiveness, exemplifies the self-report methodology.[2]

OBSERVING GROUP INTERACTION

A widely-used and time-tested scheme for observing group interaction is the Interaction Process Analysis (IPA), designed by Robert Bales in 1950. While the IPA was originally intended for formal, empirical research application, it can be adapted readily for more informal group observation. Bales's category scheme consists of twelve classes of statements that fall into four general types: positive reactions, attempted answers, questions, and negative reactions. Use the Interaction Process Analysis by observing group interaction, counting the number of statements that fall into each category and analyzing the data as it applies to that group's phase of development in the problem-solving process. As with the use of interaction diagrams and category systems, Bales's Interaction Process Analysis can reveal a great deal about the structure of small group communication.

Table 11-1   Seashore Index of Group Cohesiveness

Check one response for each question.

1. Do you feel that you are really a part of your work group?
_____ Really a part of my work group
_____ Included in most ways
_____ Included in some ways, but not in others
_____ Don't feel I really belong
_____ Don't work with any one group of people
_____ Not ascertained

2. If you had a chance to do the same kind of work for the same pay in another group, how would you feel about moving?
_____ Would want very much to move
_____ Would rather move than stay where I am
_____ Would make no difference to me
_____ Would want very much to stay where I am
_____ Not ascertained

3. How does your work group compare with other similar groups on each of the following points?

	Better than most	About the same as most	Not as good as most	Not ascertained
a. The way the members get along together	_____	_____	_____	_____
b. The way the members stick together	_____	_____	_____	_____
c. The way the members help each other on the job	_____	_____	_____	_____

Interaction Process Analysis

Table 11-2 lists Bales's categories of interaction.[3] These categories are only part of a complete Interaction Process Analysis, but they are sufficient for most informal uses.

As mentioned earlier, Bales's categories can be used informally to record and analyze interaction patterns in groups. Goldberg and Larson describe a simple but effective way of doing so:

> For simple class-related activities, you can develop a form sheet to record your observations. List the twelve basic categories down the left-hand margin of a sheet. Draw vertical lines down the sheet so that a series of columns is present. Number the columns consecutively at the top of the sheet. When completed, the sheet will consist of a large matrix, the rows defined by the twelve categories and the columns numbered across the top. Each column may be used to record a single interaction unit. When the scoring is completed, the sequence of the interaction units will be recorded and numbered in keeping with the columns. Usually, members are identified by code numbers, from one to N. Who speaks to whom can be recorded simply by a series

Table 11-2   Bales's Interaction Categories

Positive Reactions	1. Shows solidarity, raises others' status, gives help, rewards 2. Shows tension release, jokes, laughs, shows satisfaction 3. Shows agreement, shows passive acceptance, understands, concurs, complies
Attempted Answers	4. Gives suggestion, direction, implying autonomy for others 5. Gives opinion, evaluation, analysis, expresses feeling, wish 6. Gives information, orientation, repeats, clarifies, confirms
Questions	7. Asks for information, orientation, repetition, confirmation 8. Asks for opinion, evaluation, analysis, expression of feeling 9. Asks for suggestion, direction, possible ways of action
Negative Reactions	10. Disagrees, shows passive rejection, formality, withholds help 11. Shows tension, asks for help, withdraws out of field 12. Shows antagonism, deflates others' status, defends or asserts self

of coupled numbers. Remarks addressed by members to the group as a whole are indicated by a zero. Thus, 2–0 would refer to group member number 2 addressing the group as a whole.

Whether a group progresses through certain phases in problem solving, whether task and social-emotional behaviors are balanced or disproportionate, whether certain members disproportionately engage in specific forms of behavior, whether specific member's behavior vary with respect to the problem phase (orientation, evaluation, control, etc.) through which the group is progressing, whether certain members talk disproportionately to certain other members, whether group interaction assumes a particular form or pattern following decision proposals, and many other questions may be explored tentatively on the basis of your analysis and observation of member behaviors conforming to these twelve basic categories.[4]

Clearly, the use of Bales's Interaction Process Analysis can yield a great deal of information about a group's processes—information that can help you understand small group communication and attempt to make it better.

OBSERVING GROUP LEADERSHIP

The ability to lead a small group is, to a large extent, the ability to communicate effectively, to send and receive messages clearly and without disruption, to channel, focus, and interpret the communication of others so that the meanings of messages are shared by all, and to help a group avoid "anything that needlessly inflates the time and energy required to exchange meanings."[5] When you observe and evaluate leadership, then, you are analyzing the quality of communication in a small group. This section presents two rating scales, which are particularly valuable for measuring leadership in that they go beyond the descriptive properties of category systems

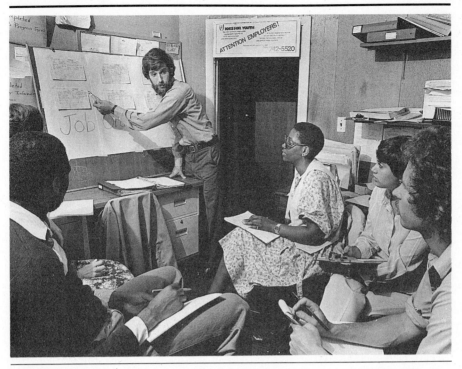

In small groups the ability to lead involves communicating effectively, being able to focus the discussion, and being able to interpret the communication of others.

by including an evaluative component that is essential for measuring the quality of communication. One scale, the Barnlund-Haiman Leadership Rating Scale, appears in Table 11-3.[6]

Leadership Rating Scale

Table 11-3 Barnlund-Haiman Leadership Rating Scale

Instructions: This rating scale may be used to evaluate leadership in groups with or without official leaders. In the latter case (the leaderless group) use part A of each item only. When evaluating the actions of an official leader use parts A and B of each item on the scale.

Influence in Procedure

Initiating Discussion

A.	3	2	1	0	1	2	3

Group needed more help in getting started		Group got right amount of help			Group needed less help in getting started

B.   The quality of the introductory remarks was:

Excellent	Good	Adequate	Fair	Poor

Organizing Group Thinking

A.   3   2   1   0   1   2   3

Group needed more direction in thinking		Group got right amount of help		Group needed less direction in thinking	

B.   If and when attempts were made to organize group thinking they were:

Excellent	Good	Adequate	Fair	Poor

Clarifying Communication

A.   3   2   1   0   1   2   3

Group needed more help in clarifying communication		Group got right amount of help		Group needed less help in clarifying communication	

B.   If and when attempts were made to clarify communication they were:

Excellent	Good	Adequate	Fair	Poor

Summarizing and Verbalizing Agreements

A.   3   2   1   0   1   2   3

Group needed more help in summarizing and verbalizing agreements		Group got right amount of help		Group needed less help in summarizing and verbalizing agreements	

B.   If and when attempts were made to summarize and verbalize agreements they were:

Excellent	Good	Adequate	Fair	Poor

Resolving Conflict

A.   3   2   1   0   1   2   3

Group needed more help in resolving conflict		Group got right amount of help		Group needed less help in resolving conflict	

B.   If and when attempts were made to resolve conflict they were:

Excellent	Good	Adequate	Fair	Poor

Influence in Creative and Critical Thinking

Stimulating Critical Thinking

A.   3   2   1   0   1   2   3

Group needed more stimulation in creative thinking		Group got right amount of help		Group needed less stimulation in creative thinking	

B.   If and when attempts were made to stimulate ideas they were:

Excellent	Good	Adequate	Fair	Poor

Encouraging Criticism

A.	3	2	1	0	1	2	3

Group needed more encouragement to be critical	Group got right amount of help	Group needed less encouragement to be critical

B.   If and when attempts were made to encourage criticism they were:

Excellent	Good	Adequate	Fair	Poor

Balancing Abstract and Concrete Thought

A.	3	2	1	0	1	2	3

Group needed to be more concrete	Group achieved proper balance	Group needed to be more abstract

B.   If and when attempts were made to balance abstract and concrete thought they were:

Excellent	Good	Adequate	Fair	Poor

Influence in Interpersonal Relations

Climate-Making

A.	3	2	1	0	1	2	3

Group needed more help in securing a permissive atmosphere	Group got right amount of help	Group needed less help in securing a permissive atmosphere

B.   If and when attempts were made to establish a permissive atmosphere they were:

Excellent	Good	Adequate	Fair	Poor

Regulating Participation

A.	3	2	1	0	1	2	3

Group needed more regulation of participation	Group got right amount of help	Group needed less regulation of participation

B.   If and when attempts were made to regulate participation they were:

Excellent	Good	Adequate	Fair	Poor

Over-all Leadership

A.	3	2	1	0	1	2	3

Group needed more control	Group got right amount of control	Group needed less control

B.   If and when attempts were made to control the group they were:

Excellent	Good	Adequate	Fair	Poor

Feedback Rating Instrument

Dale Leathers has designed a somewhat more complex scale to measure the quality of communication in a group. This scale, or instrument, examines feedback to determine whether "one's messages seem to produce confusion or tension or inflexibility or all three." It is based on the assumption that "effectiveness and efficient communication in discussion demand that the sender of a message receive feedback of maximum 'self-correcting' potential if the sender is to possess the flexibility of response so necessary in small group communication."[7] The basic unit to be observed is the "feedback event," usually a complete utterance by an individual group member that is immediately preceded and followed by statements from another group member.

> Georgette: I've been trying to figure out what the company's policy is on this issue, so I went and spoke with the first vice president.
> Roger   (facetiously): I'll bet *that* was an enlightening experience.
> Georgette: C'mon, Roger, you're not being fair to him.

The statements above constitute feedback. Roger's facetious remark is feedback to Georgette. When you look at Georgette's first statement, Roger's feedback, and Georgette's second statement, you can see a disruptive effect. Whatever it was that Georgette was going to say to the group was thwarted. Examining feedback events allows you to see their immediate effects on small group communication.

Leathers's Feedback Rating Instrument assumes that every feedback response has nine dimensions: (1) deliberateness, (2) relevancy, (3) atomization, (4) fidelity, (5) tension, (6) ideation, (7) flexibility, (8) digression, and (9) involvement. Definitions of these terms are provided on the scales in Table 11-4.[8]

In order to use the nine scales, you must approach a discussion with a strategy for selecting feedback responses to evaluate. In an ongoing group one strategy might be to rate the feedback responses of individual members over time. In a one-time observation, you might select every Nth feedback response to evaluate.

EVALUATING GROUP MEETINGS

An extremely useful tool for providing feedback to a group about its performance and progress is a post-meeting reaction sheet. These can be designed in any way that provides the most useful information for the group or group leader. They take only a few minutes to fill in, and can provide information that can dramatically improve how the group functions. An example follows.

Table 11-4 Leathers's Feedback Rating Instrument

	Symbol			Deliberateness			Signal
Scale #1	3	2	1	0	1	2	3

Symbol response represents a deliberate, carefully reasoned, logical response; signal response represents an immediate, unthinking, largely automatic, visceral response of Y to X.

	Relevant			Relevancy			Irrelevant
Scale #2	3	2	1	0	1	2	3

Relevancy—extent to which Y seeks to establish the connection between X's comment and the comment that immediately preceded X's comment.

	Unified			Atomization			Atomized
Scale #3	3	2	1	0	1	2	3

Degree to which Y's contribution involves incomplete, fragmented, or disjointed thought; includes running a number of ideas together, a number of people talking at the same time.

	Clear			Fidelity			Confused
Scale #4	3	2	1	0	1	2	3

Extent to which Y's response to X exhibits confusion as to the meaning and/or intent of X's original message; characterized by the necessity of Y's seeking clarification, definition, expansion, etc., from X.

	Relaxed			Tension			Tense
Scale #5	3	2	1	0	1	2	3

Degree to which nonverbal gestures like laughter, sighs, groans, etc., indicate Y's relative state of tension or relaxation.

	Ideational			Ideation			Personal
Scale #6	3	2	1	0	1	2	3

Ideational responses involve an appraisal or evaluation of X's ideas; personal responses represent the degree to which Y's comments involve direct or implied criticism of X, as a person.

	Flexible			Flexibility			Inflexible
Scale #7	3	2	1	0	1	2	3

Inflexible response indicates Y's unwillingness to modify his position in response to X's contribution; may include a counterassertion.

	Concise			Digression			Digressive
Scale #8	3	2	1	0	1	2	3

Degree to which Y inhibits X's immediate response, primarily by means of lengthy and discursive utterances.

	Involved			Involvement			Withdrawn
Scale #9	3	2	1	0	1	2	3

Degree to which Y seeks to avoid comment on X's contribution by attempting to withdraw from the discussion of X's contribution.

Post-Meeting Reaction Sheet

Date:

Meeting #

Was the purpose of this meeting understood clearly by all group members? Were all aware of the agenda?

How would you characterize the social climate of this meeting?

Was there relatively equal participation by all group members or did one or two monopolize the discussion?

Was there conflict during this meeting? If so, how well did the group manage it?

Did the group work through its agenda successfully?

Make three suggestions for improving the next meeting.

Any additional comments?

OBSERVING AND EVALUATING GROUP COMMUNICATION: PUTTING PRINCIPLE INTO PRACTICE

This chapter has presented a number of ways in which you can observe, measure, and evaluate small group communication processes. While most of the measures described were developed for the purpose of small group research, they can be extremely helpful in reducing uncertainty about the dynamics of any group. The

"YOU'LL NOTICE THAT WHEN SOME THINGS ARE UP, OTHERS ARE DOWN, AND WHEN THE THINGS THAT ARE UP GO DOWN, THE THINGS THAT ARE DOWN GO UP."

theories, descriptions, and examples throughout this book, and the tools presented in this chapter provide you with knowledge that will help your groups become more effective.

Take a moment before you close the book and return to the model of small group communication presented in Chapter Two. To be understood fully, all of the components of that model—goals, leadership, situation, norms, roles, cohesiveness, and speech communication—need to be seen as interconnected and as mutually influential. By necessity these components have been treated one at a time, but in reality these phenomena occur in unison—either in harmony or in dissonance. They operate all the time: in senate committees, in business offices, in families, over matters of state, over matters of business, and over matters of love.

Use your knowledge well.

PRACTICE

1. Use one of the scales presented in this chapter to observe and evaluate a group discussion (either in or out of class). Compare notes with classmates. What do your findings imply? How do you interpret the results? What recommendations would you make to this group based on your observations?

2. As a group, develop a set of criteria for selecting a measurement instrument to observe and evaluate small group communication. Under what circumstances would you use what method(s)?

3. Observe a live or videotaped group meeting. Then design a post-meeting reaction sheet that you feel would be helpful to the group or the group leader. Be able to explain the observations that led you to your choices of questions.

Notes

1. Kenneth Benne and Paul Sheats, "Functional Roles of Group Members," *Journal of Social Issues* 4 (Spring 1948): 41–49.

2. Stanley Seashore, *Group Cohesiveness in the Industrial Work Group* (Ann Arbor, Michigan: University of Michigan Institute for Social Research, 1954).

3. Robert Bales, *Interaction Process Analysis: A Method for the Study of Small Groups* (Reading, Massachusetts: Addison-Wesley Publishing Company, 1950), p. 59.

4. Alvin A. Goldberg and Carl E. Larson, *Group Communication: Discussion Processes and Applications* (Englewood Cliffs, New Jersey: Prentice-Hall, 1975), pp. 99–100.

5. Halbert E. Gulley and Dale G. Leathers, *Communication and Group Process: Techniques for Improving the Quality of Small-Group Communication,* 3rd ed. (New York: Holt, Rinehart & Winston, 1977), p. 128.

6. Dean C. Barnlund and Franklyn S. Haiman, *The Dynamics of Discussion* (Boston: Houghton Mifflin Company, 1960), pp. 401–404.

7. Gulley and Leathers; pp. 41–42.

8. Dale Leathers, "The Feedback Rating Instrument: A New Means of Evaluating Discussion," *Central States Speech Journal* 22 (Spring 1971): 32–42.

Appendix A:
Conducting Research—
Preparing
for Group Discussion

G.I.G.O. (which stands for "garbage in, garbage out") is an abbreviation that computer programmers use to illustrate that if you put the wrong information into a computer system, you will get the wrong information out of it. A problem-solving group discussion works much the same way. If members have not done their homework—have not researched and analyzed the discussion issues—the results of the discussion will be unsatisfactory. Groups don't accidentally arrive at informed solutions. Those solutions result from group members taking the time to gather facts, examples, statistics, and opinions. Groups whose members come prepared to discuss the issues have effective sessions.

You have probably had lessons in making the best use of a library. Because research is vital to an effective group discussion, this appendix reviews some of the resources and techniques that are available to you when you research and analyze issues facing your group. It will also give you suggestions for conducting your own interviews and surveys.

LIBRARY RESEARCH

By far the majority of questions that lend themselves to group problem solving also lend themselves to library research. Even questions specific to particular locales or institutions can be discussed more intelligently by group members who have researched analogous situations. For example, even though a group discussing the issue "Should Oak Park Community College become a four-year institution?" might not find any library materials about that specific question, it might find a recent magazine article that explores the advantages of a community college over a four-year college, or one that investigates another school's solution to the problem now facing Oak Park. Discussion participants exploring an issue of more widespread significance—for instance, a political, social, or ecological problem— will probably find a good deal of information in a library on their topic. In short, the library is as invaluable to a participant in a small group discussion as it is to an author of a research paper. The knowledge and skills needed to use the library are essential to anyone participating in group problem solving.

While each school's library is unique in some ways, college and university libraries do share common tools and materials. Among these are the card catalog, the stacks, periodical and newspaper indexes and holdings, the reference section, and government documents.

The Card Catalog

A library's card catalog usually consists of rows of file cabinets that contain three-by-five-inch cards, at least one card for every book and pamphlet housed in the library. Cards are arranged alphabetically by title, author, and subject, so most of the library's holdings are represented more than once in the card catalog.

The subject cards will probably be the most valuable to you as you search for information on a specific topic. Before you begin exploring the card catalog, take a few minutes to jot down headings under which you think you might find information related to your subject. Check each of these headings in turn; add to your list any subject headings listed on the library's own "See also" cards, which you may encounter when you locate your headings in the card catalog.

Each card in the catalog contains information about the work to which it refers: the author's name, the title, the publisher, the date of publication, the number of pages, a note or brief outline of the work's contents, and other headings under which the work may be located in the catalog. The call number, marked in the upper left-hand corner of the card, is most important to a researcher trying to find a work. It may be either a Dewey Decimal number or a Library of Congress reference number; in either case, it serves as your key to finding the work on the library's shelves, and you should copy it as you prepare a bibliography.

Three-by-five-inch note cards provide an efficient way to record and later assemble your bibliography. Using one card per source, record the author's name, the title of the work, the publisher, the date of publication, and the call number. Unless you are told by an instructor to record this information in a particular way, simply select and adhere to a style you find logical and easy to use. Remember, you may need to consult these cards several days or even weeks after first recording them; be sure your notations are consistent, legible, and meaningful. Once you have completed a bibliography, you may want to alphabetize the note cards by the authors' last names so that you can quickly locate any given card.

Computer Access System

In addition to the card catalog, many libraries now use computers to help researchers locate library materials. Instead of going to a card file, you (often with a librarian's assistance) type in the research topic or author's name at a computer terminal. The computer screen displays bibliographic information, and you can then decide whether you want a printed copy of the information. Libraries may charge for this service, depending on the amount of information you receive.

The Stacks

The stacks are the library's holdings. A library may have open stacks, in which you find the materials you want, or closed stacks, in which a librarian gathers materials for you. Even in a library with closed stacks, some sections will probably be open to you. There may be an open stack undergraduate library of selected titles, a reference section, periodical and newspaper holdings, and government documents. If any part of the library you are using is open stack, familiarize yourself with the library's floor plan before searching for materials. Most libraries offer floor plan sketches and tours. Keep in mind that materials in even very small libraries will be shelved by call numbers, not alphabetically by author or title.

Periodical and Newspaper Indexes and Holdings

Unless you can remember the name and the date of a periodical or newspaper in which you read an article on your subject, you will probably need to use one of the numerous periodical and newspaper indexes. The most commonly used of these is the *Readers' Guide to Periodical Literature,* an index to articles appearing in approximately one hundred popular periodicals. The *Readers' Guide* provides an alphabetical listing of authors, subjects, and titles of articles. As with the card catalog, the most convenient approach for most researchers is to look up the subject. You may consult the same headings you looked at in the card catalog. A typical *Readers' Guide* entry will include the title of the article, the periodical in which it appears, the volume and date of the issue of the periodical, and the page on which the article begins. Abbreviations, used extensively in the *Readers' Guide,* may be deciphered by consulting the key at the front of each volume. Once you understand the symbols used, you can easily transfer the information from the *Readers' Guide* to your bibliography cards.

Similar to the *Readers' Guide* are the *Social Sciences Index* and the *Humanities Index,* once combined as the *International Index to Periodicals* and later as the *Social Sciences and Humanities Index.* These works index scholarly journals and foreign periodicals not covered by the *Readers' Guide.* You may also find a number of more specialized periodical indexes useful, such as the *Education Index,* which contains articles of interest to professional educators, and the *Public Affairs Information Service Bulletin,* which indexes articles relevant to such fields as business and finance, political science, and the social sciences.

Newspapers, like periodicals, are indexed. The most widely used newspaper index is the *New York Times Index.* Most college libraries will have back issues of the *Times* on microfilm, but even in those that do not, the *New York Times Index* will prove useful. Chances are good that a news story covered in the *Times* was also covered in other major national newspapers, at least one of which your library is likely to have. The *London Times,* the *Christian Science Monitor,* and the *Wall Street Journal* are also indexed. Formats for newspaper indexes are similar to those for periodical indexes.

Each library has its own system for housing periodicals and newspapers. Although very recent editions of newspapers may still be available, back issues are usually kept on microfilm. Periodicals are frequently bound and shelved either together in one section of the library or in various stacks, according to periodical subject matter.

The Reference Section

Most libraries have an open stack reference section that houses encyclopedias; dictionaries; various book, periodical, and newspaper indexes; biographical aids, such as *Who's Who,* the *Dictionary of National Biography,* and *The Directory of American Scholars;* and numerous specialized reference works. Whatever the field of your discussion question, a library is likely to have reference works of potential value to you. Reference librarians usually are highly knowledgeable about their specialty and can be quite helpful; seek their assistance in locating reference tools relevant to your subject.

Government Documents

Like reference works, government documents are usually found in one section of a library. Although they can appear formidable to the inexperienced researcher, they are extremely valuable sources of information on many topics. Among the public documents available in most libraries are the *Congressional Record,* which records congressional debates and proceedings; various special reports and hearings of both the U.S. Senate and the House of Representatives; and bulletins and publications of various executive departments of the U.S. government. Indexes that may help you locate relevant government publications include *The Catalogue of the Public Documents of Congress and of All Departments of the Government of the United States* and the *Monthly Catalogue of United States Government Publications.* In addition, libraries usually maintain special card catalogs for their government documents. As with books, periodicals, and newspapers, transfer bibliographical information to your own bibliography cards so that you have a permanent record of the sources you discover.

While this discussion by no means exhaustively lists the ways in which a library may assist you in researching a discussion question, it may serve to remind you of sources you might not otherwise have consulted. Even small college libraries can offer you a wealth of resources if you are willing to explore them.

There are other approaches to researching a problem besides using a library. Some groups may take surveys or conduct interviews to investigate their problems. The following sections look at these two research approaches.

SURVEY RESEARCH

Survey research is useful when a group wants to sample several individuals' attitudes, beliefs, values, behavior, or knowledge of a given topic, event, or behavior. The main objective of survey research is to describe rather than to explain. Surveys are particularly effective if you are researching a local problem and can find no existing research documenting it. They are also valuable if you want to gauge how people respond to the solution of a problem. A group interested in solving the problem of an inadequate tax base to support education may decide to collect attitudes toward possible solutions. Before recommending a solution, the group may wish to determine how much of a tax increase would be endorsed by the community. A student and faculty group studying a revision of a school's required curriculum may want to survey student attitudes and suggestions for modifying academic requirements. Surveys can also help a group understand the seriousness of a problem or the probable causes, effects, and symptoms of a problem.

Bowers and Courtwright suggest that any individual or group that attempts to conduct a survey faces common problems, including: (1) developing clear, unbiased questions, (2) selecting a large enough sample to be representative of the entire population being sampled, (3) writing a questionnaire so that it is clear to the reader and efficient for the interviewer, (4) deciding on whether to interview people face-to-face, over the phone, or by mail; (5) making sure that the question-naire will answer the questions that need answers, and (6) testing the clarity of the questionnaire by administering a pilot study or mini-survey.[1]

First, the group must determine a survey's objectives. In essence, what does the group want to know that it doesn't know now? Once a group determines its objectives, it can then decide how best to ask questions that will give clear answers. **Open-ended questions,** such as essay questions, permit respondents to answer freely without any choices or constraints. **Closed-ended questions** ask respondents to choose answers from among several responses supplied by the interviewer. Examples of closed-ended questions include multiple-choice and true-false questions and questions that require respondents to rank items of importance or indicate agreement or disagreement. The answers to closed-ended questions can be more easily tabulated, but open-ended questions allow for a wide range of responses. The type of questions your group asks depends on what you want to know.

After developing and organizing questions, you need to decide on a survey method. If you primarily ask open-ended questions, it may be best to conduct face-to-face interviews so that you can probe and clarify respondents' answers. Interviewing requires listening and recording skills. If you have the time and resources, you may want to mail questionnaires. Including a self-addressed stamped envelope with each questionnaire improve your response rate. You can also stop people on campus or in your community to have them respond to a brief written questionnaire. Make sure you have permission to do this from whomever owns the property on which you distribute questionnaires. In addition, most universities have rules about conducting research on campus. If you are working on a class project, consult your instructor before making final decisions about survey methods and distribution.

Before administering your questionnaire, survey a very small sample to make sure your questionnaire is clear. Have your instructor or other members of your class examine its format and wording to see that it makes sense to those who will respond to it. This step could save you time, energy, money, and embarrassment.

Sample Questions

An example of an open-ended question is the following: What are your feelings about increasing property taxes to support local schools and other services? Examples of closed-ended questions include the following:

1.   Are you in favor of raising property taxes?

    _____ yes   _____ no
2.   Local property taxes should be increased to support our local school. Circle your response.
    strongly agree   agree   undecided   disagree   strongly disagree
3.   Select the statement that most closely reflects your feelings about tax increases.
    a.   Property taxes should be increased to support local schools.
    b.   Property taxes should not be increased to support local schools.
    c.   I am uncertain whether property taxes should be increased to support local schools.
    d.   Taxes other than the property tax should be increased to support local schools; indicate which taxes should be increased to support local schools.
4.   Rank the following sources of potential tax revenue increases to support local schools from most desirable (1) to least desirable (6).

    _____ property tax   _____ cigarette tax

    _____ sales tax   _____ alcohol tax

    _____ gasoline tax   _____ income tax

   Once you have designed and tested a questionnaire, you must make sure that you survey a broad sample of people to justify your conclusions. If, for example, you want to know if students support a 5 percent increase in university tuition, it would not be wise to ask only graduating seniors. A random sample of the entire student population at your school would provide the most adequate basis for making a decision about the acceptability of a tuition increase. You would also need to ask enough people to gauge the attitude of your entire student body. If you survey only 20 students out of 15,000, you have a greater potential for error.

Note

1.   John Wait Bowers and John Courtright, *Communication Research Methods* (Glenview, Illinois: Scott, Foresman and Co., 1984).

Appendix B: Meeting Management

MANAGING MEETINGS EFFECTIVELY

This book has covered a great deal of material about leadership that, if applied properly, can help you become a better group leader or member. This appendix will be more specific and prescriptive than usual. This section is about the nuts and bolts of managing meetings effectively as a designated leader. No matter how well-informed and sensitive you are to leadership and group dynamics, you need to know some basics.

Planning the Meeting

Designated group leaders can avoid many potential problems by careful planning. Planning is one area of leadership that is often overlooked. A number of factors are involved in planning a meeting, and these are presented here under three rules suggested by Professor Harry L. Ewbank, Jr.[1]

> Rule #1: Meet only when there is a specific purpose and when it is advantageous or desirable to solve problems and make decisions as a group.

One of your first decisions in planning a meeting is whether or not to hold it. Professor Ewbank reflects the sentiments of countless frustrated people when he says that "Any time is a good time *not* to hold a meeting."[2] You waste a lot of time in meetings that are scheduled for no particular purpose. Therefore, reflect carefully on the purpose of the meeting you are scheduling. Ask yourself whether the task to be done is the group's responsibility or if it might be accomplished more effectively through other channels.

> Rule #2: Meet with all (and only) those necessary to do the job.

If you have a choice about who is to attend a meeting, consider what resources the group will need to accomplish its task most effectively. Groups are often frustrated in their efforts when too many or too few people attend. If a group will need certain types of information, be sure the people who have the information are present; individuals who don't know why they are at a meeting usually prove to be disruptive.

Rule #3: Plan and distribute an agenda well in advance of the meeting time.

Be sure that all group members have enough advance notice of a meeting to fit it into their schedules or for you to reschedule it. Such planning is crucial, particularly when members must travel to get to a meeting. Also, let members know in advance of a discussion's agenda so that they can prepare and gather whatever resources they need. The agenda should allow time for members to introduce new business and give the time at which the meeting will end.

Plan your agendas carefully. A good agenda is realistic; it is an accurate reflection of what the group should be able to accomplish in the allotted time. A good agenda should look something like this:

AGENDA
Name of Group Meeting
Date and Time
Meeting Place

1. Call to order
2. Approve agenda
3. Approve minutes from previous meeting (in formal groups)
4. Officers' reports (if any)
5. Committee reports (if any); list separately, e.g., treasurer's report, vice president's report, etc.
6. Old (unfinished) business; list all continuing items that will be before the group for discussion and/or action
7. New business
8. Announcements
9. Adjournment

Leading the Meeting

If you are appointed or elected to serve as a group's chairperson, you should know what other members expect of you. You need a clear understanding of the purpose of your committee. You must locate a suitable meeting room, and should make sure that committee members know when and where the meetings will take place. Small group discussions generally do not need the formality of parliamentary procedure. Wagner suggests that a chairperson assume the following responsibilities:

1. Call the meeting to order.
2. Start discussion with a few comments on the nature of the problem of the committee.
3. Avoid digressions and small talk; follow the agenda.

4. Do not talk too much; draw out quiet group members.

5. When a point is saturated, move on to the next.

6. Summarize frequently so that members may keep a mental picture of their progress before them.

7. Prepare a committee report when, after one meeting or many, your group has completed its work.[3]

Different groups accept (or tolerate) different levels of direction from their designated leaders. One simple rule of thumb is this: When the leader emerges naturally from the group or leads a one-time-only *ad hoc* group, then the group will allow him or her to be much more directive. Beyond this simple rule, certain tasks are generally expected of leaders. Two of the most important are getting the meeting started and keeping the group focused on its agenda.

Beginning a meeting with "Well, group, what shall we do tonight?" is an open invitation for personal agendas and leadership battles. Assuming that the group has an agenda, the leader needs to 1) be sure that the group has enough (but not too much) time for orientation and 2) see that the group gets down to business. To initiate discussion, remind the group of its agenda and follow with an open-ended question (one that cannot be answered with a "yes" or "no").

As stressed throughout this book, members need to share an understanding of a group's goals. When this is accomplished, the group's agenda for each meeting should provide a road map for moving toward those goals. A leader often has to keep the group on course, and one of the most effective tools for doing so is summarizing. Periodically, take time to review your understanding of the group's progress and to check out that understanding with the other members. Such summaries help a group take stock of what it has done and what it has yet to accomplish. Other leadership behaviors that help the group stay on the agenda are the functional roles of initiating, clarifying, and gate keeping.

Howell and Smith[4] as reported by Mosvick and Nelson[5] offer other discussions of a committee chairperson's responsibilities. Note the following leadership responsibilities:

1. *Build a permissive climate.* Group building and maintenance, effective listening, and supportive and confirming communication promote openness within a group. Groups dominated by fear do not generate valuable ideas.

2. *Follow a plan.* Once again, an agenda is essential to effective committee functioning. Any plan is better than none.

3. *Give accurate summaries.* Summaries allow a group to clarify where it's been and where it's going, so it can see more clearly how to get there.

4. *Clarify vague statements.* Clearly defining a problem is important to problem solving. Vague statements cause needless disagreements and misunderstandings. When you hear group members make vague statements, ask them to clarify their meaning or give an example.

5. *Evaluate all generalizations.* When someone begins a sentence with "We all know that ∴.." or "It's common knowledge that . . ." this should alert you that an unsupported generalization is about to follow. Such generalizations are dangerous because, if accepted by a group, they become the building blocks upon which subsequent decisions are made.

6. *Protect minority opinion.* The opinion expressed most loudly, most often, or by the most people, is not necessarily the correct one. All ideas deserve a fair hearing and consideration. Protecting minority opinion also helps protect a group from groupthink.

7. *Minimize extrinsic conflict.* Extrinsic conflict is conflict between group members that has nothing to do with the group. When individuals use the group meeting to settle old scores or work out personal agendas, a leader should step in quickly and decisively to make such personal business out-of-bounds for a group meeting. Only conflict generated by a group's task or goal should be encouraged.

8. *Perform only necessary functions.* Many leaders tend to insert their own ideas and to impose their own structure and goals on groups, to dominate discussions, and to lead the group in all of its endeavors. This is usually a mistake, because it discourages the group from becoming a fully functioning body. The leader has plenty to do procedurally without taking on these unnecessary responsibilities.

9. *Keep your eye on the clock.* When leading a meeting constantly monitor how much time you have spent on the planned agenda and how much time remains. If your meeting is supposed to end at 3:00 P.M. and it's 3:30 you can be sure that many group members will be thinking about leaving the meeting (if they haven't already left). Begin each meeting by asking how long members can meet. If you face two or three crucial agenda items and a third of your group has to leave in an hour, you will want to make certain to schedule important items early in the meeting.

CONDUCTING FORMAL MEETINGS: PARLIAMENTARY PROCEDURE

Many of you have probably participated in groups that followed parliamentary procedure.[6] Often, organizations specify that an authority such as *Robert's Rules of Order* be used to conduct meetings. Parliamentary procedure provides an orderly way for large groups (of twenty or more persons) to conduct business, although it is less useful for small groups (in which it leads to win/lose patterns of decision making rather than consensus).

For a complete guide to formal meeting management, consult *Robert's Rules of Order* or the Sturgis *Standard Code of Parliamentary Procedure.* What follows will be enough to get you started.

Types of Motions

A motion is a proposal for action by the group. Although there are many types, motions can be divided into main motions and subsidiary motions.

Main Motions. A main motion brings an item of business before a group; it is always made when a group is considering no other motion. For example, a member might say "I move that we reschedule Homecoming Weekend from the Fall to the Spring term." Another member seconds the motion by saying "Second" or "I second the motion." Most motions must be seconded and require that at least two members wish to discuss them.

Subsidiary Motions. A subsidiary motion modifies or applies to a main motion. It is in order as long as it outranks (takes precedence over) the motion under consideration. Thus, a motion to refer is in order when a group is discussing a motion to amend, but a motion to postpone indefinitely is not. Any subsidiary motion takes precedence over the main motion.

The six subsidiary motions, in order of preference, are:

1. *The motion to lay on the table,* or simply "to table," is made to put aside the current question before a group and requires a majority vote. The question may be reintroduced at a later time by a motion to "take from the table."

2. *The motion to call the previous question* is a motion to vote immediately on the question under discussion. As soon as this motion is made and seconded, it must be voted upon; it is not debatable. This motion interferes with freedom of discussion and therefore requires a two-thirds vote for passage. If a group does not pass the motion to call the previous question, it continues debate on the motion before it.

3. *The motion to postpone to a certain day* is used to delay a decision or to move discussion to a more convenient time. This motion requires a majority vote and always clearly states where and when the discussion will be resumed.

4. *The motion to refer,* which requires a majority vote, is used to move discussion of an issue to a smaller committee where it can be analyzed in more detail at greater length. The committee then later reports to the larger group. Only the main motion (with or without amendments) can be referred.

5. *The motion to amend* is an effort to add to, delete from, or substitute words, phrases, or paragraphs in the main motion. An amendment must be relevant to the main motion you are amending.

   For example, a member might say, "Mr. Chairman, I move to amend the motion by substituting the words 'October' and 'April' for the words 'Fall' and 'Spring' in the main motion." If the motion to amend is seconded, discussion follows on the amendment only and a vote on the amendment is taken. If the amendment carries (a majority vote is required), debate returns to the main motion *as amended;* if the amendment fails, the original motion is considered further.

6. *The motion to postpone indefinitely* is used to kill discussion of the main motion for the duration of a session. It is the lowest-ranking subsidiary motion and requires a majority vote.

Chairing a Formal Meeting

The person chairing a formal meeting has five primary responsibilities in ensuring that a meeting runs smoothly:

1. *Determine a quorum.* A **quorum** is the minimum number of persons who must be present at a meeting to conduct business. Often groups have bylaws that specify the number of members constituting a quorum; in the absence of such guidelines, 50 percent constitutes a quorum.
2. *Open the meeting.* Formally call a group to order: "Will the meeting please come to order." Be on time, if possible, or as soon thereafter as a quorum is present.
3. *Control the meeting.* The chair is responsible for moving a group through its agenda in an orderly way, for asking for committee reports, for recognizing those who wish to speak, and for ensuring that the group respects individuals' rights to speak. Insisting that all debate and discussion be addressed through the chair will formalize a meeting and help to ensure fair and open discussion.
4. *Monitor debate.* As chairperson you should continually remind a group of what it is doing at a given time. Repeat motions clearly after they are seconded, and announce that debate is now open on that motion. Keep speakers on the subject at hand; do not allow debate on other subjects. Do not be led into debate yourself, since this will reduce your effectiveness. Your job is to moderate and see that the assembly considers all important aspects of every item. Control a contentious or long-winded speaker by saying "Thank you" and recognizing another speaker.
5. *Take a vote.* This is a critical skill in chairing formal meetings, one that must be performed precisely to be effective. First make sure the group knows what it is voting on. State the motion plainly, and ask if the group is ready to vote. Call first for affirmative votes: "All in favor of the motion say 'aye.' All opposed say 'no.'" You must announce the vote and decision so that the group knows what it has done. For example, a chairperson might say, "The Ayes have it and the motion is carried" or "The Noes have it and the motion is defeated." Most votes are voice votes. If you have any doubt over the results of a voice vote, ask the group to vote again or call for a standing vote or a show of hands. If anyone questions the vote, he or she may call for a "Division of the House." The chairperson immediately puts it to a standing vote. If someone calls for a ballot, the group decides about the ballot by majority vote.

A certain amount of faith is involved in successful meeting management—faith in your own ability and, more importantly, faith in the process you are managing. Meeting management is a skill that can be learned and improved with practice. The information presented in this book and the guidelines offered in this Appendix should be helpful to you.

Notes

1. Henry L. Ewbank, Jr., *Meeting Management* (Dubuque, Iowa: Wm. C. Brown, 1968).

2. *Ibid.,* p. 8.

3. Joseph A. Wagner, *Successful Leadership in Groups and Organizations,* 2nd ed. (New York: Chandler Publishing Company, 1973), p. 24.

4. William S. Howell and Donald K. Smith, *Discussion* (New York: Macmillan, 1956).

5. Roger K. Mosvick and Robert B. Nelson, *We've Got to Start Meeting Like This* (Glenview, Illinois: Scott, Foresman and Company, 1987).

6. Much of this discussion is adapted from an excellent brief guide to parliamentary procedure written by Rufus K. Broadaway, M.D., entitled *How to Run a Medical Meeting,* available from the Advertising and Communication Department of Cedars Medical Center, 1400 NW 12th Avenue, Miami, FL 33136.

Glossary

A

Adaptor.   A nonverbal behavior that helps people respond to their immediate environment.

Ad hoc committee.   A committee that disbands when it completes its task.

Affect display.   A nonverbal behavior that communicates emotion.

Affection.   The human need to express and receive warmth and closeness.

Allness statement.   A simple but untrue generalization.

Attitude.   A learned predisposition to respond to something in a favorable, neutral, or unfavorable way.

B

Belief.   The way in which you structure what you believe to be true and false—your reality.

Brainstorming.   A problem-solving technique that helps a group generate possible solutions to a problem.

Breakpoint.   A point in a group discussion when members shift to a different activity.

Buzz session.   A meeting of a few members from a larger group; the smaller group responds to a question or problem and reports back to the larger group.

Bypassing.   A barrier to communication that occurs when two people interpret the same word differently.

C

Category system.   A list of terms assigned to determine the frequency of related behaviors.

Closed-ended question.   A question that asks a person to choose from among several supplied responses.

Coercive power.   Defined by French and Raven; the ability to punish people for acting or not acting in a certain way.

Cohesiveness.   The degree of attraction members feel toward one another and their group.

Committee.   A small group given a specific task by a larger group.

Communication network.   A pattern of interaction within a group; who talks to whom.

Complementarity.   The tendency individuals have to be attracted to others who have knowledge, skills, or other attributes that they themselves do not have but that they admire.

Confirming response.   A communication response that allows a person to value himself or herself more.

Conflict.   Disagreement over available options caused by seemingly incompatible goals among group members and their thinking that others can keep them from achieving those goals.

Conflict phase.   Fisher's second phase of group interaction in which disagreement and individual differences arise.

Consensus.   All group members agree with and are committed to a decision.

Control.   The human need for status and power.

Cooperation requirement.   The degree to which a group's success depends on its utilizing member resources.

Criteria.   Standards for an acceptable solution to a problem.

D

Decision making.   Making a choice from among several alternatives.

Decision-making group.   A group whose purpose is to make a choice from among several alternatives.

Defensive communication.   Communicative behavior that arouses in another person the need to protect his or her self-concept.

Descriptive problem-solving approach.   A method of helping people understand how a group solves a problem.

Disconfirming response.   A response that causes another person to value himself or herself less.

E

Ego-conflict.   Conflict that occurs when individuals become defensive because they feel they are being attacked.

Emblem.   A nonverbal cue with a specific verbal counterpart—word, letter, or number.

Emergence phase.   Fisher's third phase of group interaction in which a group begins to manage disagreement and conflict.

Expert power.   Defined by French and Raven; the influence someone has over others because of greater knowledge and information.

Explanatory function.   The power theories have to explain things.

F

Fact-inference confusion.   Mistaking a conclusion you have drawn for an observation.

Focus group.   A group of individuals selected to discuss a particular topic so that the group's leaders can better understand how the individuals view that topic.

Forum presentation.   A discussion that directly follows a panel discussion or symposium and allows audience members to respond to ideas.

Functional perspective.   A view of leadership that assumes that all group members can initiate leadership behaviors.

G

Group climate.   The emotional environment of a group that affects and is affected by interaction among members.

Group cohesiveness.   The degree of attraction members feel toward one another and a group.

Group decision making.   The process by which a group arrives at the best decision from among available alternatives.

Group maintenance role.   A behavior that helps a group maintain its social dimension.

Group task role.   A behavior that helps a group achieve its purpose.

Groupthink.   Group members try to minimize conflict and reach consensus without critically testing, analyzing, and evaluating ideas.

I

Ideal solution format.   A problem-solving method that helps a group define a problem, speculate about an ideal solution, and identify the obstacles that keep it from achieving its goal.

Illustrator.   A nonverbal behavior that accompanies and embellishes verbal communication.

Immediacy.   A quality of nonverbal communication that refers to whether an individual likes or dislikes another person.

Inclusion.   The human need for affiliation with others.

Individual role.   A behavior that calls attention to individual contributions of group members.

Interaction diagram.   A means of identifying and recording the frequency and direction of communication networks in groups.

Interdependence.   A relationship among components in a system wherein a change in one component affects all other components.

Interpersonal need.   A human need that can be fulfilled by others.

J

Johari Window.   A model that shows the relationships between self-disclosure, self-perception, and perceptions of others.

L

Leadership.   Behavior that influences, guides, directs, or controls a group.

Leadership style.   A leader's relatively consistent behavior pattern that reflects his or her beliefs and attitudes; classified as authoritarian, laissez-faire, or democratic.

Legitimate power.   Defined by French and Raven; power derived from being elected or appointed to control a group.

Listening.   An active, complex process of selecting, attending, understanding, and remembering.

M

Metacommunication.   An aspect of a message that provides information about how the whole message should be interpreted; communication about communication.

Metadiscussion.   A statement about the discussion itself rather than about the discussion's topic.

Mutuality of concern.   The degree to which members share the same level of commitment to a group.

N

Nominal group technique.   A problem-solving method in which members work individually on ideas, rank suggested solutions, and then report their findings for group discussion.

Nonverbal communication.   Communication behavior that does not rely on written or spoken words.

Norm.   A standard that separates appropriate from inappropriate behavior.

O

Open-ended question.   A question that allows a person to respond freely, since it does not provide suggested answers.

Orientation phase.   Fisher's first phase of small group interaction in which members try to understand one another and the task before their group.

P

Panel discussion.   A group discussion intended to inform an audience about a problem.

Paralanguage.   Vocal cues such as pitch, rate, volume, and quality that provide information to other people.

Potency.   A dimension of nonverbal communication that communicates status and power.

Power.   The resources an individual has with which to exert control over others.

Predictive function.   The ability theories have to predict events.

Prescriptive problem-solving approach.   A problem-solving method that suggests specific agendas or techniques for improving group problem solving.

Primary group.   A group that fulfills people's needs to associate with others (such as the family).

Primary tension.   Anxiety and tension that occur when a group first meets.

Problem solving.   A process that attempts to overcome or manage an obstacle in order to reach a goal.

Problem-solving group.   A group that exists to resolve an issue or overcome an obstacle.

Process leadership.   Communication directed toward maintaining interpersonal relations and a positive group climate; also called group building and maintenance.

Pseudo-conflict.   Conflict that occurs when individuals disagree because of inaccurate communication.

Public communication format.   An organized group discussion presented to an audience.

Q

Quality circle.   A small group that meets on a regular basis to help with corporate decision making (to improve a product, company morale, or work quality).

Question of fact.   A question that asks whether something is true or false.

Question of policy.   A question that asks whether a group should change a procedure or behavior.

Question of value.   A question that asks the worth or desirability of something.

R

Referent power.   Defined by French and Raven; the power of interpersonal attraction.

Reflective thinking.   John Dewey's problem-solving method that identifies and defines a problem, analyzes it, suggests possible solutions for it, selects the best solution for it, and tests and implements that solution.

Regulator.   A nonverbal behavior that helps a group control the flow of communication.

Reinforcement phase.   Fisher's fourth phase of group interaction in which members express positive feelings toward a group and its decision.

Relational activity.   An activity dealing with behaviors that sustain or damage relationships among group members.

Responsiveness.   A dimension of nonverbal communication that communicates activity, energy, and interest.

Reward power.   Defined by French and Raven; the power to provide rewards for desired behavior.

RISK technique.   A discussion technique designed to assess how group members will respond to and manage a change in policy or procedure.

Role.   A consistent behavior pattern resulting from your expectations of yourself, your actual behavior, and the expectations other have of you.

S

Secondary tension.   Conflict over group norms, roles, and differences among member opinions.

Self-concept.   The characteristics and attributes an individual believes himself or herself to have.

Self-disclosure.   The deliberate communication of information about yourself to others.

Similarity.   The tendency of individuals with similar experiences, beliefs, attitudes, and values to be attracted to one another.

Simple conflict.   Conflict that occurs when each of two people knows what the other wants but neither can achieve his or her goal without keeping the other from doing so.

Simulation.   A structured exercise that creates conditions for participants that they might encounter outside of the training session.

Single-question format.   A problem-solving agenda that helps a group identify key issues and subissues of a problem.

Situational perspective.   A perspective that views leadership as the interrelationships among group needs and goals, leadership style, and situation.

Small group.   At least three people interacting with one another.

Small group communication.   Face-to-face communication among a small group of people who share a common purpose or goal, who feel that they belong to a group, and who influence one another.

Solution multiplicity.   The number of available choices that will solve a problem.

Speech communication.   The process by which people make sense of the world and share that sense with others; what people say and how they say it.

Standing committee.   A committee that remains active for a long period of time.

Status.   An individual's position of importance.

Study group.   A group whose primary purpose is to gather information and learn new ideas.

Survey research.   A method of sampling several people's attitudes, beliefs, values, behavior, or knowledge.

Symposium presentation.   A series of short speeches unified by a central issue or theme.

System.   An organic whole composed of interdependent elements.

T

Task difficulty.   The amount of mental effort required to solve a problem or complete a task.

Task leadership.   Communication directed toward accomplishing a group's task or goal.

Task process activity.   An activity a group undergoes to manage its task or its reason for convening.

Task role.   A role a member assumes to help accomplish the group's task.

Task-contingency theory.   The relationship between communication and the type of task before a group.

Task-oriented small group.   A group with a specific objective to achieve, problem to solve, or decision to make.

Territoriality.   Use of space to claim or defend a given area.

Therapy group.   A group led by a trained professional whose purpose is to help individuals with personal problems.

Topical focus.   An activity at any given time that deals with the issues under discussion by a group.

Training.   Instruction emphasizing skill development.

Trait perspective.   A view of leadership as the personal attributes or qualities leaders possess.

V

Value.   A person's perception of what is right or wrong.

Acknowledgments

Page 12 Specified two lines from "The Death of the Hired Man." Copyright 1930 by Holt, Rinehart and Winston and renewed 1958 by Robert Frost. Reprinted from *The Poetry Of Robert Frost,* edited by Edward Connery Lathem, by permission of Henry Holt and Company, Inc.

Page 32 Reprinted from "A Quantitative Analysis of Intragroup Relationships" by William M. Kephart, *American Journal Of Sociology* 60 (1950), by permission of The University of Chicago Press.

Pages 35–36 From R.Y. Hirokawa, "The Role of Communication in Group Decision-Making Efficacy: A Task-Contingency Perspective." Reprinted by permission of the author.

Pages 79–80 From *Of Human Interaction* by Joseph Luft, by permission of Mayfield Publishing Company. Copyright © 1969 by the National Press.

Page 110 Adapted from Ernest G. Bormann and Nancy C. Bormann, *Effective Small Group Communication.* Minneapolis: Burgess Publishing Company, 1980. Reprinted by permission.

Pages 130, 131–132 From *Nonverbal Communication in Human Interaction,* 2nd ed. by Mark L. Knapp. Copyright © 1978, 1972 by Holt, Rinehart and Winston. Reprinted by permission.

Pages 148–150 From R. Y. Hirokawa and Dirk R. Scheerhorn, "Communication in Faulty Group Decision-Making" in *Communication and Group Decision-Making.* Copyright © 1986 by R. Y. Hirokawa. Reprinted by permission of the author and Sage Publications, Inc.

Page 165 Table 7-1 from B. Aubrey Fisher, "Decision Emergence: Phases in Group Decision-Making," in *Speech Monographs* 37 (1970): 60. Reprinted by permission of Speech Communication Association.

Page 165 From *Interpersonal Communication: An Introduction* by Stewart L. Tubbs and Sylvia Moss. Copyright © 1974, 1977, and 1978. Reprinted by permission of McGraw-Hill, Inc.

Pages 182, 187, 192 From Brilhart, John K., *Effective Group Discussion,* 3rd ed. Copyright © 1967, 1974, 1978 Wm. C. Brown Company, Publishers, Dubuque, IA. Reprinted by permission.

Pages 228–229 From "Win As Much As You Can" by William Gellermann in Pfeiffer, J. W. and Jones, J. F. *Handbook of Structured Experiences for Human Relations Training,* Vol. II, University Associates, 1970. Reprinted by permission of William Gellermann.

Page 245 Chart from pages 26–27 in *Autocracy and Democracy* by Ralph K. White and Ronald Lippitt. Copyright © 1960 by Ralph K. White and Ronald Lippitt. Reprinted by permission of Harper & Row, Publishers, Inc.

Page 247　From "Situational Determinants of Leadership Structure" by David C. Korten, *Journal of Conflict Resolution* 6 (September 1962): 222–235. Reprinted by permission of Sage Publications, Inc.

Page 249　Adaptation of chart in "Personality and Situational Determinants of Leadership Effectiveness" by Fred E. Fiedler in *Group Dynamics*, 3rd ed., by Dorwin Cartwright and Alvin Zander. Copyright © 1953, 1960 by Harper & Row, Publishers, Inc. Copyright © 1968 by Dorwin Cartwright and Alvin Zander. Reprinted by permission of the publisher.

Pages 251–252　From Paul Hersey and Kenneth Blanchard, *Management of Organizational Behavior: Utilizing Human Resources*, 4th ed. Englewood Cliffs, New Jersey: Prentice-Hall, 1982. Reprinted by permission.

Page 269　"Seashore Index of Group Cohesiveness" by Stanley Seashore, in *Group Cohesiveness in the Industrial Work Group*, 1954. Reprinted by permission of the Institute of Social Research, The University of Michigan.

Page 270　Reprinted from *Interaction Process Analysis: A Method for the Study of Small Groups* by Robert F. Bales, by permission of The University of Chicago Press. Copyright 1950 by The University of Chicago.

Pages 271–273　"Barnlund-Haiman Leadership Rating Scale" in *The Dynamics of Discussion* by Dean C. Barnlund and Franklyn S. Haiman. Cambridge, Massachusetts: The Riverside Press, pages 401–404. Copyright by Dean C. Barnlund and Franklyn S. Haiman. Reprinted by permission of Dean C. Barnlund.

Photo Credits

Unless otherwise acknowledged, all photos are the property of Scott, Foresman and Company.

Page 13	© Susan Lapides/Design Conceptions
Page 14	David E. Kennedy/TexaStock
Page 16	Mike Boroff/TexaStock
Page 19	© 1990 by Sidney Harris
Page 30	© Susan Lapides/Design Conceptions
Page 33	George Bellerose/Stock Boston
Page 46	David E. Kennedy/TexaStock
Page 48	Richard Pasley/Stock Boston
Page 79	Ralph Barrera/TexaStock
Page 96	© Joel Gordon Photography
Page 97	Ralph Barrera/TexaStock
Page 103	Jim Pickerell/Stock Boston
Page 126	Spencer Grant/The Picture Cube
Page 133	© Joel Gordon Photography
Page 152	© Joel Gordon Photography
Page 157	Lynn Johnson/Black Star
Page 183	Lawrence Barnes/Black Star
Page 194	Milt & Joan Mann/Cameramann International, Ltd.
Page 197	© 1990 by Sidney Harris
Page 203	David Wells/The Image Works
Page 211	Anestis Diakopoulos/Stock Boston
Page 216	Ford Button
Page 239	David E. Kennedy/TexaStock
Page 241	Doug Menuez/Picture Group
Page 248	Peter Southwick/Stock Boston
Page 271	Stuart Rosner/Stock Boston
Page 277	© 1989 by Sidney Harris

Index

Active listening, 104–105, 115, 212, 213
Activities, group, 20–21
Adaptors, 125–126
Ad hoc committee, 15, 256
Affect displays, 124–125
Affection need, 47
Agendas
  hidden, 53
  for meetings, 255, 266
  for participative group problem
    solving, 178, 191, 202
Aggressor role, 65
Agreement about content response, 99
Allness statements, 106–107
Analyzing, 101
Anxiety, 6, 130, 136. *See also* Stress
Attitude, 158
Attraction
  group, 55–56
  interpersonal, 53–54
Audience, 16–18
Authoritarian leadership, 244–245, 247,
  253
Autocratic decision making, 75

Baird, John, 130
Bales, Robert, 268, 269–270
Barnlund, Dean, 29, 238, 271–273
Barnlund-Haiman Leadership Rating
  Scale, 271–273
Becker, S.W., 136
Belief, 158–159
Belongingness need, 4, 44
Benne, Kenneth D., 266, 268
Berger, Charles, 75
Bibliography, Assembly, 280, 282
Bierstedt, Robert, 73
Blanchard, Kenneth, 251, 252
Blocker role, 65
Body Language, 129

Body posture and movement, 129–131,
  140–141
Bormann, Ernest G., 66, 82–83, 169, 182,
  252–254
Bowers, John Wait, 283
Brainstorming, 184–186, 196, 198
Breakpoints in problem solving, 169
Brilhart, John K., 14–15, 187, 192
Brown, Charles T., 63
Buzz sessions, 191–192, 198
Bypassing, 106–107

Card Catalog, 280, 282
Category system, 262–266
Certainty, and group climate, 96–97
Chairperson, 111, 115. *See also* Meetings,
  managing of
Clarifying response, 99
Climate, group, 90–119
  case study, 91–93
  and cohesiveness, 107–111, 113, 115
  communication networks, 111–112,
    115
  confirming responses, 97–99, 114–115,
    264–266
  defensive, 93–97, 99–100, 114
  definition of, 91
  disconfirming responses, 97–99,
    114–115, 264–266
  and listening, 100–105
  observation of, 263–266
  and productivity, 95, 113–115
  and role uncertainty, 99–100
  self-assessment, 116–117
  and size of group, 112–113, 115
  supportive, 93–97, 114
  and verbal dynamics, 105–107
Closed-ended questions, 283
Coercive power, 74
Cognitive function, of eye contact, 132

Cohesiveness, group, 107–111, 115
  building, 109–111
  and communication, 39, 108–109
  and conformity to norms, 70
  definition of, 38, 107
  and group climate, 107–111, 113
  and groupthink, 216
  individual benefits, 108
  observation of, 268–269
  Seashore Index of, 268, 269
  and task effectiveness, 108
Committees, 14–15
Common purpose, 4
Communication
  and cohesiveness, 39, 108–109
  defensive, 93–97, 114
  definition of, 2–5
  effective, 5
  environment for, 138–140
  formats for public, 16–18
  networks of, 111–112, 115
  observation of, 276–277
  speech, 29–31
  theoretical model of, 36–39
  theoretical perspective for, 31–36
  theory, 27–31, 39
  See also Nonverbal communication
Complementarity, 54
Complexity, of communication, 30–31
Compromiser role, 65
Computer access system, 280
Condon, W. S., 131
Confirming responses, 97–99, 114–115
  observation of, 264–266
Conflict, 207–235
  and cohesiveness, 113–114
  and consensus, 222–227
  definition of, 208–209
  in descriptive problem-solving
    approach, 163–169
  and groupthink, 215–222, 226
  mediating, 211–213
  myths about, 209–211
  types of, 211–214
Conformity, factors affecting, 69–70
Congressional Record, 282
Contextual rule, 33
Control need, 47
Coordinator role, 65
Consensus, 222–227
  in decision making, 152
  and groupthink, 218
  guidelines for reaching, 223–226
  nature of, 222

Contingency model of leadership
    effectiveness, 248–250
Control, and group climate, 94–95
Cook, M., 137
Coordinating, in task leadership, 240
Coordinator role, 65
Courtwright, John, 283
Creativity, in problem solving, 184–186,
    202–203
Criteria, in reflective thinking, 180
Critical thinking, and groupthink, 217,
    219

Dance, Frank E. X., 49
Debate, in formal meeting, 290
Decision making,
    characteristics of good 149–150
    definition of, 148–149
    group methods, 150–152, 169–170,
        172–173
    as group task, 15
    and groupthink, 219–220
    See also Problem solving
Defensive communication, 93, 94
Defensiveness
    group climate of, 93–97, 114
    and uncertainty, 99–100
Delegating style, in situational leadership,
    251
Deming, W. Edward, 195
Democratic leadership, 244–245
Dependence, on group, 114
Description, and group climate, 94
Descriptive problem-solving approach,
    163–169
    conflict phase, 166
    emergence phase, 166–167
    literature on, 165
    orientation phase, 165
    process, 168–169
    reinforcement phase, 167–168
Devil's advocate, to reduce groupthink,
    220–221
Dewey, John, 179
Diagrams. *See* Interaction diagrams
Direct acknowledgment response, 99
Disconfirming responses, 97–99,
    114–115
    observation of, 264–266
Discussion
    domination of, 10–11, 66, 75
    formulating questions for, 156–161
    group members' involvement in, 224

Domination, in small groups, 10–11, 66, 75
Doolittle, Robert, 210

Education Index, 281
Ego-conflict, 213, 214
Ekman, P., 124, 126, 130, 134–135
Elaborator role, 65
Elaborating, in task leadership, 241–242
Emblems, 124
Emergence phase, 166–167
Emergent leadership, 252–254
Emihovich, Catherine A., 131
Emotions, nonverbal expression of, 123, 124–125, 133–135
Empathy
  and group climate, 96
  in listening, 101–102
Encourager role, 65
Encouraging, in process leadership, 243
Energizer role, 65
Environment, and group effectiveness, 138–140
Equality, and group climate, 96
Esteem need, 45
Evaluation
  to avoid groupthink, 220
  in brainstorming, 185
  and group climate, 94
  in leadership training, 254
  See also Observation and evaluation
Evaluator-critic role, 65
Evidence, 161–163
Examples, as evidence, 162
Eubank, Harry L., Jr., 285
Exchange theory, 32
Exercises
  conflict management, 227–234
  decision making, 171–175
  group climate, 115–118
  group communication, 20–22
  group formation, 58–59
  leadership, 257–258
  nonverbal group dynamics, 139–144
  observing and evaluating group communication, 277–278
  problem solving, 171–175
  problem-solving techniques, 198–204
  relating to others, 85–88
  small group communication, 20–22
  theory, 39–40
Expert decisions, 150–151
Expert power, 74

Expression of positive feeling response, 99
Expressive function, of eye contact, 133–134
Extrinsic conflict, 288
Eye contact, 131–134, 141

Facial expression, 123, 134–135, 141
Fact, questions of, 157, 158, 161
Fact-inference confusion, 106–107
Facts, as evidence, 162
Fast, Julian, 129
Feedback
  and eye contact, 134
  in forum presentations, 18
  in Johari Window, 81
  Leathers's Feedback Rating Instrument, 274–276
  in reaching consensus, 226
  and self-understanding, 9
  and training, 254
Fiedler, Fred, 248, 249, 250
Fisher, B. Aubrey, 163, 164, 167, 168
Focus groups, 195–196
Folger, Joseph P., 208
Follower role, 65
Formal meetings, 288–291
Forum presentations, 18
French, J. R. P., 73
Freud, Sigmund, 123
Friesen, W. V., 124, 126, 130, 134
Frost, Robert, 12
Functional perspective on leadership, 238–244
  process leadership, 242–244
  task leadership, 239–242

Galanes, Gloria J., 14–15, 192
Gate-keeper and expediter role, 65
Gate keeping, in process leadership, 243
Gender, and seating arrangement, 136–137
Generalizations, 106–107
Gestures, 130
Get-acquainted activities, 20–21
Gibb, Jack, 93–97, 114, 263
Goals
  and agendas, 255
  attracting individual to group, 56
  group, 4, 37, 48, 49–53, 56
  and group cohesiveness, 108–110
  individual, 49
  in reaching consensus, 225

Goldberg, Alvin A., 187, 189, 269–270
Goldhaber, Gerald M., 2–3
Group attraction, 55–56
Group building and maintenance roles, 65
Group formation, 42–59
  group attraction, 55–56
  group goals, 49–53
  individual goals, 49
  interpersonal attraction, 53–54
  interpersonal needs, 44–49
  mutuality of concern, 51–53
Group-observer role, 65
Group role inventory, 266–268
Groups
  advantages of, 7–9
  climate of, 90–119
  definition of, 3–4
  disadvantages of, 9–11
  and goals, 4, 37, 48, 49–53, 56
  interpersonal relationships in, 61–88
  nonverbal communication in, 120–146
  and problem solving, 8
  reasons for joining, 44
  size, 112–113, 115
  types, 12–18
  See also Cohesiveness, group
Group task roles, 64–65, 268
Groupthink, 10, 215–222, 226
  and consensus, 218
  and decision making, 219–220
  definition of, 215–216
  reduction of, 219–222
  symptoms of, 216–219

Haiman, Franklyn S., 238, 271–273
Hare, A. Paul, 107
Harmonizer role, 65
Hearing, 101
Help-seeker role, 66
Hersey, Paul, 251, 252
Hidden agendas, 53
Hirokawa, Randy Y., 35–36, 148–150, 182
Howells, L. T., 136
How We Think, 179
Humanities Index, 281

Ideal-solution format, 187–188, 198
Identity, with group, 4. *See also* Cohesiveness, group
Illustrators, 124
Immediacy, 126–127

Impersonal response, 98
Impervious response, 98
Inclusion need, 46
Incoherent response, 99
Incongruous response, 99
Indexes
  government documents, 282
  newspaper and periodical, 281
Individual goals, 49, 51, 52–53
Individual roles, 64, 65–67
Inference. *See* Fact-inference confusion
Information-giver role, 65
Information-seeker role, 64
Initiating, in task leadership, 240
Initiator-contributor role, 64
Integrative group behavior, 223
Interaction, 9, 165
Interaction categories, 262–266
Interaction diagrams, 262–266
Interaction Process Analysis (IPA), 269–270
Interdependence, in small groups, 33
Interpersonal attraction, 53–54
Interpersonal needs, 44–49
Interpersonal relationships, 61–88
Interrupting response, 98
Invulnerability, as symptom of groupthink, 217
Irrelevant response, 98

Janis, Irving, 10, 215
Johari Window, 80–82

Keller, Paul W., 63
Kelley, Harold, 54
Kelly, George, 26–27
Kendon, A., 131
Kepner, Charles H., 153
Knapp, Mark L., 130, 131–132
Korten, David, 247

Laissez-faire leadership, 244–245
Larson, Carl E., 187, 189, 190–191, 269–270
Leadership, 27, 28, 36, 236–259
  Barnlund-Haiman Leadership Scale, 271–273
  in brainstorming, 186
  definition of, 237–238
  emergent, 252–254
  functional perspective, 238–244
  and groupthink, 219

managing meetings, 254–256, 285–291
and nonverbal communication, 136,
    142
observation of, 270–273, 274–276
in problem solving, 191, 192
process leadership, 242–244
situational perspective, 244–252
style, 244–246
task leadership, 239–242
training for, 254
trait perspective, 238
Leathers, Dale, 76–77, 270, 274–276
Leathers's Feedback Rating Instrument,
    273–275
Legitimate power, 74
Library research, 279–282
    card catalog, 280, 282
    computer access system, 280
    government documents, 282
    newspaper indexes, 281–282
    periodical indexes, 281–282
    reference section, 282
    stacks, 281
Listening, 100–105
    active, 104–105, 115, 212, 213
    barriers to, 102–104
    types of, 101–102
Lying, and nonverbal communication, 130

Maier, Norman R. F., 190, 192
Majority opinion
    in group decision making, 151
    pressure to conform, 10
Maslow, Abraham, 44–47, 56, 138–139
Mediating, in process leadership, 243–244
Meetings
    evaluating, 274, 276
    managing of, 254–256, 285–291
    poorly run, 8
Mehrabian, Albert, 123, 124, 126–127,
    129–130
Membership, group, 3, 27, 43, 56
Metacommunication, 122
Metadiscussion, 167, 224–225
Miller, Gerald R., 213
Minnesota Studies, 252–254, 255
Minority role, decision making, 151–152
Mintz, N. L., 138–139
Misunderstandings, 211–212, 226
Moderators, 17. *See also* Chairperson
Monitoring function, of eye contact,
    132–133

Motions, types in formal meetings,
    289–290
Mutuality of concern, 51–53, 108

National Training Laboratories, 223
Navarre, Davida, 131
Networks, communication, 111–112, 115
Neutrality, and group climate, 96
Newspaper indexes, 281–282
New York Times Index, 281
Nominal group technique, 193
Nonverbal communication, 121–144
    body posture and movement, 129–131
    categories of, 124–126
    dimensions of meaning, 126–127
    environment, 138–140
    eye contact, 131–134
    facial expression, 134–135
    nonverbal cues, 124–127
    personal appearance, 137–138
    research applications, 127–139
    territoriality, 135–137, 141–142
    vocal cues, 135
Norms, 37–38, 67–70, 84, 87–88
    conforming to, 69–70
    development of, 68–69
    identifying, 67–68
Note cards, for bibliography, 280

Observation and evaluation, 260–277
    of cohesiveness, 268–269
    and group climate, 263–266
    of group meetings, 274, 276
    of interaction, 268–270
    interaction diagrams, 262–264
    of leadership, 270–273, 274–276
    of roles, 266–268
    and theory, 261–262
O'Connor, J., 130
Open-ended questions, 283
Opinionated statements, 162, 225–226
Opinion-giver role, 65
Opinion-seeker role, 64, 224
Orientation phase, 165
Orienter role, 65
Osborn, Alex, 184
Outcomes, 34–35
Outside observer, and groupthink, 220

Panel discussions, 16–17
Paralanguage cues. *See* Vocal cues
Paraphrasing, in active listening, 105

Parliamentary procedure, 288–290
Participants. *See* Membership, group
Participating style, in situational leadership, 251
Periodical indexes, 281–282
Personality clashes, 213, 244
Personal appearance, 137–138
Photo analysis, 144
Physical attractiveness, 48
Playboy role, 66
Policy, questions of, 159–161
Poole, Marshall Scott, 168–169, 178, 208
Position power, in leadership contingency model, 249
Potency, 127
Powell, John, 78–79
Power, 73–76, 84
  bases, 74, 75
  effects of, 75–76
  and ego conflict, 213, 214
  of group over individuals, 114
Prejudging, as barrier to listening, 103
Prescriptive problem-solving approach, 164
Prescriptive rule, 33
Primary groups, 12
Problem orientation, 94–95
Problem solving, 5–6, 8, 9, 11, 147–176
  definition of, 152–154
  descriptive, 163–169
  effective, 154–156
  formulating discussion questions, 156–161
  groups, 11, 14–15, 279
  prescriptive, 164
  types of evidence, 161–163
Problem-solving discussion questions, 156–161
  of fact, 158
  of policy, 159–160
  of value, 158–159
Problem-solving techniques, 177–206
  brainstorming, 184–186, 196, 198
  question-oriented approaches 187–192
  reflective thinking, 179–184, 196
  RISK technique, 192–196
Procedural technician role, 65
Process leadership, 242–244
Productivity, and group climate, 95, 113–115
Pronouns, group-oriented, 224
Provisionalism, and group climate, 96–97
Proximity/contact/interaction, 48

Pseudo-conflict, 211–212, 214
Public Affairs Information Service Bulletin, 281
Public communication formats, 16–18

Quality circles, 194–195
Questionnaires, 283–284
Question-oriented approaches, 187–192, 196, 198
  agendas, 191
  applying, 190–191
  buzz sessions, 191–192, 198
  ideal-solution format, 187–188, 198
  single-question format, 188–190, 198
Questions
  for active listening, 104–105
  closed-ended, 283
  discussion, 156–161
  open-ended, 283
  sample questionnaire, 284
Quorum, 290

Random choice, 151
Raven, B. H., 73
Readers' Guide to Periodical Literature, 281
Recognition-seeker role, 66
Recorder role, 65
Reference section, library, 282
Referent power, 74
Reflective thinking, 179–184, 196
Regulators, 125
Regulatory function, of eye contact, 133
Rehearsing, of response, 104
Reichert, Richard, 77
Reinforcement phase, 167–168
Reitan, H. T., 69
Relational activities, 168–169
Relationship development, 60–89
  norms and, 67–70, 84, 86–87
  power and, 73–76, 84
  in problem solving, 168–169
  roles and, 62–67, 83–84, 88
  status and, 70–73, 85
  time and, 82–83
  trust and, 76–82, 84
Research, 279–284
Responses, 97–99
Responsiveness, 127
Reward power, 74
RISK technique, 192–196
Robert's Rules of Order, 288

Roles, 38, 62–67, 83–84, 88
  diversity of, 63–64
  functional, 267
  group role inventory, 266–268
  individual, 62, 64, 65–67
  maintenance, 64, 65
  observation of, 266–268
  and self-concept development, 63
  task, 64–65
Rules, meeting management, 285–286
Rules theory, 32–33. *See also* Norms

Sample question, questionnaire, 284
Scheerhorn, Dirk R., 148–150
Schutz, William, 46–49, 56
Seashore Index of Group Cohesiveness,
  268, 269
Seating, arrangement of, 135–137
Self-actualization need, 45
Self-concept, 26, 63
Self-confessor role, 66
Self-disclosure, 77–80, 85
  and Johari Window, 80–82
Self-understanding, 6, 9
Selling style, in situational leadership,
  251
Shaw, Marvin E., 69
Sheats, Paul, 266, 268
Shimanoff, Susan, 33
Sieburg, Evelyn, 98–99, 264
Similarity, 53
Simple conflict, 212–213, 214
Simulations, in leadership training, 254
Single-question format, 188–190, 198
Situational perspective on leadership,
  244–252
  contingency model, 248–250
  factors in leadership behavior, 246–248
  Hersey and Blanchard's model, 251,
    252
  leadership styles, 244–246
  observations, 252
Size, group, 112–113, 115
Small group ecology, 136–137, 143–144
Social distance category, 141
Social exchange theory, 32
Social reality, and cohesiveness, 113–114
Social Sciences Index, 281
Solution multiplicity, 35–36
Solutions, in reflective thinking, 181
Sommer, R., 136–137
Special interest-pleader role, 66

Speech communication, 29–31, 165. *See
  also* Communication
Spontaneity, and group climate, 96
Stacks, 281
*Standard Code of Parliamentary
  Procedure,* 288
Standard-setter role, 65
Standing Committee, 15
Statistics, as evidence, 162–163
Status, 70–73, 85
  and groupthink, 216, 219–220
  and nonverbal communication, 130,
    135–136
Steinberg, Mark, 213
Stenzor, B., 136
Strategy, and group climate, 96
Stress, and personal space, 136, 142. *See
  also* Anxiety
Structurization, 69
Study groups, 12–13
Summarizing, in task leadership,
  240–241, 287
Superiority, and group climate, 96
Supportive group climate, 93–97, 114
Supportive response, 99
Survey research, 282–284
Symposium presentations, 17–18
Systems theory, 33–35

Tangential response, 98
Task-contingency theory, 35–36
Task dimension
  in descriptive problem-solving
    approach, 165
  effectiveness and cohesiveness, 108
  in emergent leadership, 252–254
  process activities, 168
Task leadership, 239–242
  coordinating, 240
  elaborating, 241–242
  initiating, 240
  summarizing, 240–241
Telling style in situational leadership, 251
Tension release, in process leadership,
  242
Territoriality, 135–137, 141–142
T-group. *See* Therapy groups
Thelen, Herbert, 113
Theory, 24–41
  of communication, 27–29
  communication model, 36–38
  explanatory function, 27

nature of, 25–27
and observation, 261–262
practical approach, 27–29
predictive function, 27–28
rules, 32–33
of small group communication, 31–36
social exchange, 32
and speech communication, 29–31
systems, 33–35
task-contingency, 36
Therapy groups, 13–14
Thibaut, John, 54
Time
as factor in leading meetings, 288
and relationship development, 82–83
Topical focus, 168–169
Training, for leadership, 254
Trait perspective on leadership, 238
Tregoe, Benjamin B., 153
Trenholm, Sarah, 251
Trust, 76–82, 84, 85
and defensiveness, 99–100

developing, 77
Johari Window, 80–82, 85–86
and positive group climate, 115
and self-disclosure, 77–80, 85

Uncertainty
and defensiveness, 99–100
speech communication to reduce,
29–30, 31
and trust, 78

Value, questions of, 157, 158–159, 161
Verbal dynamics, 105–107
Vocal cues, 135, 141
Vote, in formal meeting, 290

Wagner, Joseph A., 286
Williams, M., 130
Words, as communication barriers,
105–107. *See also* Pronouns